All Part of the Game

Violence and Australian Sport

Edited by Dennis Hemphill

Walla Walla Press
Reprint 2000

First published in 1998 by Walla Walla Press.
Reprint 2000

Walla Walla Press
PO Box 717
Petersham, New South Wales 2049
Home Page: www.asc.zipworld.com.au

Sport and Culture Group
Victoria University
PO Box 14428
MC Melbourne
Victoria 8001

ISBN 0 9587 079 3 6

Text designed and typeset by the Editing & Publishing Unit, Victoria University
Cover design by St Peters Press, Hornsby, NSW
Printed by University of New South Wales Printing Section

Cover photograph: Brisbane v Port Adelaide, 14 June 1998, The 'Gabba.
Photo courtesy Steve Holland, *The Age*.

Contents

List of Contributors

Baydon Beddoe is an amateur boxer and an Honours student in Exercise Physiology in the School of Human Movement, Recreation and Performance at Victoria University in Melbourne. His current research deals with the physiological profile of amateur boxers.

Michael Burke is a Lecturer in the School of Human Movement, Recreation and Performance at Victoria University in Melbourne. He teaches ethics in both the Bachelor of Applied Science-Human Movement and the Bachelor of Arts-Sport Administration courses. His research interests include the ethical dimensions of gender, drugs and HIV/AIDS in sport. Michael is nearing completion of his PhD program, his dissertation dealing with Rortyian pragmatism, feminism and sport.

Martin Crotty is a PhD student in the Department of History at the University of Melbourne. He has tutored in European history there, and also teaches at Trinity College. An avid sportsman and sport critic, Martin's is also nearing completion of his Ph D work dealing with the construction of manly middle-class youth in Australia during the late nineteenth and early twentieth centuries.

Roy Hay is a Senior Lecturer in economic and social history in the School of Australian and International Studies at Deakin University and is preparing a course on Sports History for offer in 1999. Recent publications include articles on the history of soccer in Victoria, on Croatian migrants and questions of identity, on relative age effects in soccer, and on industrial archaeology in Geelong. He is the soccer writer for the Geelong Advertiser and contributes regularly to radio and print media on the sport. He is President of the Victorian Branch of the Australian Soccer Media Association and Vice-President of the Australian Society for Sports History.

Dennis Hemphill is a Senior Lecturer in the School of Human Movement, Recreation and Performance at Victoria University in Melbourne. He teaches Philosophy in the Bachelor of Applied Science-Human Movement course, Applied Ethics in the Graduate Diploma in Exercise and Sport Science and the Graduate Diploma in Sport Business, and Social Theory in the Bachelor of Arts-Performance Studies course. He is the convenor of the Sport and Culture Group, and his current research is focussing on virtual reality, identity and sport.

Rob Hess is a Lecturer in the School of Human Movement, Recreation and Performance at Victoria University in Melbourne. He teaches sport history in both the Bachelor of Applied Science-Human Movement and the Bachelor of Arts-Sport Administration programs. His research interest is principally Australian Rules Football, and he is nearing completion of his PhD dissertation entitled The Development of Australian Rules Football, 1896-1908.

Brett Hutchins is a PhD student in the Department of Human Movement Studies at the University of Queensland. His research interests focus mainly on Australian rugby league, rugby union and cricket, and his PhD deals with cultural representations of Australian cricket. Recent publications of his on gender and history in rugby league are due to appear in the *Journal of Sociology* and the *Journal of Australian Studies*.

Margaret Lindley is a Lecturer in the School of History and Classics at the University of Tasmania. Her major teaching areas include Modern Europe, gender and sexuality, and revolution and dissent. Her major research area is the history of performance, particularly with regard to European theatre. In addition to being a regular football commentator for the ABC, Margaret is a member of the West Coast Eagles, the Tasmanian Cricket Association, and Member of the Board of the Tasmanian Writer's Centre.

Ian Warren is a Lecturer in the School of Social Inquiry at Deakin University. He has an ongoing interest in sport, the law, and the administration of major events, and is currently preparing a doctoral thesis examining the legal implications of security practices at the Sydney 2000 Olympic Games. He has also written extensively on police culture, private security and the law, and youth culture.

Acknowledgements

A NUMBER OF INDIVIDUALS AND ORGANISATIONS deserve recognition for their support in the production of this book. I'd like to thank the contributors for their fine papers and for their patience while I "learned the ropes" of editing and publishing. Victoria University's School of Human Movement, Recreation and Performance has been very supportive of the book and the other activities of the Sport and Culture Group. I would also like to thank Ian Syson for his valuable advice and expertise for the book layout. I am also grateful for the Victoria University-Office for Research Publication Subsidy that helped get the publication up and running, and also to Walla Walla Press for seeing it through to completion. Finally, a special thanks to those closest and dearest to me – Jennifer, Oliver and Cecily.

Foreword

THIS COLLECTION OF ESSAYS WAS DERIVED in large part from public seminars hosted by Victoria University's Sport and Culture Group, a research unit promoting multi-disciplinary study of cultural issues in Australian sport. *All Part of the Game: Violence and Australian Sport* marks the first in a planned series of thematic and multi-disciplinary sport and culture anthologies highlighting Australian issues and authorship. Future publications will include materials generated from and around the 1997 Gender, Sexualities and Sport and the 1998 Football and Culture conferences held at Victoria University.

This book of original essays, featuring authors in sport history, law, philosophy and sociology, will address to what extent violence is "all part of the game." The essays raise a number of historical, legal, ethical and aesthetic and other social questions about violence in Australian sport. Is violence more or less acceptable now than at the turn of the century? What do we stand to gain by taking a more Australian perspective? Are some sports inherently violent? Whose social interests are at stake when it comes to condemning or condoning violence in sport? These questions set the stage for the compelling and provocative essays that follow. By taking a multi-disciplinary approach, it is hoped that the essays will go some way toward generating public debate and informing social policy on this controversial issue in Australian sport.

Dennis Hemphill

'There's a Tumult in the Distance, and a War-Song in the Air'

Violence and Sport in the Australian Public School of the Late Nineteenth and Early Twentieth Century

MARTIN CROTTY

My aim in the following pages is to examine the connection between sport and violence in the late nineteenth and early twentieth century Australian public school.[1] It is the connection, in terms of a discursively and socially constructed relationship, that is my concern here. Documentation of the violence might serve some useful function in terms of assuring ourselves that even in the supposedly golden age of fair play and amateurism players and spectators alike punched and needled each other, but numerous studies already fulfill this function. Further, any connection in terms of sport logically leading to violence, or vice versa, or any examination of the processes and structures of such violence, is a matter for more sociologically-inclined historians than myself.[2] What interests me more in the public school sport context is the meaning and management of violence – the changing attitudes towards the boyish rough and tumble, and the different strategies used to direct or suppress the inclination and tendency towards violent behaviour. In essence, violence moved from being roundly condemned and repressed, to being directed to the games arena where it could be tolerated and even sanctioned, and finally to being an integral part of the strong links between public school sport and the muscular and militaristic ideals of manliness promoted in the Australian public schools in the early twentieth century.

Such developments in the attitudes towards and strategies for the management and direction of violent behaviour in the public schools were intricately bound up with the changing educational ideals of the public schools. As the educational ideals became more rugged and aggressive in the late nineteenth and early twentieth centuries, aggressive games, along with cadets, prefect systems and rigorous physical exercise, were designed to produce a hardy and resilient boy, strong of mind and body, loyal to his country and monarch, and prepared to lay down his life for a worthy cause. This was far removed from the practices and ideals of the public schools up until about 1875, so much so that it is probably fair to say that the ideal product of the public schools in 1914 would have thought his pre-1870s counterpart a 'sissy'.[3]

At Geelong Grammar, there can be little doubt that the focus in the initial twenty years after the school's opening in 1855 was firmly upon development of the intellect and religious piety. The first headmaster and his staff appear to have been uninterested in sport, the school opened and closed with prayers and a considerable amount of attention was devoted to religious instruction. There was a strict regime of examination of academic progress that involved monthly examinations along with end of year examinations which were held over several days.[4] What recreational activities the boys indulged in tended to be unorganised and dissociated from the educational role of the school.

Similarly, Wesley College's educationalists in its first thirty years, and particularly in its first twenty before the arrival of Lawrence Arthur Adamson in 1887, were predominantly men of ascetic backgrounds, deeply devoted to religion and hard work. The first President of Wesley College, for example, the Reverend Dr. James Swanston Waugh, emphasised a disciplined school life that was reflected in the tightly controlled, rigorous daily routine of the boarders, overwhelmingly devoted towards religion and scholastics.[5] The first headmaster, James Corrigan, was of a similar type. Educated at Trinity College in Dublin, Corrigan, who served at the school from 1866 until his death in early 1871, teamed with Waugh to impose strict rules aimed at getting boys to work hard and behave in an orderly fashion. The first set of rules at the school was aimed overwhelmingly at ensuring orderly, polite and respectful conduct, with no tolerance of 'boy culture'. Boys were required to be 'respectful and obedient' to authorities, were not allowed to strike each other for any reason whatsoever, and were expected to return home directly at the end of the school day. Fighting was a severe offence, even under provocation, tale telling was encouraged rather than retaliation, and boys were expected to not be rowdy, disrespectful or vandalistic, all of which could lead to expulsion. Theological examinations requiring a thorough knowledge of chapters of the Bible were held at the end of each year, boys devoted up to eight hours a week to religion, and from 1871 to 1888 the Methodist Theological Institute was a part of the school.[6] Similarly, the Act founding Sydney Grammar School stated that the school was established 'for the better advancement of religion and morality and for the promotion of useful knowledge.'[7]

This educational vision operated with only limited success. Fighting and bullying were apparently common in the early years of most of the Australian public schools, as was vandalism.[8] George Oakley Vance, for example, the first headmaster of Geelong Grammar, was reprimanded in 1859 by the trustees of Geelong Grammar for his 'inability in securing the proper behaviour of the boys out of school, as evinced in the wanton destruction of all parts of the premises', and John Bracebridge Wilson, Vance's successor from 1863, similarly had a number of discipline problems with his senior boys well into the 1870s.[9] Most schools also suffered from discouraging enrolments.[10]

The fortunes of most public schools improved markedly from the 1870s with the arrival of headmasters and assistants from English public schools, imbued with their new educational ideology which placed less emphasis upon religion and scholastics, and more upon development of the body and secular character attributes. These men set about transferring the ideals, tone and practices of English public schools to the Australian context. To develop physical fitness, fortitude, courage, discipline and a range of other qualities associated with the so-called muscular Christianity, they installed prefects, founded school magazines, and encouraged games. An over-emphasis on scholastic training was, they feared, prone to turn out 'a premature, priggish young man' when the real need of the country was for 'A body of gentlemen sturdily bred' who were 'strong of their hand' rather than 'shallow dyspeptics.'[11]

To develop the vigorous and strong boy who was 'strong of hand', men such as Edwin Bean at Sydney Grammar School (1875-78), James Lister Cuthbertson at Geelong Grammar (1875-1896), and Adamson at Wesley College (1887-1898, 1902-1932), encouraged 'manly' sports. These men tapped into the natural enthusiasm they believed most or all boys had for games and encouraged reformed, ordered and regular games as a method of instilling 'noble' qualities of fair play and discipline, but also more rugged bodily characteristics such as physical fortitude and power. Cuthbertson summed up the dual aims of games when he stated that it was wise to ensure that 'the exercises they do take and the games they play are such as will improve their health and strength and bring out their good and manly qualities.' To this end he recommended that boys play 'our noble game of cricket' and 'show their strength and pluck on the river.'[12] Games that did not teach the value of teamwork were not as valuable as those that did, but it was the 'unmanly' games that were especially scorned. For example, Cuthbertson scorned tennis as 'effeminate,' wanting it banned and giving it minimal coverage in the *Geelong Grammar School Quarterly*.[13] Tennis was also considered of less value at St. Peter's where, although the headmaster wanted to develop the game further, it was stated that 'due care will be taken that it does not unduly trespass on the more important branches of rowing, cricket, and football.'[14] The *St. Peter's School Magazine* also railed in 1905 against the habit of some boys in the upper school of playing games such as 'fly the garter' and 'glory'. The editor asked: 'If these games are going to be continued, would it not be well for the Sports Committee to try and arrange an Intercollegiate marbles match, or some such effeminate pastime?'[15]

The ruggedness of the more vigorous and violent sports was advocated because it would allegedly help guard against decline in the colonies by serving a racial imperative. Amidst fears that the colonial climate had a tendency to produce unmanly boys, games were advocated as a safeguard against effeminacy. As the *Geelong Grammar School Quarterly* reported in July 1894:

> without some hardy exercise like football boys [are] in danger of becoming effeminate. This is . . . particularly true of boys in a climate like ours, where

the tendency is to produce a tall, narrow-chested, thin-legged race without the "last" and stamina of the British pioneers who planted these Australian colonies'.[16]

The *Sydneian* maintained that 'really vigorous exercise' was an effective counter to 'that pale, tropical, weedy configuration so frequent among Australians'.[17]

What was not often explicitly stated was that the sports field would provide an acceptable outlet for excess energy which might otherwise be directed towards school fellows, masters, or the school itself. This endorsement of often violent sports amounted to tolerance of violence in one setting, and was justified on the basis of discouraging it in other settings. Boys who had let off steam by running around a football ground in their recreation time, it was thought, would have fewer urges to let off that steam in class or in the dormitories.

And there certainly was a significant level of violence in the recreations of the boys. As well as the inevitable legal violence of contact sports such as football and rugby, fighting and unnecessarily rough play occasionally broke out in inter-school contests. It was not often referred to directly in public school publications, but there are enough hints to make the conclusion inescapable. In 1886, for example, the sports committee of Sydney Grammar School briefly suspended football and cricket matches against Newington College as recent encounters had been 'productive of bad feeling,'[18] while Melbourne Grammar School in 1904 accused Wesley College of 'unfair and unmanly' unduly rough play in a recent football encounter.[19] Off the field, fights between spectators were common enough for the *Age* to refer in 1905 to 'the usual scrimmages between the boys of the two schools' after fighting had broken out between supporters of Wesley College and Melbourne Grammar football teams.[20] An informal behaviour code amongst the boys of Wesley College enforced the nominally voluntary attendance at inter-school contests by forcible duckings in a barrel in the school yard for those who did not attend.[21]

The violence boys committed and endured was held to have its benefits for its perpetrators and victims. The *Sydneian* opined that the element of physical danger inherent in sports such as football was a positive thing as 'a spice of danger is the very element, that calls forth courage and presence of mind'.[22] The *Wesley College Chronicle* ridiculed the aforementioned objections of Melbourne Grammar against the allegedly overly rough play of the Wesley footballers, suggesting that the Melbourne Grammar boys had received 'much feminine sympathy' and were being unmanly in complaining of the manner of their defeat.[23] The same journal also endorsed by implication the use of fists when opposition barrackers insulted one's school, calling this 'a manly display of self-defense'.[24] In the annals of public school sport, violence was endorsed more often than decried.

The furore surrounding the fight between supporters of Wesley College and Melbourne Grammar in 1905 is indicative of the changing perceptions of schoolboy sporting violence. The football match, played at the St. Kilda Cricket

Ground in front of several thousand spectators was expected to be somewhat 'rowdy'. In an effort to minimise fights between the rival supporters, the boys of each school were grouped at either end of the ground. The prospects of a clash at quarter time were averted by having the them move around the ground in the same direction to change ends, thus never meeting. However, at half time the Melbourne Grammar boys grouped in the middle of the ground for a photo. Wesley boys, apparently objecting to the Melbourne Grammar boys taking such symbolic possession of the arena, joined them, and a general melee ensued. According to the *Argus* report:

> Caps were torn off, and their owners knocked down when they tried to recover them. Some boys, shouting with delight, rushed round from group to group, hitting every hostile face they saw. Others picked out foemen worthy of their steel, and in a few minutes the field, like a battle-ground of long ago, was dotted all over in a series of hand-to-hand encounters.[25]

Fighting continued at the end of the game despite the efforts of police and troopers, some of them mounted, and although there were no serious injuries, the fighting took some time to subside.

There was considerable public indignation at the antics of the boys. In the letters columns of the following day's papers, 'Spectator' took exception to the 'exhibition of rowdyism' which he or she 'found painful in the extreme'. 'Paterfamilias' was similarly outraged and queried 'Must "somebody's darling" receive serious, if not fatal, injury before the responsible authorities take steps to prevent this 'upper-class larrikinism?'[26] But what is more revealing about the prevailing attitudes both to masculinity and to the issue of violence in public school sport, however, is the light-hearted and even affirmative response of headmasters, editors and other correspondents. G. E. Blanch, the headmaster of Melbourne Grammar, pointed out to the press that the same thing happened every year at the Eton-Harrow match, a point also made by Adamson. Adamson even seemed to enjoy the incident to some extent, remarking that 'we have a lot of caps – so many that I don't know what to do with them. I'm thinking of making them up into parcels, and sending them up to the Grammar School'.[27] Further, two days following the incident and one day following the indignant letters to the editor, letters of a much different nature were published, arguing that the fighting was a healthy indication of boyhood vitality, and rather harmless fun. A 'Staid Citizen of Fifty' wrote:

> One wonders if some men were ever boys? Thoughtful parents and those who fear fatal injuries to their darlings in school 'scraps' ought to put frills on their limb casings and send them to ladies' seminaries. So long as episodes such as yesterday's are not allowed to get absolutely out of hand, and too much is not made of them, little harm has ever been done or ever will be.[28]

Expressing similar sentiments, 'Ex-School' wrote:

> I fail to appreciate the tone of regret at the occurrence of the melee during half time among the school partisans, as voiced by the three correspondents in yours of to-day. On the other hand, it appeals to one as the evidence of a healthy boyish spirit and enthusiasm, and a good sign of a virile race; and though those boys would tear each other's flags and snatch each other's caps, yet I am quite certain that there is no malice in such proceedings, and no desire to injure any of the opposite side to a greater extent than the passing inconvenience of a 'black eye.'
>
> It will be a poor look-out for the British Empire when its younger school boys do not behave roughly and even rudely at times. Nations are not made or sustained by milk-sops, and so long as nothing mean or vindictive occurs in such 'cap fights' it is difficult to pass scathing criticism upon them.[29]

Editorial opinion also seemed to favour the antics of the boys. The *Australasian* stated that 'Hands were given to the youth to defend himself', and that today's feuds would only further cement tomorrow's friendships.[30] *Melbourne Punch* also devoted some attention to the incident, and saw the hardiness that boys were showing in their willingness to fight as being indicative of a proper public school training:

> part of the scholastic training is ... making men of them, not men of the skim-milk drinking, bath-bun-eating Private Secretary in the farce, but breezy, square-headed men of the world – of the world they have to battle with for bread and cheese – men who can take blows and give them ...
>
> The lad who can give and take blows in an hour of excitement and trial is likely to make a stronger man and a better one for the world's work than the other who has been carefully nurtured on the lines beloved by old maiden aunts, and who shrinks in anguish from all contests involving hard knocks ... The lads have only shown a feature of the quality that has gone to the making of good Britishers for hundreds of years. Show us a man who has made an impression on this tough old world of ours, and we will show you a man who was ready as a boy to fight for his rights ... it is a time to reflect composedly that it is very fortunate boys will be boys and not little priggish Admirable Chrichtons in knicker-bockers ... Anyway, young Australia didn't seem to suffer much from that mythical tired feeling ...[31]

By this time, violence in public school sport had moved from being a frowned-upon indication of boyish riotousness to being an implicitly, and occasionally explicitly, endorsed element in the making of rugged and tough boys who would succeed in 'the great battle of life, which taxes to the utmost the bodily and mental vigour of all.'[32] (See opposite, Figure 1)

The endorsement of violence in sport and the increasingly rugged masculine ideology it was so closely bound up with may have served the interests of those boys and masters who enjoyed the rough and tumble of the football field and the exertion of the river. However, it marginalised many within the

A RIOT OF BOYS.

Melbourne Punch, 24 August 1905, p. 266

education system. Glorification of the non-intellectual, secular, and stoic merits of athleticism and athletics went hand-in-hand with a frequent devaluation of the intellectual, the 'idle' and the religious. Idleness in particular was increasingly despised as it was portrayed as everybody's duty to work for the success of the school in one way or another. The *Geelong Grammar School Quarterly* attributed the success of the school's cricket side in 1886 to 'patriotism', which it juxtaposed against idleness. It gladly reported that 'that mysterious monster, the loafer – the over-dressed, under-couraged loafer – has disappeared of late, and long may it be before his cowardly "not good enough" whine is heard in the playground'.[33] Adamson attacked idlers in 1896 for being 'miserable spirits uninfluenced by this pulse of healthy life' who stood around 'engaging in nothing but foolish gabble, as the fatted sow lies in the sun and grunts'.[34] Albert Weigall, headmaster of Sydney Grammar School from 1867 until 1912, asked of the idlers 'what sort of selfish old women will they be when they are men!'[35] Boys who were physically or psychologically incapable of physical combat with an opponent, or unwilling to fight opposition supporters, found themselves in an increasingly 'othered' category, the opposite to the ideal of the manly schoolboy. It was not just the recipients of hard tackles or young fists that were the victims of rugged and often violent sport and its supporting ideology.

But despite its capacity to victimise less rugged boys, the connections between sport and violence was taken to new extremes in the early twentieth century. The ideals of the public schools became increasingly militaristic, devoted to turning out boys who were capable and willing to defend monarch, country and empire on the battlefield. The *Sydneian*, for example, commented in 1906 that it was just as well that the spirit of their forefathers was alive in Australian boys as 'We need men of thew and of courage and of daring for the defense of the Commonwealth in the future, by land and by sea'.[36] This was partly reflected in the increasingly violent types of games the public schools indulged in from around the turn of the century. Boxing and wrestling were frequently established, as at Wesley College in 1907 when the preparatory school decided to hold boxing and wrestling matches 'to which the fathers of the boys will be invited'.[37] The traditional gymnastic displays at speech days were supplemented with or replaced by an increasingly militaristic element, such as Geelong Grammar's annual assault-at-arms which began in 1897 and included displays of drill, horizontal bars and boxing.[38] By 1901 the programme included running drill, parallel bars, bayonet exercises, horizontal bars, dumb bells, free gymnastics, physical drill with arms, boxing, single-sticks, sword display, and vaulting horse.[39] But increased violence in the form of the new militarism also found its expression in the challenge to the hegemony of sport by military training, and in increasingly militaristic meanings and discourses of sport.

Cadets were formed in the 1870s and 1880s at most public schools, but do not seem to have captured the imagination of most boys, and usually died out. From the 1890s, however, there was a revival in interest in cadet training and new corps was formed, usually proving immediately popular. They received strong official endorsement within the schools and were portrayed as being of moral and physical benefit to the individual, as well as being for the good of country and empire. Sports and physical training were increasingly directed towards military and national purposes, and the athlete was challenged, if not displaced, by the loyal cadet as the public schoolboy model. The President of the Old Wesley Collegians Association, Major H. V. Champion, even looked forward to the day when cadets would constitute the dominant 'sport' of the public schools:

> I hope the time will soon come when military training will be considered the most important sport of any in the Public Schools. I was glad to see Wesley College win the boat race the other day, but what I want you to believe is that the most important game is the military game.[40]

The rivaling, and even displacement, of the sportsman by the cadet as the ideal type of the public schools can be seen at St. Peter's College in Adelaide. The Governor of South Australia asked at the 1908 prize-giving 'what could be better than to make themselves soldiers of the Commonwealth?',[41] while the headmaster stated at the Foundation Day Dinner of 1914, shortly before the outbreak of war, that:

> among the class we call fighting men I believe the man we know to be great – a hero – is more frequently to be found than anywhere … because they know that they must be honourable themselves first and love the honour of their country and their profession if they are to be leaders of men, to be great men, to be heroes.[42]

Here we see an attempt to redefine the hegemonic masculinity, an attempt to elevate the cadet and soldier to hero status ahead of the sportsman.

Cadet and quasi-cadet training, along with gymnastic exercises aimed at ensuring boys possessed necessary fitness and discipline for the soldierly life, came to dominate the life of the schools outside the class room. In all the Victorian public schools from 1906, even boys who were not members of their cadet corps were put through a quasi-cadet type of physical and military drill. It was compulsory for all boys over thirteen years of age, carried out with the aid of instructors supplied by the Defence Department, and designed to give them the discipline and physique necessary for soldiers.[43] At St. Peter's a drill instructor was hired in 1897,[44] drill was added to the annual gymnastic display for the first time in 1899, and in the same year the *St. Peter's School Magazine* noted that the boys 'seemed to have caught the martial instinct which is prevalent just now.'[45] Gymnastics was made compulsory in December 1901 as 'a part of the regular routine of the school' from the start of 1902,[46] and compulsory military drill was adopted in 1906, every boy drilling for about half an hour every day.[47]

Indeed, the increasing emphasis upon military training threatened the place of sport in the public schools. As the nation's needs seemed increasingly centred on military capability to defend nation and empire from the threats of German militarism and Asian expansion, sport was increasingly attacked as irrelevant and even antithetical to the national interest. Newspaper commentary and cartoons began to portray schoolboy sport in a negative light,[48] and there were also attacks on the enthusiasm for games from within the public school system. Leonard Hartford Lindon, for example, the headmaster of Geelong Grammar from 1896 to 1911, encouraged the cadet movement while seeking 'to put recreation back in its proper position' where it would be 'auxiliary to the true work of life, and not one of its leading motives'.[49] Although Lindon's attacks on the cult of athleticism did not outlast his headmastership, they were symptomatic of changing priorities that threatened the reign of athleticism.

Athleticism survived, but only by being defined in increasingly violent and militaristic terms by its proponents. Athletics and the new priorities of loyalty to country and empire were reconciled through discursively modifying the purposes of sport. These included investing it with the qualities of preparing boys for war, likening the battlefield to the games field, and playing up the connections between loyalty to team and loyalty to monarch, country and empire. In this way sport did not have to be sacrificed in the interests of militarism and imperial and national loyalty.

As early as 1879 Cuthbertson had linked, in a poem simply titled 'The Grammar', the strenuousness of the river with patriotic purpose, even to the point of sacrificing one's life for Australia in the same way that one sacrificed individualism for the good of the crew. But it was not until the early twentieth century that advocates of public school sport, in defense of games, began to consistently and emphatically emphasise the military value of sport. The discursive investment of sport with militaristic purpose was perhaps most obvious at Wesley College, where the cult of games was almost sacred under Adamson's headmastership, and which was subject to the most insistent attacks for its devotion to games. In a typical example of the elucidation of sport's military values, the *Wesley College Chronicle* reported part of the speech of Dr Watkin (former President of Wesley College) at the 1908 Speech Day:

> As they strove on the football field or the river, so it might be that in the near future they would have to fight for the motherland, their King, and the Commonwealth. He felt that the spirit of rivalry and competition engendered by these games would stand them in good stead, and that whenever Australia needed them the old boys of the Australian Public Schools, and especially those who had taken part in the games, would be side by side upholding the honour of those schools and their land.[50]

The expression of such sentiments and theories was incessant in most public schools in the years before the Great War.

Early twentieth century school songs commonly made the link between war and sport, taking on a more violent and militaristic tone. The Melbourne Grammar games song, for example, ran thus:

Some, in strife of sterner omen,
Faced the Empire's stubborn ['Afric' pre-World War One] foemen,
Fought, as erst her yeomen;
  Won a deathless name.
Praise ye these who stood for Britain
These by foreign ['rebel' pre-World War One] marksmen smitten
Praise them for their names are written
  High in storied fame.
None their ranks could sunder:
Who could shirk or blunder?
So stood they true to the Old Dark Blue'
  And all their foes went under.
Honour ye the Old School's story
Heroes, who – her sons before ye
Died or lived, but fought for glory,
  Honoured evermore.[51]

In a more metaphoric sense the language of games appears also to have become significantly more militaristic, encounters on the games field increasingly being talked of in terms of 'battle' where sides tried to 'conquer' their opponents. A good example of this is a Wesley College song by F. S. Williamson, a master at the school, titled 'Before the Boat Race, 1907':

There's a tumult in the distance, and a war-song in the air,
Where the foemen in their galleys for another fight prepare,
For they whisper in the country, and they noise it in the town,
That the Wesley colours from the mast will soon be taken down.

Chorus
Then it's forward boys, to battle – hear the bugle's thrilling tone –
With the Royal Standard borne ahead, march on to hold your own,
With the Lion proudly ramping as the Ensign flutters free,
Let the Lion keep the river, as the Lion keeps the sea.

They have raised the Light Blue Pennon, and the Flag of the Maroon,
See the Dark Blue Banner flaunting in the warm October noon.
But who careth for the menace, for it only spurs the bold,
And there are no boys that falter wearing Purple and the Gold.[52]

Similarly, a 1906 game song from Xavier College implicitly linked manliness, sport and battle in song that could easily have been written for or from the front lines of a war zone:

Oh, when the battle sweeps along, fierce and strong,
And when our luck for a moment is declining,
Like heroes let us gaily meet our defeat –
No wailing, no womanly repining.
But raise again o'erhead our standard Black and Red,
And if 'tis stained with gore, we'll love it all the more;
As if our ranks we close, once more to face our foes,
We fling them back defiance proud and strong.[53]

From about 1875 until 1900 sport had primarily meant fair play, loyalty, acceptance of victory and defeat, fortitude, discipline and obedience. It did not lose these meanings after 1900, but the meanings themselves were more allied to militaristic purposes, and sport thus became an increasingly violent activity in the sense that it increasingly came to mean preparing for war.

When World War One broke out the old boys of the public schools responded enthusiastically to their country's call to arms. Their response was seen as a vindication of the public school training they had received, imbuing them with a sense of honour, justice, devotion to a cause and self-sacrifice, qualities which Alan Gross, an Old Wesley Collegian and author of 'Young Chivalry', believed had been developed, in no small measure, upon the games field:

Because through many a bloodless field and fray
We learned the code which governs war and play;
Because our hearts were tempered in that fire
Whose flames are hot with pride and righteous ire;
Because we know for what exalted faith
Our Lion stands; and here in battle wraith
The younger breezes blow; because we hold
Our schoolboys' oath as honoured as of old –
  To play the game; to set above the fee
  Honour and Truth, Freedom and Courtesy;
And knowing well what manner of foes assail
Our King, and how our hopes can never quail;
Because of this, O Motherland, we bring
All that our lives can bear, our lips can sing.[54]

The boys who went to war were portrayed as being torch-bearers for the school and for Australia, and were proof of Australian mettle.

Sport was carried on in the public schools as usual during wartime, a continuance made possible by the militarised meaning of games. Far from being considered inappropriate, the Head of the River contest was held up as an example of the role of public school sport in training boys for the defense of the country and empire. The *Argus* waxed lyrical about the Boat Race in 1916:

> The war has claimed its thousands of young Australians, but from no source has the recruiting been so thorough as from the athletes of the public

schools, and if one must put one sport against another, I would say the public school oarsmen hold pride of place in the percentage of those who have given themselves to the Empire. Statistics show that there is hardly a boy who has rowed in these races in the last ten years who is not now in khaki. The tradition of public school devotion to a cause has been more than upheld, and we find public schoolboys almost automatically stepping from the classroom into the expeditionary forces, relinquishing everything that their names may be added to the roll of honour. Public-school sport has proved its worth to the Empire in its crisis . . . There are many men in Geelong to-day who have enjoyed the sport because they realise its value to the nation, because they know that every one of these boys is fitting himself for the greater game.

War cries and cheers resounded everywhere, and when the racing and cheering are resumed tomorrow there will be the knowledge that we have assisted at a sport which has justified its existence, and is making men for the nation fit to take their places in the army, prepared to give all, even their lives, for the sake of the land they love. It is a soldiers' boat-race year, and we can afford for once to forget the grim struggle in Europe and cheer the victors and admire the trials of the beaten.[55]

Although celebrated by the *Argus* in the above passage, the use of 'war cries' was not approved of by the headmasters of the Victorian public schools, and inter-school premiership contests were cancelled for the latter part of 1917 because of recent 'regrettable incidents'.[56] The problem was largely the use of hostile 'war cries' by the boys of different schools, which were considered unsporting and 'playing at hate' in a time of war when the brotherhood between the public schools should be at its most pronounced.[57] Sport in the right spirit, however, continued to be advocated, and the contribution of public school old boys to the war effort was hailed as proof of its efficacy in the training of loyal, devoted and brave citizens:

Now where are those people who once were predicting
Our downfall because of our fondness for sport?
They've surely concluded at last, from what's happened,
That games as we play them are just the right sort.[58]

The acting headmaster of Sydney Grammar during the later war years (the headmaster was himself serving) responded to some criticisms of the school continuing to play sport by arguing that he knew of no better preparation for war,[59] and as if to support him, the *Sydneian* published in the same issue a variation on Henry Newbolt's 'Vitae Lampada':

Nine wickets for eighty and fourteen to win,'
  Said the score-board at five forty-five.
Fifteen minutes to go! he's the last batsman in;
  "Just to stay there," they said he must strive.

He walked to the pitch in a silence intense,
There was never a clap nor a shout.
He steadied his nerves and took up his defence,
And he stuck there the quarter-hour out.

In the front of the charge 'mid the dust and the glare
He was foremost of all his platoon.
Though the shells and the shrapnel flew thick in the air,
In the heat of the blazing forenoon.

And although he was wounded, he struggled ahead
Through the storm of the death-dealing blast,
Though the ground, as he ran, with his bloods was strained red,
Still victory came at last.

He was only a soldier, but one of a host
Who, that day, had his duty to do;
But he learned, when at school, not to reck of the cost,
But just simply to carry things through.[60]

Despite the horrible carnage of the Gallipoli and the Western Front, the myth of sport as valuable training ground for war service survived beyond the war itself. In his 1921 history of Wesley College, for example, Felix Meyer, a master at the school, linked memorials to the war dead inside the Adamson Hall to the sport of the school and its training of the boys who had served:

> And the East wall bears the proudest and most numerous honour board of all – the composite group of panels containing the names of the Wesley thousand of the Great War. It stretches across the entire wall, with the names painted in gold against the polished blackwood and interspersed with shields painted with the College coat of arms. And from the opposite wall the bows of old racing eights reach inwards, like long pointers showing how the sportsmen of the River rallied to the King's Wars.[61]

In the Anzac legend the Australian nation had placed itself on the map through the endeavours of its young men at Gallipoli, and the public schools claimed their share of the glory.

From the time of the establishment of the public schools in Australia to 1920, the inter-relationship between sport, violence and the educational vision underwent major changes. There were, however, three principal constructions. In the initial years, from about 1850 to 1875, both sport and violence were antithetical to the educational vision of the ascetic and religious headmasters. These men aimed to produce religious boys who were gentle and intellectually clever, and were thus uninterested in sport and concerned to repress violence. Games were unsupervised and commonly of a violent nature, belonged to 'boy culture', and were held to do no good for either the mind or the spirit, the two principal targets of mid-nineteenth century educators. From about 1875 the public schools of Australia were directed by a new generation of headmasters and influential assistant masters. Their main aims were to improve behaviour and to ensure that the colonial public schools refocused their efforts, as the English schools had done, towards producing manly boys who were stoic and chivalrous. They endorsed and encouraged games and tolerated, and even implicitly encouraged, a certain level of violence for its cathartic and character-building effects. Violence on the football field removed the urge to be violent in less acceptable spheres; violence to oneself ensured physical fitness and mastery of one's own body; violence to an opponent showed devotion to the school; and the threat of violence from an opponent developed courage and 'pluck'. Violence was channeled away from the classroom and directed towards the development of a rugged, chivalrous masculinity, the predominant or hegemonic masculine ideal of the period. New national imperatives centred on the need for military capability developed a new, increasingly militaristic ideal of manliness in the early twentieth century, one that threatened to replace the activities of the game field with those of the parade ground. To permit the continuance of athleticism, by this stage a central element of the educational ideology and culture of almost all the public schools, the relationship between sport and violence had again to be reworked. Sport was talked about and thought about in increasingly violent terms, though the violence was no longer in terms of fights between players, but in the envisaged battlefield for which sport would serve as a prelude.

The history of violence in public school sport in the late nineteenth and early twentieth centuries is illustrative of a number of different discursive and management possibilities. It shows how violence on the games field could be repressed, or controlled and directed towards the needs of the time, and how 'boy culture' could be harnessed and enlisted in the pursuit of the changing requirements of 'adult culture'. Attitudes towards violence in public school sport were contingent upon the changing nature of the idealised public school product, itself contingent upon the dominant middle-class culture, class imperatives, national needs, and the requirements of empire.

Headmasters of the late nineteenth and early twentieth century certainly had some justification for their confidence in the ability of sport and its violent aspects to develop the sort of boys they would have considered admirable young men. Sport no doubt encouraged physical fitness, and it is difficult to see how some boys could not have grown in courage and confidence from withstanding and even triumphing in the physical combat of contact sports. Sport, moreover, may well have encouraged the enlistment rate in World War One amongst public school old boys, not because sport necessarily teaches loyalty and readiness to fight for one's side, but because it provided a forum for idealogues to incessantly proclaim the value of such characteristics. However, there was a fine line between developing positive qualities such as stoicism and loyalty, and encouraging undesirable traits such as foolhardiness or brutality. Finally, with regard to sport's alliance with militarism, I can do no better than to quote Wray Vamplew, who, when talking of English public schoolboys in the Great War, observed that 'instead of hard-tackling full backs, they ran into machine-gun fire'.[62] If the brave, courageous and loyal were all to some extent beneficiaries of the violence surrounding schoolboy sport, the reluctant, the weak, the intimidated, the brutal and the Australian dead of the Great War were all to some extent its victims.

endnotes

1 For the purposes of this paper, 'public school' is meant in the contemporary sense of the term, meaning what we would now call private or independent schools.

2 For some of the most compelling studies and accounts of violence in Australian sport, see Wray Vamplew, *Sports Violence in Australia: Its Extent and Control*, A Report for the National Sports Research Program, ASC, 1991; C. McConville, 'Football, Liquor and Gambling in the 1920s', *Sporting Traditions*, vol. 1, no. 1, November 1984, pp. 38-55; Keith Dunstan, *Sports*, Cassell, Melbourne, 1973; Bryan Jamison, 'The Sandgate Handicap Riot: Sport, Popular Culture and Working Class Protest', *Sporting Traditions*, vol. 12 no. 2, May 1996, pp. 17-48; Daryl Adair and Wray Vamplew, 'Not So Far from the Madding Crowd: Spectator Violence in Britain and Australia: A Review Article', *Sporting Traditions*, vol. 7, no. 1, November 1990, pp. 95-103; Rob Lynch, 'Disorder on the Sidelines of Australian Sport', *Sporting Traditions*, vol. 8, no. 1, November 1991, pp. 50-75; Martin Sharp, '"A Degenerate Race": Cricket and Rugby Crowds in Sydney 1890-1912', *Sporting Traditions*, vol. 4, no. 2, May 1988, pp. 134-149; and Chris Cunneen, 'An Historical Analysis of Police/Spectator Conflict at the Bathurst Motorcycle Races', *Sporting Traditions*, vol. 3, no. 2, May 1987, pp. 217-238. On the sociology of sporting violence, see Norbert Elias and E. Dunning, *Quest for Excitement: Sport and Leisure in the Civilizing Process*, Basil Blackwell, Oxford, 1986; Jeffrey. H. Goldstein (ed.), *Sports Violence*, Springer-Verlag, New York, 1983; and Michael D. Smith, *Violence and Sport*, Butterworths, Toronto, 1983.

3 For the equivalent developments in the ideals of manliness in the English educational scene, and in British children's literature, see David Newsome, *Godliness and Good Learning: Four Studies on a Victorian Ideal*, Cassell, London, 1961; Norman Vance, *The Sinews of the Spirit: The Ideal of Christian Manliness in Victorian Literature and Religious Thought*, Cambridge University Press, Cambridge and New York, 1985; Claudia Nelson, *Boys will be Girls: The Feminine Ethic and British Children's Fiction, 1857-1917*, Rutgers University Press, New Brunswick, NJ, 1991.

4 Weston Bate, *Light Blue Down Under: The History of Geelong Grammar School*, Oxford University Press, Melbourne, 1990, pp. 6, 18.

5 Geoffrey Blainey, James Morrissey and S. E. K. Hulme, *Wesley College: The First Hundred Years*, Robertson and Mullens, Melbourne, 1967, pp. 35-8, 62-3.

6 *ibid.*, pp. 30-40, 65.

7 C. E. W. Bean, *Here, My Son: An Account of the Independent and Other Corporate Boys' Schools of Australia*, Angus and Robertson, Sydney and London, 1950, p. 107.

8 Geelong Grammar School, *Church of England Grammar School, Geelong: History and Register, Jubilee 1907*, Geelong Grammar School, Geelong, chapter 6; *Sydneian*, no. 90, August 1890, pp. 6-7; John Tregenza, *Collegiate School of St. Peter Adelaide: The Founding Years 1847-1878*, The Collegiate School of St. Peter, Adelaide. 1996, p. 96.

9 *The First Annual Report of the Geelong Grammar School, April 8th 1859 and Extracts from the Minute Book of the Lay Trustees of the Geelong Grammar School August 1856 to September 1861 and Correspondence with the Lord Bishop of Melbourne*, Geelong, the Lay Trustees, 1861, p. 33. Quoted in Fay Marles, 'An Evaluation of the First Thirteen Years of the Headmastership of John Bracebridge Wilson at Geelong Grammar School, 1863 to 1875', MA Thesis, University of Melbourne, 1975, p. 56. See also Bate, p. 16, Marles, 175-8.
10 See, for example, Clifford C. Turney, *Grammar: A History of Sydney Grammar School 1819-1988*, Allen and Unwin, Sydney, 1989, pp. 49-69, *passim*.
11 *Geelong Grammar School Quarterly*, vol. 6, no. 2, July 1882, p. 20.
12 *ibid.*, vol. 3, no. 9, April 1879, p. 4.
13 Bate, *Light Blue Down Under*, p. 123.
14 *St. Peter's School Magazine*, vol. 8, no. 33, June 1898, p. 2.
15 *ibid.*, no. 57, December 1904, p. 2.
16 *Geelong Grammar School Quarterly*, vol. 18, no. 2, July 1894, p. 20.
17 *The Sydneian*, no. 13, October 1878, p. 1.
18 *ibid.*, no. 62, April 1886, pp. 5-6.
19 *Wesley College Chronicle*, no. 103, October 1904, pp. 1-3.
20 *Age*, 18 August 1905, p. 9.
21 Brian Lewis, *Our War: Australia During World War 1*, Melbourne, Melbourne University Press, 1980, pp. 188, 196.
22 *The Sydneian*, no. 123, May 1895, p. 1.
23 *Wesley College Chronicle*, no. 103, October 1904, pp. 1-3.
24 *ibid.*, no. 79, October 1898, p. 427.
25 *Argus*, 18 August 1905, p. 5.
26 *ibid.*, p. 5.
27 *ibid.*, p. 5, 19 August 1905, p. 14. Stealing the opposition's caps was a way of symbolically scalping one's adversary. In asserting that Wesley had a lot of caps, Adamson was implying that Wesley had 'won' the fight. Adamson later moderated his comments and offered assurances that he deplored the fighting, but this seems to have been more of a diplomatic response that an honestly held sentiment.
28 *ibid.*, 19 August 1905, p. 14.
29 *ibid.*, p. 14.
30 *Australasian*, 19 August 1905, p. 444.
31 *Melbourne Punch*, 24 August 1905, pp. 251, 263.
32 *Wesley College Chronicle*, no. 26, October 1884, p. 401.
33 *Geelong Grammar School Quarterly*, vol. 10, no. 1, April 1886, p. 4.
34 *Wesley College Chronicle*, no. 71, October 1896, p. 274.
35 *Sydneian*, no. 200, June 1909, p. 14.
36 *ibid.*, no. 187, May 1906, p. 1.
37 *Wesley College Chronicle*, no. 113, April 1907.
38 *Geelong Grammar School Quarterly*, vol. 27, no. 3, October 1903, p. 34.
39 *ibid.*, vol. 25, no. 3, October 1901, p. 4.
40 *Wesley College Chronicle*, no. 122, July 1909, p. 21.
41 *St. Peter's School Magazine*, no. 70, May 1909, p. 3.
42 *ibid.*, no. 86, August 1914, p. 50.
43 *Wesley College Year Book 1907*, p. 24; *Wesley College Chronicle*, no. 111, October 1906, p. 9.
44 *St. Peter's School Magazine*, vol. 6, no. 30, October 1897, p. 477.
45 *ibid.*, vol. 8, no. 39, December 1899, pp. 163-4.
46 *ibid.*, vol. 9, no. 47, December 1901, p. 337, vol. 9, no. 51, December 1902, p. 451.
47 *ibid.*, no. 62, August 1906, pp. 25-6.

48 See, for example, cartoons published in the *Bulletin*, 5 January 1911 and 20 June 1912.
49 *Geelong Grammar School Quarterly*, vol. 26, no. 4, December 1902, pp. 25-6.
50 *Wesley College Chronicle*, no. 119, October 1908, p. 5.
51 James Beacham Kiddle, *Liber Melburniensis, 1848-1936: Melbourne Church of England Grammar School Official History*, Melbourne Grammar School, Melbourne, 1937, pp. 674-5
52 *Wesley College Chronicle*, no. 115, 1907, p. 3.
53 Geoffrey Sherington, R. C. Petersen and Ian Brice, *Learning to Lead: A History of Girls' and Boys' Corporate Secondary Schools in Australia*, Allen and Unwin, Sydney, London and Boston, 1987, p. 138.
54 *Wesley College Chronicle*, no. 142, December 1914, p. 3.
55 Quoted in *ibid.*, no. 146, May 1916, p. 32.
56 *Geelong Grammar School Quarterly*, vol. 42, no. 3, December 1917, pp. 20-1.
57 Felix Meyer (ed.), *Adamson of Wesley: The Story of a Great Headmaster*, Robertson and Mullens, Melbourne, 1932, p. 181; *Wesley College Chronicle*, no. 151, December 1917, pp. 8-9. See also no. 149, May 1917, p. 19. At a meeting on 24 February the headmasters had decided to prohibit the use of 'war cries' at public functions. They agreed that if there were any 'regrettable' incidents such as the use of war cries or fighting between spectators, the remaining premiership contests would be cancelled. At a football match between Xavier and Scotch on 22 August and at a football match between Wesley and Melbourne Grammar on 24 August, war cries were used, so on 30 August the headmasters acted upon their threat.
58 *Wesley College Chronicle*, no. 150, August 1917, p. 27.
59 *Sydneian*, no. 235, March 1918, p. 6.
60 *ibid.*, no. 235, March 1918, p. 55.
61 Meyer, *The History of Wesley College, 1865-1919*, p. 162.
62 Wray Vamplew, *Pay Up and Play the Game: Professional Sport in Britain, 1875-1914*, Cambridge University Press, Cambridge, 1988, p. 8.

Analysing Sporting Violence

History, Theory, Context, and Figurations

BRETT HUTCHINS

> . . . he kneed Beath in the face and was sent straight off. I can still see Beath lying there, unconscious on the ground, the blood dripping down from his forehead and forming little pools in his closed eyes. He was really gone; they had to cart him off. (Adams, 1994: 66)

THIS DESCRIPTION OF A 1970S RUGBY LEAGUE INCIDENT indicates the possible consequences of participant sporting violence: it can be injurious and outright vicious. Yet in many of our most popular sports, various forms of violence are expected, sanctioned, rewarded, and central to competition, especially those involving regularised body contact (Bryson, 1987; Heikkala, 1993; Young, 1993). Sport provides an important site of incision for analysis of social violence norms and associated values (Sheard, 1992: 17). Important issues are raised: what do the forms and frequency of sporting violence tell us? How are fluctuations and distinctions between levels of interpersonal violence to be explained? What is the relationship between sporting violence and wider social structures? And what methods are effective in analysing violence as a social phenomenon?

Figurational sociology attempts to address all of these questions. Developed from the pioneering work of German sociologist, Norbert Elias (1978), 'Eliasian' methodology represents a tradition that selects social violence as a primary focal point of analysis, and has examined sporting violence extensively throughout its research history (Dunning, 1970; Dunning et al., 1993; Dunning and Rojek, 1992; Dunning and Sheard, 1979; Elias and Dunning, 1986a; Rojek, 1985; Rojek, 1995). This chapter attempts to present the figurational method as a useful way of investigating sport participant violence. It is far from an exhaustive account of this approach as there are already some admirable evaluations of the Eliasian methodology (Jarvie and Maguire, 1994; Layder, 1994; Mennell, 1989; Rojek, 1985). Nor is this essay a dogmatic treatise claiming that the Eliasian way is the *only* way to analyse sport violence. Rather, it is intended to highlight that the figurational method is of value in analysing sporting social relations and violence dynamically, relationally and systematically.

In the first half of this chapter, attention is given to the case of historical sociology, the two main sensitising concepts of figurational sociology, and weaknesses of this methodology. In the second half, Australian elite level rugby league violence is used as a vehicle to illustrate four components of figurational theory.

History = Sociology? Crossing Sacrosanct Borders

> ... a great deal of the opposition to theory is born of prejudice. (Tosh, 1991: 159)

Within sections of the Australian sports studies community, there has been some stern resistance to the merging of historical and sociological concerns (Booth, 1997: 191-204; Hay, 1995: 13-14; Hutchins, 1996: 11-12; Stewart, 1995: 1; Turner, 1996: 15-16; Whimpress, 1996: 12-13;). Such prejudice appears unreasonable and futile considering historical sociology has been established since the 1950s, with expositions growing from a 'trickle' at this time into a 'torrent' by the 1980s (Abrams, 1980: 4; Hunt, 1989: 1; Mandalios, 1996: 279). Figurational sociology is part of this movement. It transgresses the borders between mainstream history and sociology as it acknowledges the relative quality of "historical facts" and "social facts" (Tosh, 1991: 152). In appreciating the historicity of social relations we can come to a better understanding of how "we got from here to there" (Mandalios, 1996: 279). Many figurationalists comprehend the complexity of the historical process and suitably position it at the centre of analysis, acutely realising the necessity of empirically and substantively accounting for *long-term social processes and development*. Championing this approach, Elias (1982: 231) stressed that without historical evidence the study of social relations "remains empty and ambiguous, unless the actual dynamics of social interweaving are directly illustrated by reference to specific and empirically demonstrable changes."

Emphasis on theoretical matters indicates figurational sociology is different from 'traditional' sporting history. Figurationalists aim to avoid the weaknesses contained within many "who did what when" (Struna, 1985: 151-152) narrative histories:

> None of the richness of sport history can be gleaned from a series of descriptive chronologies piled on top of the other and very little insight into the relationship between sport and society ... revealed. (Morrow, 1983: 54)

Such chronologies fail to consider that history is not just about people and events, but it is also about the development of concepts, ideas and human knowledge (Elias, 1994: 30-31). Also, chronological histories do not always appreciate that the conception of time is fraught with difficulties. When analysing the development of human knowledge, concepts and ideas develop interdependently and simultaneously, but their germination and development often occur at distinctly different rates (Elias, 1987: 56-57; Jarvie and Maguire, 1994: 130-131; Watson, 1993: xxxii). The need for theory is further sustained on a number of fronts. Theory can throw light on social practices and change. It can help us understand people's identities and how they constitute themselves collectively (Hall, 1996: 30-31). Most importantly, theoretically fashioned history can account for social structuring within historical narrative. The perpetual unfolding of social events and human actions are interconnected to multitudes of social structures, patterns, orders and processes – all affect one another and they are ultimately inseparable. Therefore examination of the structures feeding into the historical eventuations contained in narratives is vital (Abrams, 1982: x). Significantly, Abrams (1980: 13) venerates Elias for his treatment of social structuring within social relations, declaring it "the most serious and penetrating attempt to develop the problematic of structuring outside Marxism . . . ".

Figuring Social Interrelationships

The first of the two main concepts within figurational sociology is quite simple: social life is driven by the interdependencies of human actions and relations. This is represented by the concept of human "figurations" (Elias 1970: 13-18, 128-133):

> The network of interdependencies among human beings is what binds them together. Such interdependencies are the nexus of what is here called the figuration, a structure of mutually oriented and dependent people. Since people are more or less dependent on each other first by nature and then through social learning, through education, socialization, and socially generated reciprocal needs, they exist, one might venture to say, only in figurations. That is why . . . it is not particularly fruitful to conceive of men *(sic.)* in the image of the individual . . . It is more appropriate to envisage an image of numerous interdependent people forming figurations (i.e., groups or societies of different kinds) with each other. (Elias, 1978:261)

The motivation for viewing people as figurations or interdependent linkages is to deal with the tension between human agency and social structuring. Elias sought to loosen and/or break down the "frozen dichotomies" (Goudsblom, 1987: 332) and sterile popular dualisms used in many forms of sociology. These dualisms include individual/society, agency/structure, base/superstructure and macro/micro (Elias, 1970: 130; Layder, 1994: 114). These artificial constructs reduce social life to immutable, static and mutually exclusive 'states' and 'things' (Dunning, 1986a: 9; Rojek, 1992: 14; Sheard, 1992: 8). Figurational sociology opposes such reification of social relations by jettisoning such dualisms, and views social relations as wholly inseparable and interdependently constituted. Lived social experience is captured *processually* as being dynamic, in constant flux, and driven by conflict and perpetually shifting interdependencies – in Eliasian terms "the immanent dynamics of figurations" (Dunning, 1986a: 13). Above all, figurations are an attempt to 'humanise' the social structures and relationships utilised in social analysis.

In figurational methodology, singular causal relationships, or direct cause-and-effect mechanisms are rejected (Maguire, 1993a: 35). These reductive mechanisms fail to account for the diversity of processes feeding into any social and historical development. It is put forward that social life should be studied "in the round" (Dunning, 1986a: 15); that is, it is imperative to examine any number of the many-sided and multi-polar social, cultural, political, technological, economic, psychological (or any other) part-processes applicable to social phenomena. *Inclusiveness* in analysis emphasises the pluralities and multiplicities – the micro-politics – of power in social life. Macro-political institutional unities, often used in neo-Marxist cultural studies, such as the state, class, and the economy are not rejected out of hand, but any tendency to characterise them as ahistorical superstructures is avoided (Rojek, 1992: 8-10; Rojek, 1995: 20-25). By contrast, these unities are treated as historically contingent formations processually produced through conflict, struggle and interplay of differences (Foucault, 1972: 37-39; Hunt, 1989: 10-13; O'Brien, 1989: 33-40).

Civilising Processes: Violence and Sport

The second component of figurational sociology is Elias's theory of the civilising processes. As a theory it has been heavily criticised for over-emphasising the role of violence and under developing the role of gender, the media, race, and economics in social analysis (Critcher, 1988; Gruneau, 1993; Gruneau and Whitson, 1993; Hargreaves, 1994; Hargreaves, 1992; Stokvis, 1992; Wilson, 1992; Zolberg, 1987). While some of these arguments may be valid (and will be further addressed in a later section), a countervailing argument to these is that the civilising process provides a much needed theory accounting for fluctuations and distinctions between levels of violence (Blok, 1977: 179). The theory of the civilising processes is broad and complex, and arose from Elias's study of manners and state development in Europe since the Middle Ages (Elias, 1978; Elias, 1982). What Elias attempted is to fluidly interweave analysis between *structural* social power and *interpersonal* behaviour (Dunning, 1994: 147-148; Mandalios, 1996: 293). The civilising process is about determining the historical interrelationship between socio-genesis (the structural) and psycho-genesis (the interpersonal):

> Socio-genesis examines the power structures and balances composing society. At this structural level, features of the civilising process include the centralisation of politics, and the development of government controls and regulative state apparatuses.
>
> Psycho-genesis explores the long-term changes within personality structures and conscience formations. Developments are analysed through tracing behavioural features and norms of selected populations within Western society. Since the Middle Ages, civilising process characteristics include people displaying increasing levels of self-restraint and control over aggression and violence, and less willingness to witness, engage in and find violent acts entertaining and gratifying. Accompanying these are refinement of manners, and advancing levels of shame and embarrassment, especially regarding public demonstration of bodily functions, e.g. farting, belching, defecation (Elias, 1982: 229; Dunning, 1993: 46, 53; Rojek, 1985: 166).

Sheard (1992: 12) comments on Elias's attempt to dissolve the gap between the structural and the interpersonal:

> Elias suggested that the increased social control which comes from centralisation of political power and more complex webs of interdependence is also associated with rising standards of self-control. It was his contention that the boundary between "external" social constraint and "internalised" self-control is not so distinct as is often conceived, and that this boundary gradually shifts in the course of history.

Neither the 'external' nor the 'internal' has determination over the other. They are functionally interdependent and are in no way reducible to one another (Elias, 1987: 77-78; Elias, 1986a: 52). It is the innumerable interdependencies and figurational power dynamics that intersect to produce discernible social behaviour patterns and social structures.

Sport provides a readily observable social forum for the examination of transforming violence levels. The suitability of sport for Eliasian practitioners is enhanced as it is an activity that is often intensely competitive and prone to violence (Dunning, 1986c: 227; Heikkala, 1993: 409-410), and is controlled by various regulative apparatuses such as sporting, commercial and government bodies. In light of this, sport can in no way be isolated from wider structural social development and processes, and offers a social enclave in which people's sensitivity and tolerance for violent acts is regularly and widely tested (Elias, 1986a: 41-42). Critcher (1988: 207-08) focuses upon the social context in which Western sport is conducted:

> Sport is a competitive and rule-bound physical activity, always exciting and sometimes violent. It develops alongside industrialisation and its particular organizational forms reflect an ongoing struggle for control of culture,

> affected variously by economic, political and social groups. Sport attracts such popular enthusiasm because it legitimates excitement and violence, provides a common sense of identity and purpose and lends itself to a media-defined version of public spectacle.

It is important to note that only a selected aspect of Elias's civilising theory is fully evaluated through sport: that in the course of the civilising processes, standards have developed in Western urban industrial societies showing their members have, on-balance, exercised stricter self-control over violence and aggression (Dunning and Sheard, 1979). To build a credible case for or against a long-term change in the patterns and forms of sporting violence requires the following: historical context and social context.

Contextual Analysis

The theory of the civilising processes is of most analytical value when context-driven. This claim is supported by two main propositions. Firstly, violence is a complex social phenomenon that is polymorphous in its forms and meanings (Finn, 1994: 90; Gunter, 1985: 10). Violence is then only identifiable in the context of the form and symbolic actions of the activity taking place (Dunning, 1986c: 224-44). What is perceived as 'violent' in one sport may not be in another, and tightly defined frames of social reference help negotiate this variation.

Secondly, as Mouzelis (1993: 244) powerfully argues, the theory of the civilising processes is only convincing when addressing strictly *context-bound* issues, not when trying to analyse *overall trends*:

> The ... requirement for going beyond the 'overall trend' predicament is for the theory to renounce its universalizing pretensions and to look closely at time and space. This seems to be what Elias was doing when he focused on France, but then he claimed that the connection between interdependence and civilizing conduct applies to all and any processes of social differentiation whenever and wherever they may occur ... If the aim of the theory is as all-embracing as that, one can safely predict that, like all universal theories in the social sciences, it will end up with propositions that are either trivial or wrong, in that they remain true only in conditions that remain unspecifiable as long as the theory adheres to its all-inclusive orientation.

The social features accompanying the trajectory of a civilising process are not always generalisable beyond a limited social setting. If considered in other settings, these features may indicate something quite different.

An example of a contextually driven historical and social study is Dunning and Sheard's (1979) study of the development of modern rugby football.

In this work, *specific* civilising effects come to the fore. For example, up to mid-1800s rugby was an extremely disorderly and violent game where 'stiff-arm' tackles and 'hacking' with iron-tipped boots ('navvies') were not necessarily part of any victory driven logic, but just an accepted part of playing a 'manly' game of rugger.[2] By comparison, contemporary rugby players demonstrate less propensity for excessive violence, and illegitimate violence is far more likely to be acted out only to improve the prospects of victory (Dunning and Sheard, 1979: 79-276; Dunning, 1993: 54).

In summary, if worthwhile history is the result of contextual analysis (Pearson and McKay, 1981: 69), and there is also no division between sociology and history (Abrams, 1982: x), a sociological theory such as the civilising processes must then observe the need for context in analysis in order to produce meaningful findings.

Accounting for Selected Figurational Shortcomings

Figurational theorists have often given the impression of a gang mentality due to the often "prickly" (Rowe, 1996: 128) responses to criticism leveled at them from the likes of Curtis (1986), Hargreaves (1992, 1994), Horne and Jary (1987), and Layder (1994). Some considered (and decidedly 'unprickly') response to criticism is imperative however.

Critics charge that the civilising process is a theory of unilinear human development, latent functionalism, or generalised evolutionism (Curtis, 1986: 59; Gruneau and Whitson, 1993: 179; Horne and Jary, 1987: 101; Rowe, 1996: 128) Undeniably, the term 'civilising', contains obvious teleological (and racist) impositions (Dunning, 1994: 145-49), though in fairness to Elias he viewed the term 'civilising' as quite distinct from the sociological concept of a 'civilising process':

> Elias ... explicitly recognized that 'civilization' is a value-laden term. By contrast the concept of a 'civilizing process' in his usage is a detached, technical term that refers to the shared complex of changes experienced by the major societies of western Europe as their development led, first of all their ruling groups and, later, more and more sections of the population to have the idea of themselves as 'civilized'. (Dunning, 1994: 146)

It is added that the theory is in no way developed from an idea that there has been a "zero-point" of civilisation; or the existence of an "absolutely uncivilized" human group or society (Dunning, 1989: 39-40; Dunning, 1993: 43).

> The civilising process is also not about conceptions of perpetual 'progress': Elias's theory is not marred by the drawbacks of classical evolutionism, since it neither implies progress in any moral sense of the term, nor does it claim the civilizing trend to be unilinear or irreversible. (Mouzelis, 1993: 243)

The possibility and likelihood of counter-civilising movements is declared candidly by Elias (1982: 251): "The civilizing process moves along in a long sequence of spurts and counter-spurts." De-civilising spurts are inevitable as Elias's theory is based on peoples' ability to control their environment through learning and knowledge. Furthermore, types, levels and degrees of knowledge shift over time (Elias, 1987: 56-57), and these shifts may precipitate either civilising or counter-civilising developments. Elias contended that these developments have greatly favoured the former. Thus Mouzelis (1993: 243) suggests the civilising process argument could be solidified, and many attacks nullified, by highlighting that counter-civilising developments are inevitable but have been comparatively secondary to civilising trends (Mouzelis, 1993: 243).

The other main point of attack against figurational sociology is its neglect of gender issues. Jennifer Hargreaves (1992, 1994) accurately claims that figurational sociologists have remained remarkably silent on the issue of gender and women in sport. Arguments put forward by Dunning (1986a: 12-15) of an overall trend of long-term equalising changes in the balances of power across social classes and groups (implicitly including women) in Western society[3] have been criticised for ignoring gender and lacking specifiable context (Hargreaves, 1994: 13-15). Dunning has neglected that "writing on gender is always specific and contingent" (Miller, 1990: 85). Other claims that the figurational method involves the researcher implementing Weberian notions of 'objective' analytical detachment in study (Elias, 1970: 121-122, 153-154; Mennell, 1989: 59-180; Mouzelis, 1993: 247; Rojek, 1986: 593), thus attaining a form of ethical neutrality, have been hard to sustain in the face of the "passionate objectivity" driving many feminist analyses (Hargreaves, 1994: 12). Certainly, reaching a state of 'detachment' above one's "own histories and consciousness" (Hargreaves, 1992: 162) is impossible without any guidelines on how to go about transcending your own ethical and moral reality (Rojek, 1985: 171-172). Put simply, the analytical 'detached' position is insupportable. 'Objectivity' in theory and history amounts to little more than a chimera (Tosh, 1991: 148-163); and it can only remain contentious by its openness to accusations of crude positivism (Mouzelis, 1993: 247). It can also be inferred that a 'detached' position merely masks a fear of making a commitment to a firm political, moral or ethical position (Rojek, 1986: 594). Later in this paper I hope to show that there is room within figurational sociology to analyse gender issues.

Putting Theory Into Practice: Australian Rugby League 1970 to 1995

To illustrate the use-value of the figurational method, I will examine the sport of Australian elite level rugby league between 1970 and 1995. As a body contact sport, rugby league's conduct is reliant on controlled, licensed violence. Its popularity and extensive media coverage throughout Australia (Brook, 1995: 27; Lynch, 1993: 109-114; Phillips, 1997), especially in the states of New South

Wales and Queensland, invest it with a great deal of social and cultural power (Hutchins, 1997a). Standards of violence and violence control in rugby league informs us of important social features in one of the two most prominent Australian football codes, and also points towards critical interrelationships with the wider social milieu.

There is no intention within this paper to assert that rugby league has experienced a civilising process, as the examples provided are far too few in number to ascertain such an over-arching process. Rather, the objective is to illustrate figurational concepts through an examination of the social context of rugby league violence. Furthermore, the four cases provided are intended only to serve as figurational 'snapshots' in which rugby league is situated. For more comprehensive analyses and substantive evidence on changes within rugby league violence over time (at least up to Super League), see Headon and Marinos (1996), Heads (1992), Hutchins and Phillips (1997), Hutchins (1997a, 1997b), Masters (1990), Phillips (1997), Yeates (1995) and Writer (1995).

Case One: Transformations in Patterns and Forms of Violence

A strength of the figurational method is its theorising of sporting violence. It rejects the categorical, reductive, ahistorical, biological determinism contained within catharsis theory (Dunning, 1993: 39-40; Gruneau and Whitson, 1993: 177-178; Yeates, 1992b: 131) for a more socio-cultural oriented sub-theory that emphasises the transformative features of sporting violence patterns and standards. On an interpersonal level and over the long-term, violent sporting conduct is seen to have gradually shifted from, on the whole, *expressive* and *affective* forms of violence, to *instrumental* and *rational* forms of violence (Elias, 1986a: 41-42; Dunning, 1986d: 47-48; Pilz, 1982: 47-48). Expressive and affective forms refer to violence that is spontaneous, uncontrolled, and not calculated; while instrumental and rational forms refer to violence that is deliberate, measured and purposeful. It must be remembered that these are polarised conceptualisations that have never been, nor will be, experienced in totality. As sport has become more organised and regulated over time – represented as figurational differentiation and integration to higher levels – the balance has swung away from expressive violence towards instrumental violence. Dunning has amplified this aspect of the civilising process: "It is not a simple theory about the disappearance of violence but, on the contrary, about changes in its forms and in the ways it is socially stored and used" (Dunning, 1993: 66).

Media reports[4], New South Wales Rugby League (NSWRL) Player Judiciary records[5], observation and analysis of matches, and anecdotal evidence, provide the impression that between 1970 and 1995 rugby league players have displayed advancing levels of physical and emotional control over violence (Hutchins and Phillips, 1997). The most notable transformation in patterns of violence appears to be from a fluid mixture of often illegitimate instrumental and provoked expressive violence in the 1970s, to a prevailing code of largely legitimate instrumental or rational violence in the 1990s. In the 1970s, spontaneous, illegitimate and excessive violence is evident:

> The two men grappled on the ground for several minutes, punching, kicking, butting and gouging in the shadows of the famous SCG Members' Stand. Legend has it that Piggins told team-mates after the dust had settled: "I had my finger in the bastard's eye . . . I should have flicked it out." (Adams, 1994: 79)

> If you didn't punch about six blokes in a game and tread on a couple of hands and head butt a couple of people, you weren't picked as a forward and you weren't tough enough to play the game.
> (Les Boyd quoted in, Masters, 1990: 33).

Predictably, illegal physical attacks were often met with extreme and equally violent response. Media headlines from *Rugby League Week* in the 1970s support this anecdotal evidence of extreme illegitimate player violence: 'Blood and Guts', 'Rugby League: 80 Minute Hate', 'Jump On His Head Big Jimmy!', 'Kill! Kill! Kill!' and 'Slaughter!' (Hutchins and Phillips, 1997: 163).

Compared to the 1970s, players in the 1990s display far greater discipline and respect for the rules preventing illegal violence (Hutchins and Phillips, 1997; Hutchins 1997a). One contemporary player acknowledges:

> They have taught me to control my temper even though Blocker Roach reckons I should keep the aggro . . . but in the modern game, you just can't afford to get into strife. I suppose its still there in a way, just more controlled. What I'm trying to do is harness it and use it to my advantage. (Craig Salvatori quoted in, Adams, 1994: 195)

This statement is linked to the various mechanisms that have been instituted since the 1970s to discourage players from 'losing their temper' and performing illegitimate violence. However, players have not lowered their propensity 'to get into strife' – change the way they store and use violence – independent of the sport's administration. Players interpersonal illegitimate violence has triggered measures to restrain violent on-field acts, and these measures have been implemented through the regulative apparatuses and/or administrative mechanisms (the structural level) controlling the sport. These mechanisms are both structurally and interpersonally constituted and operated, and have included:

> official policies that have increased volition of referees and touch-judges to caution, send-off or report illegally violent acts;
> the institution of a revamped player judiciary in the 1980s which handed down the severest suspensions in the game's history, and in the 1990s *insists* that players have a responsibility to ensure each others safety –

team-mate *or opponent* (Heads, 1992: 383-416; Mascord, 1995: 62);
calls for elimination of various forms of illegal violence by the media, spectators, television viewers, and officials (*Rugby League Week*, 1981-1985[6]);
and, the added threat of legal action claiming loss of income from victims of illegitimate violence (there have been at least 5 cases arising from incidents in 1985, 1987, 1988, 1991 and 1992, and one more publicly threatened in 1993[7]).

The objective of this synopsis is to highlight that processual development in forms of interpersonal rugby league player violence, be they expressive to instrumental or vice versa, must be considered historically and in the context of the overall figurational linkages at hand. Processes occurring at the structural level of rugby league social relations are interdependently linked in and through processes unfolding at the interpersonal level. They are functionally interdependent and are in no way reducible to one another (Elias, 1987: 77-78; Elias, 1986a: 52). Ultimately, a worthwhile analysis of transformations within sporting violence needs to take into account the complex web of interdependencies existing between the structural and interpersonal in social relations.

Case Two: Tension-Balance and Violence

Team sports can be understood figurationally. Attack and defence formations are dynamic units composed of players' standing, moving, passing and tackling in reaction to one another's actions: they are in constant interdependence (Elias and Dunning, 1986b: 199; Hutchins and Phillips, 1997: 170-171; Masters, 1995: 66). Players must also observe a sport's rules. Sporting regulations are seen by Elias and Dunning to control the "tension-equilibrium", or "tension-balance", of a contest (Elias and Dunning, 1986b: 201-204; Jarvie and Maguire, 1994: 134-136). Tension-balance refers to how, and to what extent, a sporting contest is regulated or de-regulated in order that a competitive match, or spectacle, is produced. The regulations of a sport are a pivotal mechanism in this production. For example, the rules control the polarities and dynamics between attack and defense formations in order that an even contest is played out (Dunning, 1986b: 208). Elias (1986b: 134-136) has highlighted that the rules significantly influence levels and degrees of sporting violence. This is particularly the case in rugby league, a code of football in which interpersonal violence is a key element in the game's competitive logic. The challenge for rugby league administrators is to maintain safety while allowing physicality (Stoddart, 1994: 29). It is therefore necessary to see how the elasticity and fixity of the rules (Dunning, 1986b: 208) over time has controlled and/or de-controlled player violence.

Up to 1995, a defining feature of rugby league is that its regulatory content and internal controls have remained remarkably fixed throughout the long-term developments of commercial and television involvement (Hutchins and Phillips, 1997). While Australian sports such as cricket, surf-life saving, and triathlon have substantially altered their content and form for these commodifying elements (Goldlust, 1987: 159-178), rugby league has been resistent to major rule alterations. The most significant modifications occurred prior to the game's rapid commodification in the 1970s, and since then changes have been comparatively minor (Phillips, 1997). It is paradoxical then, despite relative rule content stability, that violence is an area of rugby league where the tension-balance has been significantly re-adjusted. This has come about by the elimination of what Smith (1981: 6) terms 'borderline' violence, that is,

> ... assaults which, though prohibited by the official rules of a given sport ..., occur routinely and are more or less accepted. To wit: the hockey fistfight, the late hit in football, the high tackle ... These practices are tolerated and justified on a number of grounds, most of which boil down to some version of the "part of the game" argument.

Such borderline violence was a stable part of rugby league throughout the 1970s with referees and touch-judges only willing to act on extreme illegitimate acts such as vicious brawls and seriously injurious head-high tackles. Reinforcing this permissible violence was a judiciary handing out light sentences (Hutchins and Phillips, 1997; NSWRL Player Judiciary Minute Books 1970-1987).

The transformative forces in changing borderline violence standards did not come through major rule modification. Such major regulatory change, including the introduction of the 'play-the-ball' rule (1920s) and limited tackle football (1967), came prior to the 1970s (Phillips, 1997) – a time when social histories of the game depict rugby league as an often brutally violent sport (Moore, 1996; Writer, 1995). Critically, the rules necessary to lower violence were already largely in place, but policed laxly. The major impetus for tension-balance adjustment came through external controls of the game such as the judicial policy of the NSWRL, and its implementation of video taping of all games. Overall, the NSWRL utilised a stable rule structure, instructed referees and touch judges to be more vigilant in enforcing these rules, and strengthened external regulative mechanisms to revamp the game's tension-balance.

Case Three: Unplanned Consequences

Central to understanding figurational dynamics is the method by which Elias went about the problematic of social change. The sheer multiplicity of interdependent relationships connecting people and their actions dictates that social processes have many unanticipated and unintended consequences (Elias, 1970: 146). That is, unintended consequences inevitably flow from planned actions as no one actor or group has complete control of resulting social features (Dunning, 1992: 276). Elias explains that with

> the interweaving of innumerable individual interests and intentions – be they compatible, or opposed and inimical – something eventually emerges that, as it turns out, has neither been planned nor intended by any single individual. And yet it has been brought about by the intentions and actions of many individuals. And this is actually the whole secret of social interweaving – of its compellingness, its regularity, its structure, its processual nature, and its development; this is the secret of socio-genesis and social dynamics. (Elias, 1970: 12; Curtis, 1986: 58-59)

It needs to be qualified that this "relative autonomy" (Kilminster, 1991: xii; Mennell, 1989: 165-166) of social processes does not imply that figurational patterns and shifts are totally random or accidental (Sheard, 1992: 11). They are not. They are discernible and their trajectory can be traced over the long-term, thus explaining the need for historical examination. What the 'relative autonomy' of figurational processes highlights is that social power is viewed as micro-politically constituted through relentless change, flux and conflict, and no one group, individual, or even nation (Sheard, 1992: 11) can claim complete command of social relations, their negotiation, and outcomes.

For the NSWRL rugby league, an example of unintended consequences flowing from strategically planned actions occurred between 1980 and 1984. At the end of the 1970s junior footballers were preferring other codes, crowds were dropping, television popularity had slumped to its lowest point in 1977 with Walt Disney's 'Disneyland' consistently out-rating the match-of-the-day, and most clubs were technically financially insolvent (Masters, 1990: 33; *Rugby League Week*, 9 April 1977: 5[8]). The NSWRL accepted that the game had an image problem for several interlinked reasons, with a major one being the perception that the game was excessively violent. A 'crackdown' on 'thuggery' ensued. The player judiciary chairman, Jim Comans, sent an unambiguous message to illegally violent players: "If the offence is serious, it might happen once, even twice. But I assure you there will not be a third time for that player. He will be out of the game forever." (*Rugby League Week*, 20 May 1982: 8[9]). Importantly, the use of a video camera in every fixture gave the judiciary the means to police violence to an extent never before possible, and the highest average suspension in the game's history was enforced (Hutchins and Phillips, 1997; NSWRL Player Judiciary Minute Books, 1980-1984). The NSWRL General Manager also visited all clubs lecturing players on their responsibility in building rugby league's image through proper conduct (Heads, 1992: 405). Unfortunately for the NSWRL, these actions produced quite unanticipated consequences in terms of public opinion on rugby league violence. The extensive action to counter and discourage violence helped to produce a negative feedback cycle (Dunning, 1986a: 14-15; Elias, 1987: 48-49). In paying explicit attention to violence, the NSWRL instead contributed to a perception that the game was actually more violent than ever. A long-term ally of rugby league, *The Catholic Weekly* (7 March 1982), published a damning editorial, entitled 'Commercialism and football violence', and engaged in an acrimonious public exchange with the NSWRL President (*Catholic Weekly*, 21 March 1982). The nationally circulated *Sun-Herald* newspaper followed with a front-page report crying, "Catholics Slam League Violence" (Stewart, 1982: 1). In addition, a 1983 *Rugby League Week* (19 May 1983: 18-19[10]) Readers Poll showed only 22% of respondents believed the game had a good image, with declining crowds reinforcing this negative outcome. The lowest average crowd for any season on record, 6557, occurred in 1983 (*Rugby League Week*, 10 Sept 1986: 6[11]). The causes for this slump were principally ascertained in a research report on the NSWRL competition. It found that a popular image of rugby league was "of an aggressive, violent sport", and that *perceived* violence was a primary reason for people not choosing to support the code (Granville Management Syndicate, 1984). Another finding of this report was that media coverage over-emphasised individual violent incidents, rather than skill, tactics and team play.

The NSWRL actions to curb violence did not produce intended outcomes, at least in the short term, as they were subject to a multiplicity of interpretations and responses by millions of people, in this case the media and general public. In essence, the NSWRL experienced the 'relative autonomy' of interdependent social relationships. Despite what the intentions of social groups and individuals may be, consequences are governed by the innumerable power balances and interdependencies that govern social experience.

Case Four: The Media-Sport Production Complex

The most recent and substantial additions to figurational sociology literature have come through Joe Maguire and his work on sport commodification, globalisation, and the media. A touchstone of his approach is what he terms the 'media-sport production complex' (Jarvie and Maguire, 1994: 150-151, 233-234; Maguire, 1994: 251-254; Maguire, 1993b). It comprises three main figurationally constituted groups: sports organisations, media and marketing organisations, and media personnel. It is concerned with cultural flows and interdependencies at both the local and global levels, and more particularly, those generated within 'mediascapes'. By situating the nexus between media/sport/capital (Maguire, 1993b: 35) at the heart of the complex, it aids negotiation of the complicated interrelationships that constitute sports forms, products and images, and how these are projected and sold to large audiences. The following case study expands the scope of the 'media-sport production complex' to accommodate the issues of violence and gender in Australian rugby league. It is also hoped to demonstrate that figurational methodology is useful when adopting an interdisciplinary approach. In this instance, Maguire's media-sport production complex is bolstered by drawing upon key conceptualisations contained within Connell's (1987, 1995) theory of the 'gender order'.

When examining the development of rugby league media coverage into and through the 1990s, two themes rise to the fore: violence and masculinity. Gendered values play a crucial role in the interdependent dynamics and polarities of power in the media system (Creedon, 1994: 5). Therefore it is necessary to recognise the homosocial character of the Australian media, and its function in deciding "what the people get" (McKay and Middlemiss, 1995: 43). In rugby league, the assumed make-up of the 'people' and what they receive, by and large, excludes female involvement, experience, and opinion.[12] Privilege, glamour and respect are awarded to the male-only preserve of rugby league with its rationalised and normative aggression, violence, domination, toughness and injury (Hutchins, 1997a).

Resistance to the hyper-masculinity acted out on the football arena is effectively framed out by the sacred status accorded to rugby league within Australian sport and the media. To resist is to violate a firmly entrenched gender order[13] (Connell, 1987: 98-99). The disheartening experience of Australian female academic, Helen Yeates, when she sought to challenge the "shrill and insistent form of brash, heterosexual sporting masculinity in football reporting" (Yeates, 1995: 35), and the ex-nomination[14] (O'Sullivan et al, 1994: 110-111) of female experience within football and sporting discourse, is a telling case study. It also indicates how deeply this form of ex-nomination is embedded within the discursive practices of the sporting media.

Yeates (1992a: 17-20) wrote an article in *Social Alternatives*, entitled 'Women, the Media and Football Violence', which focused on an allegedly violent, off-the-field incident involving Queensland State of Origin players. The article also perceptively condemns the rugby league media for celebrating, trivialising or ignoring violence, using traditional phallocentric terms in reporting, and articulating images and representations of masculine superiority and strength, contributing to the "symbolic annihilation" (Hall, 1996: 41) of female experience in the media. It provoked strong negative reaction from a number of print, radio and television outlets, which regarded Yeates' article as an attack on rugby league, and Australian men in general. Yeates comments on the experience:

> My views were diluted, distorted, trivialised, overlooked and satirised. According to the media, I represented a threat to Australian manhood. I dealt with a volatile subject, the sacred cow of Rugby League, not fully understanding the passion and interest within certain sections of the community. (Yeates, 1992b: 135)

Sections of the media were disillusioned that someone, especially a woman, dare question their biological determinist and reductive view of violence and masculinity. As the *Courier-Mail* announced, Yeates was "A woman who won't play the game" (Brown, 1992: 15). Even those who agreed with the need to condemn aspects of rugby league violence often "appropriated it on their own terms" (Yeates, 1992b: 133), paying scant attention to anything Yeates had said about masculinity and violence from her critical feminist perspective, reverting instead to nebulous, simplistic explanation.

Media response to Yeates' article demonstrates the gendered character of the media-sport production complex (Hutchins, 1997a). It is not possible to isolate gender within the innumerable social and cultural interdependencies and processes flowing between sport and media institutions, or any other social institutions (Connell, 1987: 120). Currently, the sporting (and rugby league) gender order power balance is heavily weighted towards masculine values and ideals, and these are protected vigilantly, both implicitly and explicitly, by media personnel. Yeates' experience shows that there is a good case to be made that male dominance and monopolisation of sporting and media power relations privileges the "aggression/force/violence" tripartite. Interrelatedly, this serves to legitimise, and naturalise, the inferiorisation and marginalisation of women and their activities (Bryson, 1987: 356-359).

Conclusion: Strengths and Unities

Attempting to unravel the complex, multi-faceted social processes contributing to sporting violence, its standards, regulation, contemporary social make-up, and historical trajectories, is a difficult exercise. What has been offered here is an outline of a social theory seeking to traverse this terrain. Figurational sociology is an approach demanding historical evidence to provide substance to theoretical hypotheses. The brief analytical 'snapshots' of rugby league attempt to show how historical evidence complements theoretical concepts. Certainly, a theme of this paper has been to suggest that a socio-historical method can reveal more than may be otherwise concealed by a 'traditional' narrative historical method, or an ahistorical theoretical approach.

Figurational sociology offers valuable insight into a selection of issues, particularly violence, revolving around social relations and their processual character. It is reasonable for critics to be suspicious of possible inferences in the term 'civilising', lack of attention to gender issues, and commitments to analytical 'detachment' by some Eliasian practitioners. However, the question remains: is there any point in completely dismissing this voluminous and rich body of theory, and social and historical information on sport, and sporting violence? As a researcher, it is far more constructive to concentrate on strengths and unities between theories and methodologies, rather than weaknesses and disunities.

endnotes

1. Thank you to Janine Mikosza and Murray Phillips for their helpful comments on drafts of this chapter.
2 While this point in Dunning and Sheard's study has not been challenged for its accuracy, the historical basis of some of their findings have. See Collins (1995, 1996).
3. This is identified as a functional democratisation process.
4. Predominantly from *Rugby League Week*.
5. (a) From 1970-1987 – NSWRL Player Judiciary Minute Books.
   (b) From 1988-1995 – League Information Services Pty. Ltd.
   For full details of these sources see: Hutchins and Phillips, 1997.
6. P. Peters, 'Mortimer cover-up', *Rugby League Week* 19 March 1981, p.1; P. Peters, 'Truce! Wests-Manly war must end', *Rugby League Week* 2 April 1981, p.1; P. Peters, 'Easts Star "Blinded": new terror tactic', *Rugby League Week* 23 April 1981, p.1; I. Heads, 'Proof!', *Rugby League Week* 18 July 1981, p.1; P. Peters, 'Forrest kayo: "Filthiest ever!"', *Rugby League Week* 30 July 1981, p.1; P. Peters, 'Damn the wall of silence', *Rugby League Week* 13 August 1981, p.1; F. Hyde, 'Savagery!', *Rugby League Week* 11 March 1982, p.1; P. Peters, 'Head Hunters Beware!', *Rugby League Week* 3 March 1983, p.3; J. Harker, 'Ad Ban on "Brohman Incident"', *Rugby League Week* 31 May 1984, p.6; J. Harker, 'Gouging', *Rugby League Week* 19 July 1984, p.5; N. Waller, 'Exit a Champion', *Rugby League Week* 21 March 1985, p.1; I. Heads, 'Easy Prey', *Rugby League Week* 21 March 1985, p.7, and; I. Heads, 'Jack-Hammer! "Police spear tackle before someone gets a broken neck"', *Rugby League Week* 19 July 1985, p.5.
7. See: J. Curtin, 'Football "assault" settled', *Sydney Morning Herald* 16 April 1996; M. Gunn, '"Gouge" Threat', *Rugby League Week* 23 June 1993, p.5; J. Harker, 'Rogers to Sue Bugden', *Rugby League Week* 11 April 1985, p.5; P. Kent, 'Mario sued over tackle', *Sun-Herald* 21 Jan 1996, p.46; P. Kogoy, 'At last! Shearer awarded $60,000 for French "kiss"', *Sun-Herald* 12 Jan 1997, p.56; D. Page, 'Cry Foul!', *Rugby League Week* 3 July 1991, p.12.
8. G. Prenter, 'Disneyland out-rates TV league', *Rugby League Week* 9 April 1977, p.2.
9. B. Cummins, 'Gentleman Jim', *Rugby League Week* 20 May 1982, p.8.
10. 'The Facts: How YOU voted in THE POLL', *Rugby League Week* 19 May 1982, pp.18-19
11. *Rugby League Week* 10 Sept 1986, p.18.
12. For discussion of the exclusion of female involvement in media coverage of Australian Rules Football see: Poynton and Hartley, 1990.
13. The 'gender order' is defined by Connell (1987: 98-99) as "a historically constructed pattern of power relations between men and women and definitions of femininity and masculinity."
14. Ex-nomination: "A term coined by Barthes . . . to show how the economic determinants of a society are absent from representations of that society . . . The concept of ex-nomination can be extended to encompass other aspects of modern cultures, and in doing so further implications can be worked out. Just as capitalism is ex-nominated in the movement from economics through politics to ideology, so we find that there are ex-nominating processes involved in representations of gender, race and nation." (O'Sullivan et al., 1994: 110-111)

Abrams, P. (1980). History, Sociology, Historical Sociology. *Past and Present*, 87, 3-16.
Abrams, P. (1982). *Historical Sociology*. Somerset: Open Books.
Adams, T. (1994). *Hit Men: A tribute to league's tough guys*. Sydney: Ironbark.
Blok, A. (1977). Selbsthilfe and the Monopoly of Violence. In P.R. Gleichman, J. Goudsblom & H. Korte (Eds.), *Human Figurations: Essays for Norbert Elias* (pp.179-190). Amsterdam: Amsterdams Sociologisch Tijdschrift.
Booth, D. (1997). Sport History: What Can Be Done? *Sport, Education and Society*, 2(2), 191-204.
Brook, H. (1995) Queer Football: Feminism, Sexuality and Corporeality. *Critical inQueeries*, 1(2), 25-45.
Brown, P. (1992, April 22). Shaping up the big league. *Courier-Mail*, p.15.
Bryson, L. (1987). Sport and the Maintenance of Masculine Hegemony. *Women's Studies International Forum*, 10(4), 349-360.
Catholic Weekly. (1982, March 7). Commercialism and football violence. p.6.
Catholic Weekly. (1982, March 21). Two Sides of the League Controversy. p.11.
Collins, T. (1995). Rugby's Road to 1895. *Sporting Heritage*, 1(1), 36-51.
Collins, T. (1996). Myth and Reality in the 1895 Rugby Split. *The Sports Historian*, 16, 33-41.
Connell, R.W. (1987). *Gender and Power*. Cambridge: Polity Press.
Connell, R.W. (1995). *Masculinities*. St Leonards, NSW: Allen & Unwin.
Creedon, P.J. (1994). Women, Media and Sport: Creating and Reflecting Gender Values. In P.J. Creedon (Ed.), *Women, Media and Sport: Challenging Gender Values*. California: Sage.
Critcher, C. (1988). Sport and Society. *Leisure Studies*, 7(2), 201-208.
Curtis, J. (1986). Isn't it Difficult to Support Some of the Notions of 'The Civilizing Process'? Response to Dunning. In C.R. Rees and A.W. Miracle (Eds.), *Sport and Social Theory* (pp.57-65). Champaign: Human Kinetics.
Dunning, E. (1970). *The Sociology of Sport: A selection of readings*. London: Frank Cass.
Dunning, E. (1986a). Preface. In N. Elias & E. Dunning, *Quest For Excitement: Sport and Leisure in the Civilising Process* (pp.1-18). Oxford: Blackwell.
Dunning, E. (1986b). The Dynamics of Modern Sport: Notes on Achievement-Striving and the Social Significance of Sport. In N. Elias & E. Dunning, *op. cit.* (pp.205-223).
Dunning, E. (1986c). Social Bonding and Violence in Sport. In N. Elias & E. Dunning, *op. cit.* (pp.224-244).
Dunning, E. (1986d). The Sociology of Sport in Europe and the United States: Critical Observations from an 'Eliasian' Perspective. In C.R. Rees & A.W. Miracle (Eds.), *op. cit.* (pp.29-56).
Dunning, E. (1989). The Figurational Approach to Leisure and Sport. In C. Rojek (Ed.), *Leisure for Leisure: Critical Essays*. Hampshire: MacMillan.
Dunning, E. (1992). Figurational Sociology and the Sociology of Sport: Some Concluding Remarks. In E. Dunning and C. Rojek (Eds.), *Sport and Leisure in the Civilizing Process: Critique and Counter-Critique* (pp.221-284). Toronto: University of Toronto Press.
Dunning, E. (1993). Sport in the Civilizing Process: Aspects of the Development of Modern Sport. In E.G. Dunning, J.A. Maguire & R.E. Pearton (Eds.), *The Sports Process: A Comparative and Developmental Approach* (pp.39-70). Champaign: Human Kinetics.
Dunning, E. (1994). The Social Roots of Football Hooliganism: a reply to the critics of the 'Leicester School'. In R. Giulianotti, N. Bonney & M. Hepworth (Eds.), *Football, Violence and Social Identity* (pp.128-157). London: Routledge.
Dunning, E.G., J.A. Maguire & R.E. Pearton (Eds.)(1993). *The Sports Process: A Compara-*

tive and Developmental Approach. Champaign: Human Kinetics.
Dunning, E. & Rojek, C. (1992). *Sport and Leisure in the Civilizing Process*. Toronto: University of Toronto Press.
Dunning, E. & Sheard, K. (1979). *Barbarians, Gentlemen and Players: A Sociological Study of the Development of Modern Rugby Football*. Oxford: Martin Robertson & Co.
Elias, N. (1970). *What is Sociology?* London: Hutchinson.
Elias, N. (1978). *The Civilizing Process: The History of Manners*. Oxford: Basil Blackwell.
Elias, N. (1982). *The Civilizing Process: State-Formation and Civilization*. Oxford: Basil Blackwell.
Elias, N. (1986a). Introduction. In N. Elias & E. Dunning, *op. cit.* (pp.19-62).
Elias, N. (1986b). The Genesis of Sport as a Sociological Problem. In N. Elias & E. Dunning, *op. cit.* (pp.126-149).
Elias, N. (1987). *Involvement and Detachment*. Oxford: Basil Blackwell.
Elias, N. (1994). *Time: An Essay*. Oxford: Basil Blackwell.
Elias, N. & Dunning, E. (1986a) *Quest for Excitement: Sport and Leisure in the Civilising Process*. Oxford: Blackwell.
Elias, N. & Dunning, E. (1986b). Dynamics of Sport Groups with Special Reference to Football. In N. Elias & E. Dunning, *op. cit.* (pp.191-204).
Finn, G.P.T. (1994). Football Violence: a societal psychological perspective. In R. Giulianotti et al., *op. cit.* (pp.90-127).
Foucault, M. (1972). *The Archaeology of Knowledge*. London: Tavistock Publications.
Goldlust, J. (1987). *Playing for Keeps: Sport, Media and Society*. Melbourne: Longman Cheshire.
Goudsblom, J. (1987). The Sociology of Norbert Elias: Its Resonance and Significance. *Theory, Culture and Society*, 4(2-3), 323-337.
Granville Management Syndicate (1984). *Rugby League: The Management Ballgame*. Research Report. Granville: Granville Management Syndicate.
Gruneau, R. (1993) The Critique of Sport in Modernity: Theorising Power, Culture, and the Politics of the Body. In E. Dunning et al., *op. cit.* (pp.85-109).
Gruneau, R. & Whitson, D. (1993). *Hockey Night in Canada: Sport, Identities and Cultural Politics*. Toronto: Garamond Press.
Gunter, B. (1985). *Dimensions of Television Violence*. Aldershot: Gower Publishing.
Hall, M.A. (1996). *Feminism and Sporting Bodies: Essays on Theory and Practice*. Champaign: Human Kinetics.
Hargreaves, J. (1992). Sex, Gender and the Body in Sport and Leisure: Has There Been a Civilizing Process?. In E. Dunning and C. Rojek (Eds.), *op. cit.* (pp.161-182).
Hargreaves, J. (1994). *Sporting Females: Critical Issues in the History and Sociology of Women's Sport*. London: Routledge.
Hay, R. (1995). Sporting Traditions X – Another Viewpoint. *Victorian Bulletin of Sport and Culture*, 5, 13-14.
Headon, D. & Marinos, L. (1996). *League of a Nation*. Sydney: ABC Books.
Heads, I. (1992). *True Blue: The Story of the New South Wales Rugby League*. Sydney: Ironbark.
Heikkala, J. (1993). Discipline and Excel: Techniques of the Self and Body and the Logic of Competing. *Sociology of Sport Journal*, 10(4), 397-412.
Horne, J. & Jary, D. (1987). The Figurational Sociology of Sport and Leisure of Elias and Dunning: an exposition and critique. In Horne, J., D. Jary & A. Tomlinson (Eds.), *Sport, Leisure and Social Relations* (pp.86-112). London: Routledge.
Hunt, L. (1989). Introduction: History, Culture, and Text. In L. Hunt (Ed.), *The New Cultural History* (pp.1-22). London: University of California Press.
Hutchins, B. (1996). History Versus Sociology – Nascent Impressions. *Bulletin of Sport and Culture*, 9, 11-12.
Hutchins, B. (1997a). Mediated Violence: The Case of State of Origin Rugby League. *Sporting Traditions*, 13(2), 19-39.

Hutchins, B. (1997b). *Five Yards, a Cloud of Dust and a Bucket of Blood: Australian Rugby League Violence 1970 to 1995*. Unpublished Masters thesis. Canberra: University of Canberra.

Hutchins, B. & Phillips, M.G. (1997). Selling Permissible Violence: Australian Rugby League and Commodification 1970 to 1995. *International Review for the Sociology of Sport*, 32(2), 161-176.

Jarvie, G. & Maguire, J. (1994). *Sport and Leisure in Social Thought*. London: Routledge.

Kilminster, R. (1991). Editor's Introduction. In N. Elias, *The Symbol Theory* (pp.vii-xxv). London: Sage.

Layder, D. (1994). *Understanding Leisure Theory*. London: Sage.

Lynch, R. (1993). The Cultural Repositioning of Rugby League Football and Its Men. In A.J. Veal (Ed.), *First Steps . . . Leisure and Tourism Research in Australian and New Zealand* (pp.105-119). ANZALS Leisure Research Series, Vol. 1. Sydney: Australian and New Zealand Association for Leisure Studies.'

McKay, J. & Middlemiss, I. (1995). 'Mate Against Mate, State Against State': A Case Study in the Constructions of Hegemonic Masculinity in Australian Sport. *Masculinities*, 3(3), 28-45.

Maguire, J. (1993a). Bodies, Sportscultures and Societies: A Critical Review of Some Theories in the Sociology of the Body. *International Review for the Sociology of Sport*, 28(1), 33-50.

Maguire, J. (1993b). Globalization, Sport Development and the Media/Sport Production Complex. *Sport Science Review*, 2(1), 29-47.

Maguire, J. (1994). American Labour Migrants, Globalization and the Making of English Basketball. In J. Bale and J. Maguire (Eds.), *The Global Sports Arena: Athletic Talent in an Interdependent World* (pp.226-255). London: Frank Cass.

Mandalios, J. (1996). Historical Sociology. In B. Turner (Ed.), *Blackwell Companion to Social Theory* (pp.278-302). Oxford: Blackwell.

Mascord, S. (1995, August 16). Moore gets two for high tackle. *Sydney Morning Herald*, p.62.

Masters, R. (1995, Sept. 23). A Ray of Light. *Sydney Morning Herald*, p.66.

Masters, R. (1990). *Inside League*. Sydney: Pan Books.

Mennell, S. (1989). *Norbert Elias: Civilization and the Human Self-Image*. Oxford: Basil Blackwell.

Miller, T. (1990). Sport, Media and Masculinity. In D. Rowe and G. Lawrence (Eds.), *Sport and Leisure: Trends in Australian Popular Culture* (pp.74-95). Sydney: Harcourt Brace Jovanovich.

Moore, A. (1996). *The Mighty Bears: A Social History of North Sydney Rugby League*. Sydney: MacMillan.

Morrow, D. (1983). Canadian Sport History: a Critical Essay. *Journal of Sport History*, 10(1), 52-79.

Mouzelis, N. (1993). On Figurational Sociology. *Theory, Culture and Society*, 10(2), 239-253.

New South Wales Rugby League Player Judiciary Minute Books, 1970-1987.

O'Brien, P. (1989). Michel Foucault's History of Culture. In L. Hunt (Ed.), *op. cit.* (pp.25-46).

O'Sullivan, T., J. Hartley, D. Saunders, M. Montgomery & J. Fiske (1994). *Key Concepts in Communication and Cultural Studies*. London: Routledge.

Pearson, K. & McKay, J. (1981). Sociology of Australian and New Zealand: State of the Field Overview. *Australian and New Zealand Journal of Sociology*, 17(2), 66-75.

Pilz, G.A. (1982). Changes of Violence in Sport. *International Review of Sport Sociology*, 17(4), 47-72.

Phillips, M.G. (1998). From Suburban Football to International Spectacle: The Commodification of Rugby League in Australia. *Australian Historical Studies*, Vol. 29, No. 110, 27-49.

Poynton, B. & Hartley, J. (1990). Male-Gazing: Australian Rules Football, Gender and Television. In M.E. Brown (Ed.), *Television and Women's Culture* (pp.144-157). Sydney: Currency Press.

Rabinow, P. (Ed.) (1984). *The Foucault Reader*. Victoria: Penguin.

Rojek, C. (1985). *Capitalism and Leisure Theory*. London: Tavistock Publications.

Rojek, C. (1986). Problems of Involvement and Detachment in the Writing of Norbert Elias. *British Journal of Sociology*, 37(4), 584-596.

Rojek, C. (1992) The Field of Play in Sport and Leisure. In E. Dunning and C. Rojek (Eds.), *op. cit.* (pp.1-35).

Rojek, C. (1995). *Decentring Leisure: Rethinking Leisure Theory*. London: Sage.

Rowe, D. (1995). *Popular Cultures: Rock Music, Sport and the Politics of Pleasure.* London: Sage.

Rowe, D. (1996). Quest for Excitement: Sport and Leisure in the Civilizing Process. *Australian and New Zealand Journal of Sociology*, 32(3), 127-129.

Rugby League Information Services Pty. Ltd., Judiciary Statistics, 1988-1995.

Rugby League Week (1977-1993).

Sheard, K. (1992). *Boxing in the Civilizing Process*. Unpublished Phd. thesis. United Kingdom: Anglia Polytechnic.

Smith, M.D. (1981). Sports Violence: A Definition. *Arena Review*, 5(1), 2-8.

Stewart, A. (1982, March 7). Catholics Slam League Violence. *Sun-Herald*, pp.1-2.

Stewart, B. (1995). Editorial. *Victorian Bulletin of Sport and Culture*, 4, 1-3.

Stoddart, B. (1994). Sport, Violence and Modern Thought. *Sport Report*, 14(2), 29.

Stokvis, R. (1992). Sports and Civilization: Is Violence the Central Problem?. In E. Dunning and C. Rojek (Eds.), *op. cit.* (pp.121-136).

Struna, N.L. (1985). 'In Glorious Disarray': The Literature of American Sport History. *Research Quarterly for Exercise and Sport*, 56(2), 151-160.

Tosh, J. (1991) 2nd edition. *The Pursuit of History: Aims, Methods & New Directions in the Study of Modern History*. London: Longman.

Turner, N. (1996). Sporting Traditions X Revisited. *Victorian Bulletin of Sport and Culture*, 7, 15-16.

Watson, B. (1993) *Frank Zappa: the Negative Dialectics of Poodle Play*. London: Quartet Books.

Whimpress, B. (1996). Sporting Traditions X – The Debate Continues. *Victorian Bulletin of Sport and Culture*, 6, 12-13.

Whitson, D. (1986). Structure, Agency and the Sociology of Sport Debates. *Theory, Culture and Society*, 3(1), 99-107.

Wilson, J. (1992). Cleaning up the Game: Perspectives on the Evolution of Professional Sports. In E. Dunning and C. Rojek (Eds.), *op. cit.* (pp.65-95).

Writer, L. (1995). *Never Before, Never Again: The Rugby League Miracle at St George 1956-66*. Sydney: Pan MacMillan.

Yeates, H. (1992a). Women, the Media, and Football Violence. *Social Alternatives*, 11(1), 17-20.

Yeates, H. (1992b). The State-of-Origin: The Media State of Play. *Australian Journalism Review*, 14(2), 130-136.

Yeates, H. (1995). The League of Men: Masculinity, the Media and Rugby League Football. *Media Information Australia*, 75, 35-45.

Young, K. (1993). Violence, Risk, and Liability in Male Sports Culture. *Sociology of Sport Journal*, 10(4), 373-396.

Zolberg, V. (1987). Elias and Dunning's Theory of Sport and Excitement. *Theory, Culture and Society*, 4(2-3), 571-575.

A new look at soccer violence

ROY HAY

ACADEMIC INTEREST IN VIOLENCE AND SOCCER, like academic study of the game itself, is a very recent phenomenon. Until the late 1960s, football or soccer violence was not a matter of serious concern in academic or official circles in the English speaking world. The popular consensus, which had not been intellectually challenged, was that soccer violence only occurred in South America, southern Europe and Scotland. In the first two areas, a hot blooded Latin temperament and a general lack of self control was a sufficient explanation, while north of the border the religious divide between Catholics and Protestants underlay most of the violence. In England, the demise of folk football, prior to or during the industrial revolution, had put an end to the connection between football and violence and any subsequent outbreaks had a peculiar and specific rather than a systematic and structural explanation.

Soccer, deviance and the breakdown of social control

Concern with violence at an official level became evident in the late 1960s following a series of pitch invasions and scuffles involving rival groups of football fans.[1] Probably the first academic study appeared in 1971, when Ian Taylor, who had spent a year in the Sociology Department at Glasgow University, wrote an article for Stanley Cohen's *Images of Deviance*.[2] Taylor's focus was originally on Scotland though by the time this version appeared he was covering England as well and his thesis, in its original and unvarnished form, was that the football clubs had grown out of the working class and had been 'owned' in a fundamental sense by the working class who made up the vast bulk of the support. Since you did not commit *chien lit*, you did not shit in your own bed, people did not get involved in violence on their own turf. The collective forces of social control operated effectively. As the commercial possibilities of football became fully appreciated and football became a business, then the ownership of football clubs was gradually wrested from the punters by a new business class of owners. Deprived of their control, the fans lost the kind of respect for the turf which had previously guided conduct, and protest, accompanied by violence, followed. Taylor speculated that this response was an attempt to restore a traditional sense of control, in the absence of the kinds of reform which might have met the aspirations of the fans. It was an attractive, if simple, thesis, which owed a lot to the popular sub-Marxist critique of society of the time. Later criticism was to demolish both the empirical basis of the argument, because football clubs had always been business firms from the start of the professional game in the 1880s and there had been plenty of violence in the nineteenth century, and the theoretical underpinnings, as the sociology of deviance was challenged by other more hard-nosed paradigms.[3] But Taylor's prophetic conclusion that 'the soccer hooligan may begin to organise' was to be borne out in spades.

Ritual aggression and tribal anthropomorphism

In England, the successes of English clubs and the national team in the World Cup in 1966 led to an upsurge of intellectual interest in the game. This took various forms including the radical chic which led A J 'Freddie' Ayer, the philosopher, to the stands at White Hart Lane, and a more anthropological concern as Peter Marsh, Elizabeth Rosser, Rom Harré and colleagues left the dreaming spires for the wilds of Cowley and Headington to study the strange tribes who supported Oxford United.[4] The Oxford group were responding to what has also been seen as an offshoot of the 1960s revival of soccer and the general mood of liberation and popular protest, the appearance of violence on the terraces of England. The word 'appearance' is used here in a double sense. Marsh and his colleagues were interested in the rituals of behaviour, seeing much of the apparent violence as forms of posturing and display rather than actual, physical confrontation. Subsequent developments were to undermine this relatively comforting conclusion. But the question whether violence was appearing or re-appearing also needs to be addressed.[5] Was the post-Second World War period unique with its high attendances and apparently little violent behaviour? Desmond Morris continued the anthropological strand with his glossy illustrated work *The Soccer Tribe*.[6]

Failure of the civilising process

At the University of Leicester, Eric Dunning, joint author of a celebrated study of rugby union, *Barbarians, Gentlemen and Players: A sociological study of the development of rugby football*, published by ANU Press in 1979, turned his attention to association football and violence in the 1980s. He attributed the rise in violence to the failure of the civilising process The theoretical underpinning of the explanations advanced for the form of English soccer hooliganism from 1966-7 onwards by Dunning was the figurational sociology of Norbert Elias. Elias's argument was there had been a long-run decline in interpersonal violence associated with what he described as 'the civilising process'. It is a very complex middle level theory with strong empirical content.[7] Dunning strongly resists charges that the theory is evolutionary either in content or tendency.[8] As applied to football, especially soccer, by Eric Dunning and Patrick Murphy, it was used to explain the levels of violence and the form that violence took in the periods before the First World War and after 1966-7 as primarily resulting from the norms and the social conditions faced by groups of unincorporated young lower working class males. Where the processes of state formation produced a stable monopoly of the use of force, then citizens could operate in an environment in which overt force was neither required nor tolerated. The lower ranks of the working class were deprived to some extent of this experience. The 'ordered segmentation' of these communities produced a set of characteristic features among the young male members.[9] Their manliness depended on a willingness to fight in defence of local, parochial or tribal concerns. The particular form that the violence took was also shaped by government policies and political tactics, the media and the police. The level of violence was sometimes amplified and at other times played down by these authorities.[10]

Having embarked on a study of contemporary problems, Dunning and his colleagues also pursued the historical origins of football violence. The work of Tony Mason, John Hutchinson and Wray Vamplew had alerted them to the existence of soccer-related violence in earlier periods of the modern organised game.[11] So in a mixture of sociological and historical research they claimed to have discovered the roots of football hooliganism around the turn of the twentieth century when 'a much larger proportion of the British working class appears to have been less "civilised" than tends nowadays to be the case'.[12] Growing incorporation reduced the levels of violence in the period down to the 1950s (at least in England). The post-1960s explosion of violence was attributed to the growing power of the working class and a shift in intergenerational power, plus the advertising of the game as a place where fights and incidents regularly take place, thus making the game more attractive to rougher working class males.[13] Dunning's work has been challenged on theoretical and empirical grounds by R W Lewis, who argues that existing theories, including Dunning's, fail to place football adequately in its historical and social context. Moreover the statistical evidence compiled by Dunning and his associates involves double counting of incidents, inadequate categorisation, and misinterpretation of examples and leads to some inadequate speculation, thus exaggerating the extent of violence before 1914. Lewis also provides some Lancashire evidence which he asserts indicate that incidents of hooliganism were 'few and untypical'.[14] Dunning and his colleagues have responded with an extended critique of Lewis's article as 'bad history and bad sociology', characterising Lewis as empiricist and arguing that many of the latter's examples were open to more than one reading.[15]

Participant observation and the violent masculine style

The Leicester group was, however, the amalgam of two distinct styles, which have recently shown signs of bifurcating again. John Williams, a mainstream sociologist, was the man who did the field work among the fans for his thesis, while Eric Dunning was a collaborator with Elias.[16] Williams's participant observation of English fans at the 1982 World Cup finals in Spain, at the European championship game between Denmark and England in Copenhagen and Aston Villa supporters who went to the 1982 European Cup final against Bayern Munich in Rotterdam provided the centrepiece of the first book to appear from Leicester, *Hooligans Abroad*.[17] Williams was not the first participant observer of football hooliganism. Peter Marsh spent three years on the terraces from Southampton to Middlesborough, though the bulk of his work was done at Oxford and Milwall.[18] Williams, however, was the first to study the international dimensions of the interactions between fans of different nationalities and the authorities in a range of countries. His reporting, in conjunction with Dunning and Murphy, was based on a reading of the English and local press and some consultation with police and other agencies abroad, and the book itself concluded with a series of recommendations for policy changes to control football hooliganism, including the control of tickets for overseas matches, monitoring of travel arrangements, segregation of fans and a new role for stewards accompanying fans on away trips. This piece of social engineering was to bear fruit in the next few years, though its outcomes were not always as the Leicester group had wished or predicted.

In his most recent work Williams has become increasingly critical of the original Leicester paradigm. After aligning himself with those who criticise 'the latent evolutionism' of the Eliasian approach partly because of his reassessment of earlier episodes of football hooliganism, Williams suggests that the aura of 'irrefutability' surrounding the work of Dunning leads to an underplaying of important national and cultural differences in patterns and forms of hooliganism.[19]

> The theory underplays the more general importance of culturalist approaches, perhaps particularly those which examine the nature of, and shifts in, the cultural significance of the game in this country, and those structuralist perspectives which highlight key aspects of the constantly changing relationship between the state, football and the football audience.[20]

Needless to say, Dunning has responded vigorously, and one might think convincingly, to these charges.[21]

The Williams-Dunning-Murphy work was historically and sociologically informed and pioneering, though some of its limitations are becoming apparent. It was followed by some more controversial participant observational work by Gary Armstrong and Rosemary Harris among the fans of Sheffield, the Blades and the Owls, United and Wednesday. A proposed article by these two researchers provoked a response among referees (academic, rather than the football variety) which eventually led to an issue of the *Sociological Review* being devoted to the cultural aspects of football in August 1991. Part of the controversy arose from the trenchant criticism by Armstrong and Harris of previous work and their failure to provide a convincing theoretical justification for their own research. While it extended the coverage of ethnographic research, the typicality of Sheffield was much disputed and there was derision for the rather lame conclusion that the focus should be shifted to why some young men are drawn into groups which indulge in hooliganism and others are not. That these groups might have provided a supplement or substitute for the family for people drawn from all social classes did not appear to be a world-shattering revision of existing theory. The notion that football hooligans were a totally acephalous tribe was also criticised by Bert Moorhouse among others.[22]

Participant involvement

If participant observation was a key feature of the research of the 1980s another genre which emerged in the latter part of the decade can be described as 'participant involvement' represented by the work of Colin Ward, Jay Allen, Bill Buford and the Brimsons.[23] Ward, Allen and the Brimsons claimed to be the autobiographical works of self-described football hooligans, but Buford's account was a deliberate piece of slumming by the American editor of the Cambridge literary magazine *Granta*.[24] This is a shocking book, deliberately so. The author became involved after witnessing fans taking a train apart in Wales and then devoted eight years to an inside study of English hooliganism. Yet it is also a quite conscious attempt by the author to come to terms with his own feelings about violence. In describing the ways in which crowd behaviour escalates from collective solidarity into demonstrative behaviour and eventually what appears to be anarchy, Buford recounts his own dissociation from his normal values as he abandons himself into this moral void. He portrays the nihilism of the violent actions, relating it to feelings he had not had since he was a teenager. "Violence is one of the most intensely lived experiences and, for those capable of giving themselves over to it, is one of the most intense pleasures. What was it like for me? An experience of absolute completeness."

Buford's sources, apart from his own observation, are members of the various organised groups of fans who attached themselves to clubs, such as Manchester United's Red Army, newspaper cuttings services and contacts in the National Front. Aside from its description of the mentality and social experience of some soccer hooligans, the book makes some large claims. One of these is about the disappearance of the English working class. Nothing is left but a bankrupt style and violence for its own sake. As a kick at some sacred cows this is one thing, but as serious sociological observation, it is ludicrous. Pete Davies described *Among the Thugs* as a "meretricious, misleading, morally repellent piece of work" and it is hard to disagree.[25] The quotation comes from his book which is a much better guide to what soccer is all about. It has a much more balanced, if less involved, assessment of hooliganism too.

Allen's account is distinct from the others since it is the first inside story from a new group who apparently emerged in the later 1980s, the so-called 'casuals' for whom style and the voyeurism of violence were a major part of life. As police surveillance and crackdowns targeted the increasingly penned in working-class football fans, so street-wise kids treated the challenge to a series of finely orchestrated series of responses, which involved the emergence of the 'firms' and the 'casuals' – football-supporting and hooliganism became post-modern.

Reading the football hooligan, soccer becomes postmodern

Inevitably the study of football hooliganism became bound up in the development of postmodern critiques of society, though it is arguable whether there were any gains to be made as a result. There was some highly effective criticism of the solipsist tendencies of the postmodernist project at the Sport, Philosophy and the Olympics Conference at De Montfort University in 1996.[26] It is easy to guy postmodernism when applied to soccer hooliganism, and it is hard to resist this extract taken more or less at random from Giulianotti:

> Unlike the Scots, the Irish did not attempt to construct a symbolic "fusion of horizons" between themselves and other teams, which would have provided them with greater scope for popular cultural colonisation of those teams encountered in Genoa. The pre-eminence of secondary sub-discourse of instrumental sociability and self-regulation amongst team members when performing to the local, media and *prima facie* opposing teams has been noted consistently.[27]

My preference is for a more accessible account:

> 'We walked down to the Scotland versus Holland game with a couple of young Scots supporters and they said they were getting on famously with the Dutch. Evidence of this appeared when we got to the ground as a group of Dutch supporters in orange hair, orange faces, orange tops and kilts appeared. "Can you not make up your mind what you are?" I asked. In reply, one lifted his kilt and crossed his legs. Just as well, for he had nothing on underneath. "Dutch hermaphrodites", I said to Tony Mason.[28]

The work of Steve Redhead, Stuart Cosgrove and Giulianotti has not been without its value. Redhead, in particular, in teasing out connections between football, popular music and youth culture has helped in the process of demolishing simplistic connections between the sartorial style of football fans and a predilection for fascism.[29] Redhead argues that carnival rather than fighting has become fashionable at British sporting events, though this was written before the England match in Ireland last year, when there were reports of considerable neo-fascist involvement. Also a claim that most English, Scottish and Irish fans at Italia 90 behaved more like Italian spectators can be a somewhat double-edged compliment when you remember what the Ultras and the Tifosi get up to, or the Juventus fans when they met Manchester United in 1996.[30]

Manipulation from above and tackled from behind

Gary Armstrong and others have revived some of the manipulative models of society which were common in the 1960s and 1970s in relation to football hooliganism.[31] They argue that the authorities, particularly the police, have used a socially sanctioned campaign against football hooliganism to introduce surveillance methods and techniques which would otherwise have been pilloried and exposed by the civil libertarians. Most of this comment relies on Armstrong and Hobbs' article in the Giulianotti volume, since unsuccessful efforts were made to get hold of Armstrong's London PhD thesis 'Fists and Style' which is the basis of much of his evidence on the topic.[32] When Armstrong's arguments were put to police representatives at the *Football, the Law and Civil Liberties* Conference in Glasgow they were met by a response that the police were always fully accountable and a cautionary tale about what happened when a match commander who believed in treating fans like human beings was put in charge of a contentious game.[33] Subsequently the appearance of Armstrong's *Football Hooligans: Knowing the score* in early 1998 has provided a much more extended and nuanced account of the Sheffield experiences, though his publishers' claim that this is the first anthropological study of football hooliganism is ludicrous.[34] A biographical appendix of the Sheffield United "Blades" compiled on the way to an away game in April 1987 is designed to illustrate that there was no stable membership to this particular supporters group, though it is not clear how a single survey can illustrate dynamic and fluid cohorts over time.

Critiques and displacement, moral panics

Bert Moorhouse has always been very sceptical of much of the interpretative writing on football hooliganism in England, both because of his work on Scottish fans, particularly those who made the biennial pilgrimage to Wembley for the England versus Scotland game until that ended in 1989, and on general sociological grounds. The Scots got drawn into a moral panic and an English labelling process even though their behaviour had not significantly altered over the years.[35] More seriously though Moorhouse argues,

> 'The sober truth is that football violence is not a particularly large segment of all recorded violence and that one theoretically puzzling issue is why, given a high value on masculinity norms, heavy drinking and pre-existing social antagonisms in British society, football hooligans have not been a lot more violent'.[36]

Recent research tends to support this conclusion. 'It may be that even at their highest levels, arrest and ejection rates are representative of "run of the mill" behaviour at these events which requires official police intervention'.[37]

Cross-cultural comparisons

Moorhouse opens up the possibility of international comparisons of which there have been several of varying quality and depth in recent years. A pioneer was Alan Roadburg who tried to account for differences in level of violence associated with sport in the Britain and the United States. He was one of the few social scientists whose predictions were borne out in practice as he said there was no reason to expect that English football hooliganism would flourish in the United States in connection with the National Soccer League.[38] But that was true only because the league folded!

Bill Murray had done a piece of detailed work on the Old Firm, Rangers and Celtic, in Scotland and their fans, including a chapter on disturbances.[39] This is careful historical research with no taste of sociological concern or theorising, but it makes the point that the bulk of disturbances in Scotland seemed to have been linked to the Old Firm and religious rather than class differences. A highly polemical response to Murray's research by Gerry Finn adds a great deal of heat but little light to the topic.[40]

The work of Janet Lever for Brazil, Eduardo Archetti for Argentina and several Italian studies also have much to contribute, making evident the parochialism of much of the English analysis. H H van der Brug wonders why football hooliganism has taken on in Holland, Germany and England to a greater extent than in other European countries, but again the situation is neither as clear cut nor as static as this view implies.[41] A full comparative study has not really been attempted, though Philippe Broussard's *Génération supporteur: Enquête sur les ultras du football* comes closest from a journalistic perspective.[42]

Australian themes

i Perceptions

The Age
1 June 1985, p. 40

The study of sports violence and soccer violence in Australia is in its infancy. Wray Vamplew was one of the first in the field. His informants were a non-random selection of sports coaches, participants, administrators and academics researching in the area. He used a questionnaire which included the following questions: "In your opinion is the current level of violence in your sport 1 acceptable 2 excessive". Violence among players was defined by example as including foul language, racial or ethnic abuse, sexual harassment, verbal abuse of officials, physical abuse of officials, verbal abuse of other players, kicking, eye gouging, punching, biting, elbowing, head high tackles, tripping and other. For spectators, the examples were: foul language, racial or ethnic abuse, sexual harassment, verbal abuse of officials, throwing of missiles, drunkenness, running on to pitch, vandalism (Note the absence of physical abuse of officials or players from the categories of spectator behaviour). In each case respondents were asked to compare current experience with that of five years ago and in regard to spectators they were invited to rate spectator violence as 'no problem, exists but acceptable, excessive'.[43]

He analysed 906 responses, 675 males and 231 female, with 54 from soccer, 143 Australian rules, 69 cricket. 34 per cent of soccer respondents thought spectator misbehaviour was excessive, compared with 19 per cent for rugby league, 18 for rules, 16 for basketball and 10 for netball. Soccer was perceived as being particularly bad for throwing missiles, running onto the pitch, foul language, racial and ethnic abuse and abuse of officials. These are perceptions. Perceptions of more or less well informed people involved with the various sports, but they are not measures of the actual level of such incidents. Since perceptions are important in forming attitudes to games these may not be ignored but while they help identify a perceived problem, they don't necessarily give a firm statistical grasp on the issues identified.

In the media, the association of soccer violence has become a journalistic cliché producing some almost Pavlovian reactions. The Roth cartoon captures a widely held perception that Australian Rules is more violent than soccer on the field.

ii Balkan politics and displaced person syndrome

Phil Mosely has done some excellent detailed work on violence in soccer in Australia concentrating on the importation of Balkan politics in the post-war period.[44] More generally, in his original thesis and in subsequent work, he has linked violence in Australian soccer to the experience of the first generation of immigrants from war-torn Europe, with all their ethnic hatreds, and the idea of a 'displaced person's mentality' arguing that the disorientated and anomic individual was more prone to violence than settled members of Australian society.[45] Soccer as a sport which attracted the first generation migrants accordingly picked up the violence as part and parcel of the migration process. Different styles of play involving migrants from Britain and the continent also provoked conflict. This kind of work has moved the argument a long way forward, and by concentrating on certain key groups it has focussed research in a very interesting way. But there are problems. The Maltese had a deserved reputation for violence in Australian soccer. George Cross was suspended on occasion in Victoria and St Georges in New South Wales. The former drew referees' bans and so on. But the majority of Maltese were not DPs, had no great reputation for violence at home at matches, and political problems only with Germans and Italians, which one might understand, but Maltese violence does not seem to have been limited to those groups. More generally the recitation of a number of incidents and a brief examination of each based largely on newspaper reports carries certain inherent biases which need further exploration.

iii The BBB and Croatian identity

John Hughson in his PhD thesis has taken up the running with a close ethnographic study of the Sydney Croatian Bad Blue Boys, who model themselves on their counterparts in Zagreb, who followed Dinamo, now Croatia Zagreb renamed by President Tudjmann.[46] The original BBB are the subject of some fascinating analysis by Furio Radin, Minister for the Italian minorities in the Croatian Parliament, as they began to form a key part of the Croatian identity and independence movement, and later became a focus of the democratic opposition to Tudjmann.[47] Hughson has also produced a number of articles on the BBB and Croatian involvement in soccer violence and claims on that basis that Australian multicultural policy should be brought into question. The evidential base for this large demand is somewhat tiny, even within the Sydney

United club.[48] Similarly discussion about violent incidents involving Croatian and Greek fans needs to take account of the political context of Victorian politics as is done below.[49]

A new look?

Having spent much of the last five or six years trying to quantify changes in violence associated with soccer in Victoria using all the available sources, I have come to the conclusion that there is a strict limit on what can be achieved by this approach. There are no consistent series of records belonging to the soccer associations; the referees records are even more patchy; newspapers only report selected cases and even the specialist soccer press, when it exists, cannot be relied on to have covered each relevant incident. Police records do not distinguish soccer related incidents and it is only by a close recalculation of data at the watch-house level and the application of some fairly arbitrary judgment that one could construct anything from this material. For an attempt to make sense of some recent data see the work of my colleague Ian Warren.[50] There is the further set of puzzles related to the questions of variations in control and policing of incidents.

As a result I have turned back to what one might regard as traditional historical techniques for my new look at soccer violence. I now tend to believe that it is only be very careful and more wide ranging investigation of specific incidents that one can to a closer understanding of the dynamics involved. To give a flavour of that, the rest of the discussion is a consideration of three sets of incidents, in 1972 and 1994 and those in England in 1996.

The first of these might easily but misleadingly be categorised as a simple case of ethnic violence with a crowd invasion and an attack on a referee at a match between Croatia and Hakoah in Melbourne. However to understand the events of 1972, it is necessary to appreciate that changes in the structure of Victorian soccer in the 1960s had put the clubs in control. Collectively the clubs had great difficulty in disciplining members since they relied heavily, as many still do to this day, on a support base, particularly for finance, drawn from one specific community. Yet clubs and the Victorian Soccer Federation were prepared to act and several members were suspended for varying periods for various kinds of irregularities including on and off-field violence. Geelong (Italian) was suspended for four or five weeks in 1955, George Cross (Maltese) in 1949, Croatia in the most significant and controversial case in 1972.

There is a considerable range of sources available for the study of the last of these incidents, which has not been seriously examined before. There are newspaper reports, the transcript of court proceedings before Mr Justice Newton in the Supreme Court of Victoria, which cites the essence of the deliberations of the various Victorian Soccer Federation disciplinary bodies, the oral memories of participants on and off the field which have been recorded and those of Victorian Soccer Federation officials some of whom were key figures in the proceedings.

On 30 July 1972, Croatia played Hakoah at Olympic Park, which was Croatia's home ground at the time, in front of 1700 spectators. Croatia was fighting for a place in the top four, as was Hakoah. Jimmy Brennan was the referee.[51] Fifteen minutes into the second half, he sent off a Croatian full back Hugh Gunn. It appears that Gunn had made a series of strong tackles on the Hakoah winger, Bobby Saunders, who formerly played with AFC Bournemouth. The winger was described as a 'jumper' by his team manager Hedley Copeland. He made a meal of the tackles and Brennan decided to take action against Gunn.[52]

Two minutes later Brennan gave another foul against Croatia. According to Tony Vrzina, an eye-witness and an influential figure in the Croatian community and coach of several successful teams, Brennan then warned the Croatian player who had perpetrated the foul that a repetition would result in him being sent off too, and when he signalled this to the player by pointing towards the dressing rooms, the crowd interpreted the gesture as an indication that this player too was being dismissed.[53] The crowd invaded the pitch and the referee, the linesmen and some officials and players were punched and kicked (There was no mention of any weapons)[54]. According to Hedley Copeland, the players on both sides lined up to protect the referee, landing a few blows on spectators who were trying to get at him. The match was abandoned. There were five police in attendance, who were unable to prevent the assaults, but more police were summoned and matters were brought under control and the ground was cleared.

Frank Burin, an eye-witness and later team manager of Croatia, says that the young Croatian captain was in the mood to take his team off the field and waved in the direction of the Croatian youth on the terraces, perhaps inviting them to come over the fence. The trouble-makers were known to the club. Frank thinks it was inexperience on the part of the captain, Benec, or perhaps he was set up.[55] The first fans over the fence may well have been connected to the Croatian Youth in Carlton, which had had trouble with the police.

At the VSF Tribunal, chaired by Justice O'Connor, on Thursday 3 August 1972, Croatia was charged that it had failed to control its spectators resulting in the abandonment of the game and an assault on the referee and linesmen. The club criticised the referee. 'Because of his poor umpiring the public was upset and invaded the playing area'. Croatia had five paid police and officials who were themselves assaulted. No club would have been able to control the spectators. The Club deplore and 'are very sorry about these incidents which only harm our club's welfare and soccer in general'. The Tribunal unanimously found, 'Croatia Club failed in its responsibility to control the spectators and ordered that Croatia be disqualified from membership of the VSF. To the decision, the tribunal added, 'The tribunal feels that if strong action is not taken to compel soccer clubs to control spectators the day is not far distant when such behaviour will result in the death or serious injury of some persons.'[56]

Croatia appealed against the decision, but the Appeal Board on Tuesday, 8

August 1972 found Croatia guilty and disqualified the club from membership until the conclusion of the 1972 season. Thereafter it was specifically allowed to apply for re-admission, with the decision on that application being determined by the VSF in accordance with its Constitution and Rules.[57] Croatia did apply on 22 August 1972 in writing, but this application was refused.[58]

After a considerable debate within the club, Croatia then appealed to the Supreme Court of Victoria that the decisions of the Tribunal and the Appeal Board were invalid, that the club was still a member of the State League and that the club had not been guilty of an 'offence' in respect of which the Tribunal or the Appeal Board were empowered to impose any penalty on the club.[59] Mr Justice Newton found for the VSF and awarded costs against Croatia.

Whatever the outcome of the expulsion, many people connected with the clubs were convinced that Croatia had been victimised. Martin Groher of North Geelong Soccer Club believes that Croatia was set up, particularly by Tony Kovac, who was associated with the Footscray JUST club, and the fact that the match was against Hakoah, and hence seen by some as Nazi sympathisers (Ustashe) versus Jews, was significant.[60] The former Executive Director of the VSF, George Wallace, denies that Croatia was set-up and says that the matter was handled by the book by the VSF, as was proved in the subsequent court case. Both may be right. However, it seems that there were equivalent incidents that year which did not result in expulsion or comparable penalties, for example Sunshine George Cross versus Footscray JUST on 7 May 1972.[61] Enver Begovic was reported to have said that it was humanly impossible for club officials and police to stop a determined group of troublemakers from creating a disturbance at any sporting event. 'It has happened at four different State League rounds this season, yet charges have not been brought against any other club', he said. 'To disbar Croatia for an incident which it could not possibly prevent is both unjust and a threat to other properly administered clubs'.[62]

In the transcript of his judgment in the Supreme Court of Victoria, Mr Justice Newton referred to eight cases from a large bundle of case records submitted by the VSF. His references related to whether the charge against Croatia constituted an offence, and hence the selection and comment on these cases has to bear that in mind. Of the eight cases cited however, only one, that against Victoria Park Soccer Club, for an incident on 16 July 1972, dealt with on appeal by the Federation Tribunal on 2 August 1972, resulted in the disqualification of the club. In this instance it was from the District League for the remainder of the 1972 season. During the incident which led to the charge against Victoria Park supporters armed with knives, iron rods, umbrellas, stones and broken bottles invaded the ground and attacked the referee and opposing players. In the other seven cases dealt with, the penalties, for offences which all involved spectator incursions, ranged from fines of up to £100 to reprimands and requirements to supply two policemen to subsequent home games. In the case of one club, Kingsville, it was the second offence which resulted in a $50 fine and the instruction to supply police.[63] Now these cases may well exclude others where more severe penalties were applied including expulsion.[64] Fred Hutchison, referee and secretary of the Ringwood Wilhelmina club said that other clubs had been expelled and it was the fact that Croatia was regularly in trouble which led to the severe penalty in its case.[65] However, it is at least arguable that Croatia was treated with disproportionate severity in 1972. On the other hand Laurie Schwab and Craig Mackenzie's claim about 1972 that 'Everything went smoothly until there was crowd disturbance during a match at Olympic Park against Hakoah', will not stand up.[66]

There were politically inspired incidents after the Ampol Cup final between Croatia and JUST which led to an unprecedented VSF decision to have the league matches between Croatia and JUST played behind closed doors at a venue to be announced to the players only 24 hours before the game.[67] Both clubs appealed against the decision and it was eventually rescinded, leading to the resignation of the Chairman of the VSF John Gorton. He was reinstated a week later.[68] The two clubs were also required by the VSF to change their names to those of the districts in which they played. JUST protested on the grounds that following the amalgamation with Footscray it was now known as Footscray JUST.[69] So Croatia was in the VSF's bad books before the expulsion.

Tony Vrzina says that he went to the club and offered to negotiate with the VSF to ensure that Hakoah got the points from the game and that Croatia was not punished severely. This offer was turned down because it was said that Vrzina was only out to do down the reputation of the club following his resignation. Vrzina had recruited a star player from Croatia who had suffered a head injury and had drink problems. He was accused of not playing the new player, whom some believed should become coach. This was part of the reason for Vrzina's resignation.

It has been put to me several times that if Croatia had agreed to Hakoah getting the points then the expulsion would never have come about. But the leadership of the Croatian club, especially Enver Begovic, believing in the rightness of their cause refused to countenance such a concession. We shall probably never know for certain whether there was decisive political pressure to expel Croatia in 1972. It is however hard to accept that the expulsion of Croatia from the State League, North Geelong from the Provisional League and North Geelong from the Ballarat and Geelong District League in 1972 was just a series of coincidences.

The Croatian community was stunned by the expulsion. Many people severed their involvement with the game at this point and some never came back. Players, whose suspensions were lifted early in August, left for other clubs.[70] Billy Vojtek joined Sydney Croatia, Mackay went to Sydney-Hakoah, Bill McIntyre to Hellas and Kondarios, Turicar and Hadiavdic to Keilor-Austria.[71]

Others Croatians were equally determined to keep the community identity to the fore and continued to hold meetings every Tuesday even though the club no longer existed as a competitive entity. Subsequently, however, those involved changed tack and came back into soccer through Essendon Lions which was gradually taken over by the Croatian community.[72] Tony

Vrzina became President-Manager with Duze Zemunik as coach. Eventually Essendon Lions evolved into Essendon Croatia and then Melbourne Croatia, then Melbourne CSC now the Melbourne Knights, champions of the National League, the Ericsson Cup in 1994-5 and 1995-6.

Because Croatians had been using the soccer club as a focus for political campaigns, the expulsion incidentally proved effective in the sense that since that time Croatian clubs have been careful to maintain their opposition within the boundaries set by the national and state federations. One interesting point has been raised to me. There was no real ethnic conflict with Hakoah. Hakoah actually spoke for Croatia in the VSF tribunal. Conflict, if it existed, was with Serbians represented in VSF by Tony Kovac. Kovac died before I could interview him and so I have nothing from his perspective on why the ban was imposed. VSF sources deny any departure from the rules or ethnic bias. Fred Hutchison remembers it as the culmination of a long series of incidents and said the VSF was tired of Croatia. But what about George Cross, which was also involved in a series of incidents? It was Maltese. With whom did they have ethnic conflict? Italians or Germans?

The next pair of games I want to look at took place in 1994 at the same venue, involving teams from areas involved in territorial disputes in south east Europe, which had very different receptions, though as I will try to show, it was events off the pitch which gave them that. The first game I want to consider was a National Soccer League game on 6 March 1994 between South Melbourne (formerly South Melbourne Hellas) and Melbourne Knights (previously known as Melbourne Croatia) ended peacefully in a one-all draw. There was a crowd of 15,000, close to capacity at Middle Park, South Melbourne's home ground for over 30 years, though it has now been displaced to the Lake Oval (the Bob Jane Stadium) to make way for the Grand Prix. After the game, as the crowds left the stadium, a scuffle among a small group of supporters broke out and an elderly fan was struck 'by half a brick thrown into a crowd'.[73]

On the Monday headlines in the press included 'Racial row spills on to soccer field', (*Geelong Advertiser*), 'Violence erupts after soccer match (*Age*), but the context was more clearly given in the *Herald-Sun*, which had 'Kennett offer on feud' above a colour photograph of the injured Alex Karamitros in an extensive report on page three.[74] The front page repeated the photograph in close-up under the heading 'Fan felled, ten held in flare-up', which put the focus back firmly on the soccer. The match, far from being the cause of inter-ethnic violence, was rather caught up in what had erupted over the previous months in large part as a result of political decisions made by the Federal government in Canberra and the State government in Victoria. The rumbles following the terms of the recognition of Macedonia as the Former Yugoslav Republic of Macedonia on the one hand and Mr Kennett's apparent endorsement of the Greek position on the other came in the midst of, and helped to contribute to, rising tensions in the two communities in Melbourne. The Croatians had absolutely nothing to do with this in a political sense.

The soccer match however guaranteed a huge crowd as the two Melbourne teams vied for top spot in the NSL with an advantageous position in the play-offs at stake. The match was very exciting and could have been decided three minutes into injury time, but Australian skipper Paul Wade, of South Melbourne, fired a penalty kick wide of the goals. During the match, despite warnings from the soccer authorities to both teams and their fans, provocative banners were raised, very tentatively, by spectators. The Croatian youth flew Macedonian banners, while the Greeks, the Hellas Hooligans perhaps, had a Serbian flag on display albeit briefly. Both sets of younger supporters indulged in some fairly pointed chanting and there was a great deal of passionate support, but most of it directed at the result of the game. There was a stronger than usual police presence at the ground and virtually no trouble while the match was in progress.

At the end of the game, both sets of fans are inevitably intermingled on the bankings opposite the main grandstand and in the car park area. There is very little traffic control after major sports events in Melbourne, with the crowds usually left to sort themselves out. According to the *Herald-Sun* report there was a huge shouting match around 5 pm, about ten minutes after the end of the match, and some youths were throwing rocks, which are plentiful around the back of Middle Park. 'A man was charged with recklessly causing injury, while another nine between 17 and 63 were charged with resisting arrest, obstructing police and riotous behaviour'. The young reporter sent by the *Herald-Sun* had very little experience of soccer matches and according to the soccer correspondent behaved very naively.

The contrast needs to be drawn with the Victorian Soccer Federation Premier League final played on 25 September 1994, when the political atmosphere in Victoria had cooled considerably. This match involved Preston (Macedonian) and Port Melbourne (Greek) and once again was played at Middle Park, before a much smaller crowd, perhaps a tenth of that for the National League game. There was some shouting and chanting, some banging of the back of the stand, a couple of flares, a provocative banner, quickly confiscated, and one small disturbance during which a youth in a Macedonian top ran into a group of Greek fans in front of the social club, then sprinted away to the top of the banking where he quickly removed his top and put on another nondescript one. I thought at the time that this was the action of an agent provocateur. No arrests were made and the Preston, the minor premiers, won the match comfortably and were well received at the finish.

The lesson which I hope is emerging from this is that politicians have to be careful about their interventions in these areas, as do the police. If soccer was an independent dynamic and a cause of violence in an earlier generation, and I think that is very arguable, then it no longer is and has become more the victim of, rather than the trigger for socio-political issues. The image of the game remains, despite the best efforts of the Associations and the clubs, which have accepted the process of downplaying traditional symbols, including long time club names, even if somewhat reluctantly at first. Commercial pressures, sponsorship, and the critical need to manage a successful transition from the generations who built up the sport in Australia in the 1950s and 1960s to younger people, born in Australia, to whom the game inevitably means somewhat less, are combining to encourage clubs to go down the path of community and locality identification, rather than ethnic exclusiveness. Examples include Morwell Falcons, Wollongong Wolves, Brisbane Strikers and the revived Newcastle Breakers. Even the big city clubs like Croatia, now the Knights in Melbourne and United in Sydney, Olympic and South Melbourne are setting off down the same road.

I suggest that we need to adopt a similar approach if we are to make sense of the Trafalgar Square riots during the European Football Championships in England in June. After England's defeat in the semi-final by Germany there was a major gathering in central London that night and what began as a wake ended up with police baton charges and mayhem. In several other parts of England there were reports of riotous incidents and a young Russian student was stabbed because it is said his assailants thought he was German. Frank Keating has recently claimed that the violence was covered up by the media and authorities, by the former in shame at the ways in which they had contributed to fomenting the xenophobia surrounding the later stages of the championship. I can only report that I had copies of all the material relating to the violent incidents in my files within forty-eight hours of the events and did not see any signs of a cover up, more something which could be explained by timing, since the troubles occurred too late to be picked up by the morning papers and there are very few afternoon editions in England these days.

In a recent study David Waddington has developed what he calls a flashpoint theory of social disorders to explain how public gatherings sometimes turn into riots.[75] Waddington admits that football hooliganism does not fit his model.[76] He finishes with a quote from Dick Holt about the difficulty of disentangling old and new in social history. Yet the kind of approach Waddington's work represents seems to me suggestive.

I believe we do need thick description in Geertz's sense, and close historical analysis. Riots and hooliganism are seldom, if ever, reducible to a single historical cause. Riots change in character as they proceed because of the interactions between the rioters, bystanders and authorities and hence the perceptions of the various groups can be very different, thus producing the greater likelihood of escalating conflict and certainly differing accounts of what transpired. The external context for hooliganism may be vital. This can include structural factors and direct interventions by politicians and the media which raise the temperature making trouble more likely. Here I think there is a link to Waddington's flashpoint theory. Then again fashions change and people respond. Today's violence will not be the same as yesterday's. The problem with soccer of course is that it is just too popular.

Nowadays there is bound to be one incident of violence associated with soccer somewhere in the world on any given day. It will be picked up by the news services and chances are that it will be the item which will appear on soccer in the Australian mainstream press. Even the sending off of an Argentinian polo player for violent conduct in a match involving Kerry Packer's team somehow turned up in the *Herald-Sun* under the heading 'Soccer' and a soccer ball logo. Is the link between soccer and violence so deeply buried in the sub-editor's psyche that this is the result, or is there a more prosaic explanation?

Herald Sun, Thursday, June 17, 1993

SOCCER

BILLIONAIRE Kerry Packer's star player, Argentinian Gonzalo Pieres, is facing a heavy fine and a possible worldwide suspension for recent bad behavior.

Pieres allegedly committed an act of "dangerous riding", after which countryman Sebastian Merlos lay sprawled on the turf, while playing for Packer's Ellerston White team against the Black Bears in the Queen's Cup final at Windsor on June 6.

endnotes

1 *Soccer hooliganism: A preliminary report to Mr Dennis Howell, Minister of Sport*, by a Birmingham Research Group, Directed by Dr J A Harrington, Bristol, John Wright and Sons, 1968; *Report of the working part on crowd behaviour at football matches*, London, Ministry of Housing and Local Government, 1969.

2 Ian Taylor, 'Soccer Consciousness and Soccer Hooliganism', in Stanley Cohen, ed., *Images of Deviance*, Penguin, London, 1971, pp. 134-164.

3 Taylor modified his original thesis in the light of subsequent research, see 'On the sports violence question: Soccer hooliganism revisited', in John Hargreaves, ed., *Sport, Culture and Ideology*, London, Routledge and Kegan Paul, 1982.

4 Peter E Marsh, Elizabeth Rosser and Rom Harré, *The rules of disorder*, London, Routledge and K. Paul, 1978

5 Geoffrey Pearson, *Hooligan: A history of respectable fears*, London, Macmillan, 1983, pp. 29-31, concludes, 'The realities of pre-war football do not find agreement with post-war nostalgia'.

6 Desmond Morris, *The soccer tribe*, London, Cape, 1981.

7 For a very brief introduction see, Eric Dunning, 'The social roots of football hooliganism: A reply to critics of the Leicester school', in Richard Giulianotti, Norman Bonney and Mike Hepworth, eds, *Football Violence and Social Identity*, Routledge, London, 1994, pp. 145-49; See also, Norbert Elias and Eric Dunning, *Quest for excitement: Sport and leisure in the civilising process*, Oxford, Blackwell, 1986.

8 Dunning, *Reply*, pp. 145-149.

9 Drawing on the theories of Gerald Suttles, *The social order of the slum: Ethnicity and*

territory in the inner city, Chicago, University of Chicago Press, 1968; *The social construction of communities*, Chicago, University of Chicago Press, 1972.

10 Eric Dunning, '"Culture", "Civilisation" and the sociology of sport', *Innovation in Social Sciences Research*, 5, No. 4, 1992, pp. 7-18.

11 Tony Mason, *Association football and English society, 1863-1915*, Sussex, Harvester Press, 1980; John Hutchinson, 'Some aspects of football crowds before 1914', *The Working Class and Leisure*, Conference of the Society for the Study of Labour History, Sussex, 1975; Conference report, *Society for the Study of Labour History Bulletin*, 32, Spring 1976, pp. 10-12; Wray Vamplew, 'Ungentlemanly conduct: The control of soccer crowd behaviour in England 1888-1914', in T C Smout, ed., *The Search for wealth and stability: Essays in economic and social history presented to M W Flinn*, London, Macmillan, 1979, pp. 139-154.

12 Eric Dunning, Patrick Murphy and John Williams, *The roots of football hooliganism : an historical and sociological study*, London, Routledge, 1989, p. 230.

13 This is a close paraphrase of ibid, pp. 232-234. Liberal and progressive ideas and decriminalising legislation also had to bear a share of the blame.

14 R W Lewis, 'Football hooliganism in England before 1914: A critique of the Dunning thesis', *International Journal of the History of Sport*, 13, 1996, pp. 310-339.

15 Patrick Murphy, Eric Dunning and Joseph Maguire, 'Football spectator violence and disorder before the First World War: A reply to R W Lewis', *International Journal of the History of Sport*, 15, 1998, pp. 141-162.

16 Norbert Elias and Eric Dunning, *Quest for excitement: Sport and leisure in the civilising process*, Oxford, Blackwell, 1986.

17 John Williams, Eric Dunning and Patrick Murphy, *Hooligans abroad: The behaviour and control of English fans in continental Europe*, London, Routledge and Kegan Paul, 1984.

18 Peter Marsh, 'Life and careers on the soccer terraces', in Roger Ingham et al, *'Football Hooliganism': The wider context*, London, Inter-Action Inprint, 1978, pp. 61-81.

19 J Horne and D Jary, 'The figurational sociology of sport and leisure of Elias and Dunning: An exposition and critique', in J Horne, D Jary and A Tomlinson, eds, *Sport, leisure and social relations*, London, Routledge, 1987, p. 100.

20 John Williams and Steven Wagg, eds, *British football and social change: Getting into Europe*, Leicester, Leicester University Press, 1991, p. 177.

21 Eric Dunning, 'The social roots of football hooliganism: A reply to critics of the Leicester school', in Richard Giulianotti, Norman Bonney and Mike Hepworth, eds, *Football Violence and Social Identity*, Routledge, London, 1994, pp. 137-155.

22 H F Moorhouse, 'Football hooligans: Old bottles, new whines?', *The Sociological Review*, 39, No. 3, August 1991, p. 500.

23 Colin Ward, *Steaming in: Journal of a football fan*, London, Simon and Schuster, 1989; Jay Allan, *Bloody Casuals: Diary of a football hooligan*, Famedram, 1989; Bill Buford, *Among the thugs*, New York, Vintage Departures, 1993, Originally published London, Martin Secker & Warburg, 1991; Dougie and Eddy Brimson, *Everywhere we go: Behind the matchday madness*, London, Headline, 1996.

24 In what follows I am plagiarising my review of Buford in *Mattoid*, 48, 1994, pp. 259-260.

25 Pete Davies, *Twenty-Two Foreigners in Funny Shorts*, Random House, New York, 1994, p. 268.

26 Roy Hay, *Sport, Philosophy and the Olympics*, Second annual conference on Philosophical Issues in Sport and Physical Education, Maryland College, Woburn, 15 to 17 March 1996, Centre for Applied Sports Philosophy and Ethics Research (CASPER) at De Montfort University's Bedford Campus, sponsored by International Centre for Research on Sports History and Culture, De Montfort University,

Leicester, *Victorian Bulletin of Sport and Culture*, Victoria University of Technology, 7, June 1996, pp. 11-12.
27 Richard Giulianotti, 'Scotland's tartan army in Italy: The case for the carnivalesque', *The Sociological Review*, 39, No. 3, August 1991, p. 515.
28 Roy Hay, 'Euro 96 Diary Day Three', *Australian and British Soccer Weekly*, 25 June 1996, p. 23.
29 Steve Redhead, 'Football and youth culture in Britain', in John Williams and Steven Wagg, eds, *British football and social change: Getting into Europe*, Leicester, Leicester University Press, 1991, pp. 145-159.
30 'Manchester United fans want action from UEFA after claiming they were subjected to violent treatment during Wednesday's European Cup match against Juventus in Turin'. Manchester, England Sep 13, 1996 – 15:17 EST, (c) 1996 Copyright Nando.net (c) 1996 Reuter Information Service.
31 Gary Armstrong and Dick Hobbs, 'Tackled from behind', in Richard Giulianotti, Norman Bonney and Mike Hepworth, eds, *Football Violence and Social Identity*, Routledge, London, 1994, pp. 196-228.
32 In April 1997, I was told by the Graduate Studies section of University College, London that the thesis was currently not available for consultation because it contained 'sensitive material'!
33 Roy Hay, *Football, the Law and Civil Liberties*, Royal Scottish Academy of Music and Dance, Renfrew Street, Glasgow, Tuesday 26 March 1996, Scottish Council for Civil Liberties and the Scottish Trades Union Congress, sponsored by the *Scotsman* newspaper, *Victorian Bulletin of Sport and Culture*, Victoria University of Technology, 7, June 1996, pp. 12-14.
34 Gary Armstrong, *Football hooligans: Knowing the score*, Oxford, Berg, 1998.
35 H F Moorhouse, 'Scotland against England: Football and popular culture', *International Journal of the History of Sport*, 4, September 1987, pp. 189-202; H F Moorhouse, 'Football hooligans: Old bottles, new whines?', *The Sociological Review*, 39, No. 3, August 1991, pp. 489-502.
36 ibid. p. 493.
37 Ian Warren, *Cultures of control: Law, Enforcement and public order at sporting events: A comparative approach*, University of Melbourne MA, 1996, pp. 26-7.
38 Alan Roadburg, 'Factors precipitating fan violence: a comparison of professional soccer in Britain and North America', *British Journal of Sociology*, 31, 1980, pp. 265-276.
39 Bill Murray, *The Old Firm: Sectarianism, sport and society in Scotland*, Edinburgh, John Donald, 1984, Chapter 7, 'The riots and the fans', pp. 163-189.
40 G P T Finn, 'Racism, religion and social prejudice: Irish catholic clubs, soccer and Scottish society – I The historical roots of prejudice, *International Journal of the History of Sport*, 8, 1991, pp. 72-95; G P T Finn, 'Racism, religion and social prejudice: Irish catholic clubs, soccer and Scottish society – II Social identities and conspiracy theories', *International Journal of the History of Sport*, 8, 1991, pp. 370-397.
41 H H van der Brug, 'Football hooliganism in the Netherlands', in Richard Giulianotti, Norman Bonney and Mike Hepworth, eds, *Football Violence and Social Identity*, Routledge, London, 1994, pp. 174-195.
42 I owe this reference and much else besides to Bill Murray. For a sane discussion of the issue of hooliganism see his *The World's Game: A history of soccer*, University of Illinois Press, Urbana, 1996, pp. 162-171.
43 Wray Vamplew, 'Sports crowd disorder: An Australian survey', in John O'Hara, ed., *Crowd violence at Australian sport*, ASSH Studies in Sports History, No. 7, Australian Society for Sports History, Campbelltown, 1992, pp. 79-111.
44 Philip Mosely, 'Balkan politics in Australian soccer', in John O'Hara, ed., *Ethnicity and soccer in Australia*, ASSH Studies in Sports History, No. 10, Australian Society

for Sports History, Campbelltown, February 1994, pp. 33-43; Philip Mosely, *Ethnic involvement in Australian soccer, 1950-1990*, Canberra, Australian Sports Commission, 1995, Chapter 6, Violence – a case study of the Balkan communities, pp. 64-72.

45 Philip Mosely, 'European immigrants and soccer violence in New South Wales, 1949-1959', *Journal of Australian Studies*, 40 March 1994, pp. 14-26.

46 John E Hughson, *A feel for the game: An ethnographic study of soccer support and identity*, Ph D, University of New South Wales, 1996.

47 Roy Hay, *Football in Europe*, Sir Norman Chester Centre for Football Research, University of Leicester and the International Centre for Sports History and Culture at De Montfort University, hosted the Football in Europe Conference at Leicester City Soccer Club, 30-31 May 1996 *Bulletin of Sport and Culture*, Victoria University of Technology, 8, September 1996, pp. 10-12.

48 John Hughson, 'The Bad Blue Boys and "the magical recovery" of John Clarke', in Gary Armstrong and Richard Giulianotti, eds, *Entering the Field: Studies in World Football*, Oxford, Berg, 1997, pp. 239-259; John Hughson, 'Football, folk dancing and fascism: diversity and difference in multicultural Australia, *Australia and New Zealand Journal of Sociology*, 33, 1977, pp. 167-186.

49 Hughson, *Football, folk-dancing and fascism*, p. 183, fn. 8.

50 Ian Warren, *Cultures of control: Law, Enforcement and public order at sporting events: A comparative approach*, University of Melbourne MA, 1996.

51 According to George Wallace, Brennan was much affected by these events, though he continued to referee. He is alleged to have committed suicide in 1984 or 1985.

52 Hedley Copeland in conversation at meeting of Victorian chapter of ASSH, Adam Street, Burnley, 4 October 1993. Copeland attended the subsequent meeting of the tribunal and spoke on behalf of Gunn and Croatia. At the tribunal Gunn was acquitted when he appeared on a charge of violent conduct. *Sun*, 10 August 1972, p. 62.

53 Discussion with Tony Vrzina at Fawkner, 5 September 1993, following the Premier League semi-final. Vrzina had resigned as coach of Croatia earlier in the year after recruiting players from overseas during a pre-season trip. There was disagreement among the committee according to the *Age*, 17 April 1972, p. 22. Vrzina had been with the club for two seasons and he won the Ampol Cup with Croatia at the start of the season, beating JUST 2-1 in a violent final. *Age*, 11 March 1972, p. 28. The replayed semi-final with George Cross also had fiery incidents. *Age*, 4 March 1972, p. 27 and 9 March 1972, p. 28.

54 According to the AUP report in the Geelong Advertiser, 500 people stormed on to the ground. The referee was escorted from the ground by police, he was not injured. No arrests were made. The police locked the gates and ushered people out of the ground. 'The treasurer of the Croatia club Mr Husein Plecic said yesterday his club's followers were tired of unfair refereeing'. *Geelong Advertiser*, 31 July 1972.

55 Interview with Frank Burin, 31 Jan. 1994, tape recording in possession of the author.

56 *ibid*, p. 19

57 Decision of the Appeal Board of the VSF 8 August 1972, VSF Files at Soccer House. See also *Sun*, 10 August 1972, p. 62; *ibid.*, 11 August 1972, p. 48.

58 Enver Begovic and others v Michael Parker and others, Judgment by Mr Justice Newtown of the Supreme Court of Victoria, 3 May 1973, pp. 2-3.

59 *ibid*, p. 3

60 Harry Mrksa also believes that Kovac, JUST and the Yugoslav authorities were instrumental in putting pressure on the VSF directly and through Jewish members

of the Federation, interview with Harry Mrksa, 27 May 1993, tape recording in possession of the author.

61 *The Age*, 8 May 1972.

62 *Sun*, 10 August 1972, p. 62.

63 Enver Begovic and others v Michael Parker and others, Judgment by Mr Justice Newtown of the Supreme Court of Victoria, 3 May 1973, pp. 21-3 and 29-34.

64 Geelong Soccer Club, playing as IAMA was suspended for four weeks in 1955, *Geelong Advertiser*, 25 July 1955 and Goodchild Soccer Club was expelled in June 1956 "for failure to comply with League requirements on club management and other matters". *Soccer News*, 30 June 1956, p. 4.

65 Interview with Fred Hutchison, tape recording in possession of the author.

66 *Soccer Action*, 19 October 1983, pp. 8-9.

67 Jack Pollard, *Ampol's Australian Sporting Records*, 1968, p. 250.; *Age*, 22 April 1972, p. 27.

68 Pollard, *op. cit.*, p. 250. The meeting of the Tribunal was scheduled for Monday, 15 May 1972, *Age*, 3 May 1972, p. 24.

69 *Age*, 26 April 1972, back page.

70 *Sun*, 11 August 1972, p. 48.

71 *Soccer Action*, 19 October 1983, pp. 8-9.

72 Tony Vrzina was invited to coach Essendon Lions in July 1974. He saved the Ukrainian team from relegation and during the next season he was instrumental in the Croatian players and officials taking over, paying their predecessors $25,000 for the clubrooms and facilities at Montgomery Park. Notes on an interview with Tony Vrzina at Hilton Hotel prior to AC Milan press conference, 17 June 1993.

73 *Age*, 7 March 1994, p.

74 *Geelong Advertiser*, *Age*, and *Herald-Sun*, 7 March 1994.

75 David P Waddington, *Contemporary issues in public disorder : a comparative and historical approach*, London, Routledge, 1992.

76 ibid, p. 138.

Order and Disorder at Sporting Venues

IAN WARREN AND ROY HAY

Introduction

THE MAINTENANCE OF PUBLIC SAFETY at large-scale events in Australia will be a key issue in the next few years. World attention will be focussed on Sydney for the Olympic Games in the year 2000 and the safety of athletes and visitors during the games will be a major concern in the build up to this event.[1] Many of the approaches to order maintenance in this environment will be drawn from existing practices at popular domestic events, where, comparatively speaking, Australia has witnessed only sporadic incidents of disorder throughout history.

The maintenance of order and crowd safety at major sporting events presents several dilemmas for public and private law enforcers, and event organisers. An extensive body of literature has attempted to identify the precise causes of spectator violence at major public events, and has produced a wide variety of explanations for crowd violence.[2] These explanations have considerable influence on the way in which spectator behaviour is viewed by authorities and the broader community, and on the measures adopted to avert the possibility of crowd disorder at sporting events.

Defining and measuring the incidence of spectator violence is difficult. Police statistics on charges laid under the authority of the criminal law provide the clearest measure of the frequency of violent incidents, which are deemed to require official action in the sports environment. Trivizaz[3] analysed a total of 652 charges laid by police between 1974 and 1976 in the London metropolitan region. He found that only 52 (8%) of these charges were for criminal assaults, 50 of which were assaults on police. Warren's research at Australian Rules football matches at the Melbourne Cricket Ground and Football Park in Adelaide shows a similar pattern.[4] Of the 760 charges or ejections recorded by police at the Melbourne Cricket Ground between 1991 and June

1994, 39 (5.2%) involved criminal assaults. Of 465 arrests and ejections at Football Park over the same period, 25 (5.4%) involved criminal assaults. However such data needs to be treated with caution, as they may be a better reflection of police activity rather than an indication of the overall pattern of violence amongst sports spectators. Police decisions to arrest, charge, or merely warn an individual are based on a combination of factors, including the content of the law, the demeanours of the citizen and police member, and the potential threats the incident presents to those nearby.[5] In addition, most findings from these studies involve records of contacts between the police and individuals designed to prevent or minimise the prospect of collective violence. Most routine interactions between police and sports spectators involve responses to minor disorder, rather than collective or criminal violence.

Studies such as those by Cunneen[6] Cashman,[7] Dunning, Murphy and Williams,[8] Vamplew,[9] Cantelon and Gruneau,[10] and Giulianotti[11] all indicate that mass disorderly behaviour can and often does occur at sporting events. Debate remains about the frequency of collective violence, and there are numerous problems with predicting when such behaviour will occur. Many incidents of collective deviance are glorified in spectator folklore, or are the subject of considerable media publicity or political debate. This can distort the way in which each incident transpires in its specific context, and may lead to unduly negative or uninformed political decisions and community perceptions about the nature of spectator behaviour in certain sports. Many of the approaches to the study of spectator violence disregard the specific dynamics of collective disorder at each event site, and are laden with various political or cultural biases which may affect the ways in which incident is interpreted by the public. This can have both positive and negative effects on the perceptions of crowd behaviour at sporting events in different time periods or in various political circumstances.

For example, after a series of 'riotous' events in Melbourne during the 1997 National Soccer League elimination finals,[12] local concern was raised about the extent to which European 'hooligan' culture was permeating Australian soccer. In these depictions of Australian soccer, comparisons are frequently made between the deviance of soccer spectators, and the good behaviour of Australian Rules or Rugby League crowds.[13] Such accounts, as Hay suggests,[14] have the potential to distort our understanding of the true frequency of spectator violence at various sports, and our perception of the causes of, and the factors, which might contribute to these incidents.

Cunneen et al[15] indicate that there is a complex interplay of factors which need to be considered when examining collective behaviour at sporting events. Any critical understanding of spectator violence should go beyond examining the behaviours of spectators alone.[16] Spectators, police, security personnel, and stadium managers interact in various ways at various times in the context of each event. These interactions are influenced by broader social, political, and cultural features which influence the type of spectator attracted to any particular sport, and the way in which crowd behaviour is interpreted by stadium management, crowd controllers, and the media. The environment in which the event occurs, including the time of day or year in which the event is held also influences crowd behaviour. Each of these features have an important bearing on the way various state and private authorities approach their respective crowd management functions at each sporting event, and the ways in which these functions can be evaluated by the broader public once the event has concluded.

This paper provides some insights into the various features of crowd management and their impact on analysing spectator behaviour and order maintenance at sporting events. The paper is only partially concerned with the question of why spectators engage in violence.[17] The authors see this as only one element in a more complex equation involving the management of spectator behaviour at sporting events.[18] The paper is mainly concerned with mapping out the impact of various features which interact with spectators to assist in preventing, dealing with, or in some cases promoting crowd violence. The considerable differences in the cultures of various sports events, the practices of police and security personnel, and the role managers at various sporting events are highlighted to illustrate the complexity of the order maintenance function. The paper concludes with a discussion of the importance of these matters in understanding crowd management practices in the context of each site, and an outline of some possible future directions for research into crowd disorder at sporting events, which recognises the interrelationship of these issues with their broader cultural, social and legal contexts.

Classes of public events

Different sports generate a variety of cultures of support. The crowd at an international tennis or golfing event will differ greatly from that of a soccer or boxing match.[19] Crowds can be gendered, with high numbers of women as a total proportion of spectators, or high concentrations of women and men in different areas within the stadium.[20] Some crowds may consist of large numbers of young men who may be more predisposed to engage in violent behaviour than a similar sized crowd with a higher average age or more even sex composition.[21] The composition of the crowd, which creates and responds to the culture of each sporting event, is important in assessing whether spectator violence is likely to occur in any particular setting. This matter becomes central to developing methods of order maintenance, which are sensitive to the specific needs of each class of patron at each event.

History indicates that context is also a key factor in understanding the dynamics of spectator violence. As Smith and others indicate, spectator antagonism at refereeing decisions has been a common cause of disorderly behaviour at different events in different countries.[22] One of the more fascinating features of crowd behaviour is the interaction between spectators and competitors.[23] This becomes particularly important in team sports at either a domestic or international level. The rivalries inherent in team competition can be heightened where long standing geographical, cultural and ethnic features might influence spectator composition. Law enforcers or event organisers when devising strategies to prevent crowd violence can cater for such factors. However, when combined with less predictable factors, such as the emotion of the event, seemingly biased umpiring, or cheating and violent rule breaking by athletes, the prospect of collective spectator violence may be heightened.[24] Not all sporting cultures will tolerate such reactions, and the cultures of some events encourage spectators to applaud the opposition, or to engage in other behaviours, which might temper spectator agitation at on field events.[25] Situational context is therefore an important variable when examining the patterns of spectator behaviour at various events and at various times. Such is the importance of this variable, that even the same class of event, such as a motorcycle race, which is held in the same venue at different times can lead to extreme variations in the character of spectator behaviour.[26] This can make it extremely difficult for event managers or law enforcement agents to predict exactly when or how spectator disorder is likely to occur.

Stadium design is also an important means of averting the risk of danger to spectators.[27] This has been particularly prominent in England since the Hillsborough disaster in 1989 where 95 people were crushed to death in a metal enclosure designed to segregate opposition spectators and prevent pitch invasions. Both official[28] and unofficial[29] inquiries into the disaster stressed the danger of this crowd control measure. Coleman et al[30] and Scraton et al [31] indicate that the public discourse on the harmful behaviour of football supporters ultimately led to the introduction of stadium design measures, which compromised spectator safety. Thus, while the cultures of sports spectatorship and the environmental characteristics of sports stadia can often interrelate in broader debates about spectator violence, this incident demonstrates that public debates can generate negligent and often dangerous stadium design measures aimed at curtailing the threat of collective disorder.

Sport can often be a site for the expression of local, national or international political sentiments.[32] In Australia, the demonstrations against the Springbok Rugby tour in 1971,[33] the legislative activity in Queensland designed to suppress Indigenous Australian protest during the Brisbane Commonwealth Games in 1982,[34] and the recent publicity surrounding the status of Indigenous Australian athletes in domestic[35] and international competition,[36] are all testimony of the power of sport to generate and transmit political messages to the broader community. Politics and sport are often closely linked. Broader cultural attitudes regarding the connection between politics and sport, combined with the highly political nature of some legislative and police responses to spectator behaviour can all impact on the frequency of, and responses to the crowd activity within and beyond contemporary sport. As Waddington[37] indicates, not all political protests lead to violence, and often the perception of public threat generated by politicians and law enforcers can unnecessarily trigger violence during political demonstrations. Sports spectating and political protest are collective activities and this problem has the potential to cause friction between authorities and the public, which can influence the nature and extent of collective disorder in both environments.[38]

Each of these factors has a different impact at various sports events at different times. This means that it is important to take a relative approach to examining crowd violence from a comparative perspective. Even though some events may have global or extensive international appeal, such as soccer or rugby union, the different cultural contexts in which these events take place can lead to significant differences in the character of spectator behaviour. This is despite the generic similarities of these events and their crowd compositions. This can make generalisations about spectator violence and its pervasiveness in various domestic and international sports difficult to sustain. The literature on crowd disorder and policing practices in British football illustrates this point. Given the specific cultural and legal climates governing soccer and the control of spectators in Britain in the last three decades, the trends in soccer violence may, or may not, parallel Australian experiences. Australia has developed its own pattern of spectator attraction and crowd control responses to spectator disorder.[39] This may mean that international comparisons are of little value in analysing the problem of violence in the Australian context. While some global similarities may appear between the cultures of various sports, generalisations on the overall pervasiveness of these similarities must be treated with caution.

Each of these considerations may seem relatively obvious to those familiar with the issue of sports crowd behaviour. However, when examining the causes of crowd violence it is necessary to come to terms with the varying characteristics of each sporting event, and the importance of the various sports cultures in identifying measures to deal with the behaviour of spectators. Each event will have its own specific crowd characteristics. The factors which influence sports crowd behaviour at each event site cannot be divorced from the various situational, environmental and political features which surround each event and which influence the status of the sport in broader society. These issues are of particular significance when assessing the various approaches to preventing or dealing with spectator violence at sporting venues. The range of cultural traits of sports spectators outlined above all have some impact on the approaches to order maintenance in various sports at various times. Further, each factor needs to be considered in the context of the specific roles, cultures and obligations of each agency, which provides order maintenance services at sports events. The impact of the roles and functions of various agencies in charge of crowd management at sporting events is the subject of the next three sections of this paper.

The police role

State policing has maintained a pivotal role in order maintenance at sporting events throughout history. Evidence suggests that, in the most part, the police have conducted this function successfully, with minimal harm ensuing to patrons at most routine sporting events. However, a growing body of literature in Australia[40] and the United Kingdom[41] indicates that police tactics at some sporting events can be highly confrontational, and have the potential to heighten the prospect of collective spectator violence. Law enforcers can adopt a variety of crowd control tactics at each event site. The successes and failures of these tactics depend largely on what is deemed to be an 'appropriate' police response by patrons and the broader community in any given event setting. High arrest rates may be evidence of police vigilance at a particular sporting event. However high levels of arrests may also be evidence of a policy of saturation policing, which can alter the character of the event. This might deter prospective patrons from attendance, or might conflict with the wishes of event managers.[42] Low levels of violence leading to police action may be considered as evidence of efficient or effective policing. However, in some circumstances, this may also be evidence of police exercising their discretion within the sports stadium and 'turning a blind eye' to certain sorts of behaviour, which are legally actionable or socially harmful.[43] Too much police activity may unduly restrict the behaviour of patrons. Not enough police intervention may lead to allegations that police are compromising spectator safety.[44]

The police are ultimately directed by law to maintain public order, and to prevent crime. Converting legal definitions of orderly or disorderly behaviour into police practices can be a complicated task, and gives rise to one of the most problematic aspects of the law enforcement function: police discretion. Within the extremes of a rigid, legalistic approach to crowd control, and a highly discretionary, non-interventionist approach, police have the difficult task of assessing which forms of behaviour warrant informal and formal intervention, and how such intervention should take place. In some circumstances, the individual police officer, or the institution of policing more generally, may be subject to retaliatory attacks from individuals or groups, based primarily on the way they have approached their role.[45] The range of cultural characteristics in various sports requires flexibility in the police approach.[46] Not all police tactics will be appropriate in all environments. These issues need to be recognised by those involved in police operations at the site itself, and by police managers co-ordinating and administering the provision of policing services at each event.

The distinction between managerial and operational policing functions is critical in understanding the multi-faceted nature of state policing tasks. As the table below indicates, police managers deal primarily with the macro-policy issues relating to order maintenance and the provision of policing services. These include resource allocation, training for operational personnel, the development and application of technologies of order maintenance such as radio communication or video surveillance, deployment of personnel within the stadium or to protect players, umpires and other officials, the supervision and accountability of operational personnel, and evaluating the efficiency and effectiveness of each of these tasks. Operational police deal with the implementation of managerial directives. Their role involves interaction and liaison with the public and detecting and responding to public complaints of disorderly behaviour when they arise. While managerial and operational roles are not mutually exclusive, the table indicates that each has the potential to generate a variety of issues in the policing environment, which have different impacts on the police role at different event sites

Outline of managerial and operational policing roles

Managerial policing roles	Operational policing roles
Resource allocation	On site law enforcement
Technology development and deployment	The use of technology
Implementing appropriate training regimes	Converting training directives into operational practice
Organisational discretion (involving deployment, budgetary considerations, pre-event planning, and compliance with Equal Opportunity and Occupational Health and Safety provisions)	Operational discretion (involving interpersonal contacts with members of the public, decisions to warn or charge individuals, and operationalising legal definitions of order and disorder)
Supervision of operational personnel	Supervision of patron behaviours
Identifying and monitoring displacement causes and effects	Implementing displacement policies on the ground
Co-ordinating law enforcement responses at various event sites	Gathering evidence to sustain criminal or summary prosecutions
Implementing accountability mechanisms in the event of public complaints	Identifying operational issues regarding occupational health and safety
Macro performance evaluation and statistical assessments of police activity	Micro performance evaluation including self assessment and review of colleagues' behaviour

Each of these roles adds further degrees of complexity to the analysis of the police role at sporting events. Police managers need to be highly sensitive to issues such as resource allocation and budgeting given the high costs of training police personnel, developing and implementing the use of technologies of law enforcement, and the increasing public demand for the provision of effective and efficient police services in times of government cutbacks to public sector budgets.[47] These issues become further complicated when there is a threat or prospect of disorder at a particular stadium, or where violent behaviour is associated with a particular sport. The British case of *Harris v. Sheffield United Football Club Ltd*[48] indicates that police agencies in Britain can charge football clubs for 'additional policing services' above and beyond what is generally agreed by police and event organisers in the course of their pre-event planning. There are only limited provisions in Australia for the direct billing of clubs or individuals for policing services.[49] Nevertheless, police managers are often involved in a complicated balancing act. While 'sufficient' police resources might be required to maintain order within the stadium environment, and traffic control in the immediate vicinity of the event, police managers must also be sensitive to the needs of the community who are not in attendance. To saturate one environment might lead to a diminution of resources in another environment, and may also give rise to allegations that a particular sporting event is being either over- or unnecessarily policed at the broader community's expense.[50] Moreover, unintended consequences may arise from police activities, which need to be considered by stadium managers. The recent tendency for aggrieved individuals to sue individual police or police organisations for harms sustained as a result of alleged police negligence may have long term effects on police budgets, particularly where compensatory or punitive damages are awarded by the courts to aggrieved individuals or groups of spectators.[51] In addition, various other forms of external[52] and internal accountability mechanisms may be instigated by members of the public who may be aggrieved by the practices or decisions of operational or managerial police personnel.[53]

Technologies of crowd control are an additional source of concern for the state police. Police training can be a costly exercise,[54] particularly where sophisticated crowd control technology is involved. However, the use of video cameras and police radios at sporting events can be a useful means of detecting spectator misbehaviour or issuing instructions to operational personnel to quell crowd disturbances. Research from the United Kingdom,[55] and Australia[56] indicates that such technologies may however exacerbate tensions between police and the community. In the case of video technology, there are serious questions about the storage and use of video material after it has been collected. These raises concerns about how police agencies are using the information they have gathered after the event has occurred. The potential for video footage to be used for purposes which infringe individual rights and civil liberties may compromise the effectiveness of this order maintenance initiative. Further, as Palmer et al[57] have found from interviews with cricket spectators in Melbourne, only 3% of respondents felt that police video cameras were necessary to promote spectator safety. This means that the costs of this technology may be better utilised through some other means, such as the deployment of more police at the stadium, or devoting more attention to monitoring the displacement effects of patron behaviours after the event has completed.[58]

Operational police are concerned with implementing managerial policies in practice. This involves many complex factors that are learned through a combination of formal police training and direct experience at various sporting events. Most routine operational tasks are conducted by general duties police members who are usually relatively inexperienced and who undertake crowd control functions at sporting events as part of their day to day operational role. Despite the existence of specialist squads which undertake para-military riot control functions when mass disorder occurs at major public events,[59] or which engage in covert surveillance to prevent seditious disorder or terrorism,[60] the absence of any defined career path for specialisation in crowd control, other than for special operations or reactive para-military divisions[61] can have several negative outcomes. Police training may devalue the importance of specialist and ongoing instruction on routine public order policing at sporting events. Those best suited to public order maintenance, or those with the greatest understanding of the dynamics of sports crowds, may not be deployed to these events by police managers. This can be particularly significant at events where the cultures of sports spectators differ from the dominant social or policing cultures. Where there is evidence that certain sports have characteristics, which require an inside policing knowledge of the culture of the event, failure to cater for this feature may compromise the safety of patrons. In addition, the absence of specialisation for general duties crowd controllers can impinge on police accountability. This is particularly important given the emphasis in contemporary policing on community based policing strategies.[62] Specialist squads are frequently criticised for their use of unnecessarily coercive or interventionist order maintenance tactics.[63] There are also ethical and legal ramifications associated with the use of overt force and covert surveillance. It is possible that many of these difficulties could be overcome with greater recourse to specialist crowd control work, based on principles of community policing, which removes the need for using reactive, para-military or covert tactics.

It is imperative for police managers and operational personnel to maintain ongoing communication before, during and after each event. Management instructions to operational personnel must to be clear and flexible, outlining the potential order maintenance problems which might arise, and the range of measures which may be employed to deal with these problems. Communication however is a two way process. Many concerns regarding order maintenance from an operational perspective can be overcome through ongoing communication between operational and managerial personnel. This is particularly important in assessing the effectiveness of crowd control technologies, police interactions with patrons, and the environmental characteristics of sporting event sites that might affect the safety of operational personnel and patrons. Communication on these matters from the bottom up can help to reduce the overall costs of policing operations, particularly where workers' compensation claims may be incurred for injuries sustained by operational personnel. In addition, ongoing and open communication within policing ranks can assist in maintaining accountability operational procedures, and may prevent allegations of police mismanagement, inadequate police training, or operational malpractice by members of the public. If lines of communication within police services are maintained, public accountability for order maintenance policies and their implementation can be enhanced.[64]

The ultimate effectiveness of the police role is largely based on the context of the event and the maintenance of good relations between individual police members, police organisations more generally, and sports spectators. Economic considerations, including the costs of police services and the overall returns for staging the event are also relevant. The balance between a flexible, responsive police presence, and a confrontational or intrusive approach to order maintenance is a delicate one, and both managerial and operational police functions require flexibility in order to ensure that the various characteristics of spectator behaviour can be catered for in each environment. Undue rigidity, or a lack of police understanding of spectator dynamics in each environment can lead to crowd violence being directed specifically at police members,[65] or allegations of negligence or impropriety which may cause irreparable damage to police relations with various community groups.[66]

Private security

This aspect of public order maintenance is a growing issue of concern in most entertainment and sporting environments. Despite a lack of evidence on the roles, functions, and theories underpinning private policing in contemporary society, recent Australian[67] and overseas[68] literature indicates that this aspect of order maintenance at public events is fraught with legal and operational difficulties. Studies by the Victorian Community Council Against Violence,[69] Homel and Tomsen,[70] and Tomsen,[71] indicate that around 30% of incidents of violence in pubs and clubs in Australia are either initiated by, or involve private security personnel. Similar concerns about the order maintenance tactics of security personnel at Australian sporting events have emerged in recent years.[72] The major problem with the private security sector is the uncertain legal status of the roles of security personnel at each event site. This is particularly problematic where event organisers contract with security corporations to provide security functions. Unlike 'in house' security, which are directly employed by and are accountable to stadium managers, contract security are theoretically independent of the direct oversight and accountability of venue management. This creates a degree of confusion regarding the legal status of individual security personnel, or their corporate employers.[73] Whilst some jurisdictions have opted for increased state regulation in an attempt to 'clean up' the industry, the precise roles of the security sector stem from a complex range of common law and statutory rules, in areas such as employment law, contract law, property law, corporations and partnerships law, and the laws of civil wrongs. These diverse legal origins of the security functions differ greatly from the centrally mandated roles of state policing and complicate the security task from the outset.[74]

There are three aspects to the provision of security services at sporting events. The first is the managerial or corporate function. This role parallels the police management function. The major difference between the two is the different legal authority governing the private security sector which complicates the provision of security services and the accountability processes governing management liabilities for the behaviour of security personnel. The second is the operational function of private crowd controllers. Again, there are various situational characteristics that impact on relations between private security personnel and spectators that are similar to those governing the operational role in state policing. The principal differences between the two lies in their sources of legal authority, and the underlying philosophies governing the operational tasks of police and private security. While the former are mandated to prevent crime and violence for the overall public benefit, security functions are based on minimising harm or losses to the employers or contractors of security services. Therefore, the conceptual differences between private and state police can lead to different legal outcomes governing the rights, liabilities, and activities of each branch of crowd controller *vis a vis* the public. However, in principle, both state and private police share similar operational functions that require similar training and interpersonal skills to deal with patrons at each event. Crowd controllers must liaise closely with patrons and be sensitive to the various cultures of sports crowds and the wide range of possible scenarios that can occur in the context of each sporting event.[75] This ensures that security practices are adequately geared to the needs of various classes of patron at each venue. Third, private security is becoming increasingly involved in the protection of individual athletes or officials. This is a particularly important security function, given the tendency for elite athletes to employ security guards for personal protection. This development has significant implications for the safety of athletes, and the legal authority of private police at domestic or international sporting events.[76]

There has been a rapid expansion in the use of private crowd controllers at sporting events in Australia and overseas. However, caution must be exercised in comparing the legal authority or practical functions of security personnel with the state police. Private security has a private law mandate. As such, despite operational similarities, the private security sector is ultimately accountable to private contractors or employers, rather than the general public. This can create numerous difficulties for individuals aggrieved by the actions of security personnel, particularly where an individual, a security firm, or a sporting event organiser is not covered by indemnity insurance. Despite concerns about the tactics of security personnel in some public event settings, not all sporting events will be characterised by violent or overly intrusive security practices.[77] Each setting will produce different security responses, some of which are appropriate to deal with the crowds in attendance, and others that may be questionable. Private security may at times be more efficient and effective than the state police. The various environments where security are employed lead to different degrees of specialisation amongst security personnel which might overcome the problems policing faces with the lack of specialisation in order maintenance service provision at sporting events. Where security personnel have a good rapport with event organisers and a detailed understanding of the various cultures of sporting events, their degree of specialisation can be an asset in preventing spectator violence. However, problems may also exist in the provision of security functions. As with state policing, effective security provision requires clear and reciprocal communication between operational personnel and security managers, adaptability to the various situations that arise at each event, and a non-confrontationist approach to crowd management.

Event organisers and venue managers

Event managers and organisers are in the best position to co-ordinate the various order maintenance agencies, and play a critical role in determining the types of security or law enforcement required for any particular event. Some managers may organise a range of different sporting events in particular event sites. Others specialise in particular sports, conducted in the same environment at various times. Event organisers or venue managers will have their own expertises and perceptions of how best to deal with sports spectators, based on the nature of the events they organise, their understanding of patron concerns, and the characteristics of the particular venue or event under their control.

The most critical concern for event organisers is the issue of stadium design, and the maintenance of stadium amenities. The legal liabilities which directly impact on stadium managers,[78] combined with the potentially dangerous effects of poor stadium maintenance,[79] place event organisers in a critical position in the context of designing environmental measures which reduce spectator frustration and minimise the risks of injury to patrons. Official inquiries into the Hillsborough disaster, the events at Heysel stadium in Brussels where 38 people were crushed beneath a collapsed retaining wall,[80] and the fire in a football stand at Bradford in England which led to the deaths of 56 people,[81] highlight the importance of event organisers ensuring the ongoing maintenance of sports stadia. Various situational measures can be adopted to ensure that sports stadia are designed and maintained in a way that minimises the potential of harm to patrons, athletes, police, and security personnel.[82] The adoption of preventative measures can minimise the prospect of harm and violence occurring during the course of a sporting event, thus minimising the costs of potential litigation and compensation to victims.

An outcome of the major stadium disasters in Europe and the concerns about public order maintenance strategies in the United Kingdom has been a series of major changes in various aspects of football crowd behaviour, management and the design of the facilities in which matches take place. The Taylor Report was a catalyst for this process though there were several other elements that contributed to these developments.[83] The Thatcher government continued to treat the issue as largely one of public order and tried unsuccessfully to introduce an identity card system which would have resulted in potential spectators having to produce a membership card to gain access to stadia where top level football matches were being played. Strong opposition from the clubs, fans and the media, the difficulties of policing the system and the costs involved combined to thwart this strategy. The costs and outcomes of saturation policing, a tactic commonly adopted to deal with British counter culture during the 1980s and 1990s,[84] and the shock of the narrow escape the police had from prosecution over the Hillsborough disaster led to a reappraisal of the then current strategies. The Taylor report directed attention at the need to reconstruct stadia to improve the control and the safety of spectators. Much discussion of Taylor's recommendations was on the introduction of all-seated stadia, but his brief was much wider. Funds from the revenue generated by the successful football pools gambling were channelled through the Football Trust into the rebuilding of stadia, a process which has seen the majority of Premier League clubs in England completely overhaul their existing stadia or move to new purpose built locations usually on the fringes of urban areas. These stadia have changed the patterns of crowd behaviours in significant ways and indeed have sometimes reduced the level of vocal and demonstrative support to the extent that fans and clubs have become discontented. There were slighting references to 'Highbury: the library' during and after the rebuilding of the Arsenal stadium in North London. Public address systems are now routinely used to generate ersatz crowd noises and singing, and the new minister for sport in the United Kingdom has talked about the reintroduction of standing areas at major grounds for domestic matches.[85]

Stadium management can also co-ordinate briefings and communication between police and security personnel prior to a sporting event. Managers are also charged with training 'in-house' security personnel, the employment of stewards or marshals, and the employment and maintenance of medical personnel and facilities at each event. The risk of civil actions for negligence in providing necessary services at each event site is an important incentive for event managers to deal with these issues vigilantly. Each of these features will differ depending on the nature of the event, the characteristics of the event site, the crowd composition, and the range of law enforcement and security services available at each event. Event and site managers are perhaps in the best position to ensure that law enforcement and crowd control services are co-ordinated, and that any potential safety concerns for the various people in attendance are addressed at the pre-event planning stage.

Additional considerations

There are several additional considerations that influence the analysis of spectator behaviour at sporting events. Many of these issues draw on themes already outlined in this paper. However, the significance of these examples in determining how spectator behaviour is to be viewed by official regulatory and crowd control warrants attention.

One of the major influences on the pattern of spectator behaviour in the United Kingdom has come from the fans themselves as small but significant groups sought to reclaim the game from the 'hooligans'. This took various forms from the fanzine movement, the revival of the Football Supporters Association by Rogan Taylor and others and their attempts to have their voice heard at official and club level and the less organised but equally significant distancing of fans from the rowdy behaviour which provoked or provided the excuse for police intervention. This could take the form of pointing out violent or abusive characters to the authorities or a silent response to attempts to stir up over-the-top behaviour. There has been a decline in the numbers of arrests at football in the United Kingdom in recent years, though debate continues as to the extent to which this is the outcome of the end of saturation policing, a change in crowd composition, or a more general trend in violence in society.[86]

The role of sports participants in contributing to perception of and actual violence at public events has also been the subject of considerable public debate in the United Kingdom and Australia.[87] A series of well publicised incidents some involving high profile public performers, Eric Cantona,[88] Duncan Ferguson, Paul Gascoigne and others has led to an attempt to set out the ground rules for police intervention. One example is the Scottish Lord Advocate's instructions on policing and discretion, which attempts to guide the behaviour of police at major sporting events.[89]

Pre-event publicity has also been acknowledged in contemporary Australian research to be important in the context of major public events.[90] Responsible pre-event publicity can highlight the enjoyable features of the event and may lead to events that attract patrons who are unlikely to engage in disorderly behaviour. Associated with this feature are issues relating to ticketing,[91] alcohol provision, and the communication of relevant event regulations and codes of conduct for patrons. This latter point helps to ensure that norms of acceptable behaviour are clearly established well before the event. Minimising possible sources of frustration to large numbers of spectators, such as long queues for entry or cumbersome ticketing and entry procedures, and creating a climate where spectators are aware of their rights and obligations at the event, can assist in preventing spectator anxiety and the prospect of collective spectator disorder. Moreover, as an element of the pre-event planning process, it is imperative that event organisers and stadium managers consult with various state and private law enforcement agencies, to assist in developing necessary communication and crowd monitoring procedures. This is particularly important in terms of identifying possible aspects of trouble which might occur at the event, and in minimising the costs of security provision by avoiding any duplication of resources which compromise the effectiveness and efficiency of crowd control services.

Discussion: Implications for research into crowd control

Effective and efficient crowd management at sporting events involves much more than analysing the behaviour of spectators. As this discussion suggests, several variables have bearing on the provision of law enforcement and order maintenance services, each of which require a detailed understanding of the cultures of each event, and the characteristics of those who might be in attendance. The intersection of policing, private security and stadium management functions raises several questions relating to order maintenance policies and the procedures to be adopted in various sports environments to ensure crowd safety. It also has significant bearing on the questions that inform future research into the crowd control function.

As Hay indicates[92] the generalisations which have informed many of the theoretical explanations for spectator behaviour have tended to create a myopic view of the problem of order maintenance at sporting events. Rather than looking at the context of specific incidents in depth, research into disorder at sporting events tends to assume that all incidents within particular sports have generically similar characteristics. The result is that research questions and the interpretation of research data are too generalised. Soccer is a sport which is therefore viewed as attracting a particularly violent, young male crowd, which can potentially lead to disorder at all soccer matches.[93] Rugby on the other hand is commonly viewed as an orderly spectator sport.[94] Each of these views is partially correct, and partially incorrect. Soccer and rugby crowds are violent some of the time. However, most soccer and rugby matches in most jurisdictions transpire without major incident. Thus context, rather than the nature of the sport in and of itself, is the key variable when examining crowd behaviour in various sports.

The material presented above presents a new gloss on this issue. It has already been mentioned that an understanding of order maintenance involves considerably more than interpreting or analysing the behaviour of sports spectators. Police, security personnel and event organisers have a range of interrelated tasks which all have different influences in different sporting contexts. The task of assessing the successes or failures of various crowd control measures is further complicated by the varied environmental, social, cultural and political issues which influence the order maintenance function and crowd composition at each event. Features which are both internal to order maintenance within the sport itself, and which also involve external judgements of sports crowds and their behaviour, have significant bearing on the various approaches to order maintenance and their effectiveness in dealing with spectator violence and preventing harm in each sports site.

This gives rise to two possible roles for research in understanding spectator violence and order maintenance at sporting events. The first is to take a narrow view of the characteristics and functions of each individual agency involved in crowd control at each event. Through a research agenda which forges a detailed understanding of the roles of operational and managerial police, security and event organisers separately, it is possible to obtain a detailed understanding of the dynamics of order maintenance from the various perspectives of each agency in own right. This approach has several benefits. Police organisations for instance can assist in providing critical and reflective information of their performance and its evaluation as an additional element of their order maintenance role. This would help develop measures to professionalise the police role in crowd control as a specialist division within contemporary police ranks. Similar procedures could be applied to the private sector either as a marketing tool for selling their services in other public order settings, or for developing new initiatives in training and order maintenance provision in the security industry. Informed knowledge from those entrusted with the security provision roles can equally assist with private and public police accountability for the actions and policies of those undertaking crowd control tasks. For event organisers, publicising safe environments becomes a selling point for attracting further sporting or other public events. This feature is particularly crucial in contemporary society, given the competition between cities, states and nations for holding major domestic and international sporting events. Informed research into crowd safety is a selling point which can only enhance this competition process, and can act as a possible defence to allegations of negligence in the provision of order maintenance or crowd safety services.

The difficulty with this approach is that it can lead to each organisation duplicating research and performance evaluation resources and conducting research for their own interests. This might lead to each organisation ignoring the broader concerns of order maintenance and spectator safety at the expense of producing findings which make each organisation appear to be comparatively more efficient and effective than the others. A more contextual approach to analysing order maintenance services would focus on each organisation and their interrelationships within the context of each sporting event. This could appear to be an onerous task, particularly given the legal and methodological complexity and the volume of data stemming from such work. Nevertheless, an approach, which focuses primarily on the context of the event and the roles of key players in order maintenance provision, can provide a holistic approach to evaluating the effectiveness and efficiency of crowd control functions. Understanding the contexts of order maintenance services and their impact on the various agencies and their crowd control methods in various sporting environments can lead to several benefits which impact on all agencies and their inter-related functions. In addition, such an approach can cater for the variances in crowd control policies and their efficiency and effectiveness in different sports, at different venues, in different time periods. This can assist in avoiding unwarranted generalisations about the overall efficient and effective nature of each agency's function, or about the positive or negative behaviour of spectators who only constitute part of the order maintenance equation in each environment.

In concluding, the issue of crowd violence at sporting involves an understanding of cultures, contexts, and the ways in which organisations entrusted with order maintenance provision carry out their functions before, during and after each event. By acknowledging this range of variables the content of future research into crowd behaviour at sporting events will be enhanced for the benefit of all organisations and the capacity for order maintenance services to achieve their ultimate aim of providing a safe environment for sports spectators will be more readily understood by the broader community and the various classes of sports fans.

endnotes

1 See A. Thompson (Ed) *Terrorism and the 2000 Olympics*, Australian Defence Studies Centre, Canberra, 1996.

2 See R. Hay 'A new look at soccer violence', in this volume.

3 E. Trivizaz, 'Offences and Offenders in Football Crowd Disorders', *British Journal of Criminology*, 20, 1980, p. 276.

4 I. Warren, *Cultures of Control: Law, Enforcement and Public Order at Major Sporting Events*, Australian Society for Sports History, Sydney, forthcoming.

5 See Lord Advocate's Instructions to Chief Constables in Scotland, 1997, copy in possession of Roy Hay.

6 C. Cunneen, M. Findlay, R. Lynch and V. Tupper, *Dynamics of Collective Conflict: Riots at the Bathurst 'Bike Races*, Law Book Company, Sydney 1989.

7 R. Cashman, *Ave A Go Yer Mug: Australian Cricket Crowds From Larrikin to Ocker*, Collins, Sydney 1984.

8 Eric Dunning, Patrick Murphy and John Williams, *The roots of football hooliganism : an historical and sociological study*, London, Routledge, 1989

9 W. Vamplew, 'Unsporting Behaviour: The Control of Football and Horse Racing Crowds in England 1857-1914', in J.H. Goldstein (Ed), *Sports Violence*, Springer-Verlag, New York 1983; W. Vamplew, 'Sports Crowd Disorder: An Australian Survey', J. O'Hara (Ed), *Crowd Violence at Australian Sport,* Studies in Sports History, No. 7, Australian Society for Sports History, Campbelltown 1992; W. Vamplew, 'Violence in Australian Soccer: The Ethnic Contribution' in J. O'Hara (Ed), *Ethnicity and Soccer in Australia,* Studies in Sports History, No. 10, Australian Society for Sports History, Campbelltown 1994.

10 H. Cantelon and R. Gruneau, *Sport, Culture and the Modern State*, University of Toronto Press, Toronto 1982.

11 R. Giulianotti, N. Bonney and M. Hepworth, *Football, Violence and Social Identity,* Routledge, London 1994.

12 Editorial, 'No Room for Hooligans', *Herald Sun*, 6/5/1997, p. 18; Editorial, 'Soccer's Biggest Challenge' *The Age*, 6/5/1997, p. A14; M. Fyfe 'Fans Score Own Goal' *The Age*, 6/5/1997 (Metro, p. C1); M. Gleeson 'War on Soccer Thugs', *Herald Sun*, 6/5/1997, p. 8; F. Hudson and G. McMahon) 'Soccer thugs on rampage', *Herald Sun*, 5/5/1997, p. 4; J. Koutsoukis and J. Rouw 'Soccer fans leave trail of destruction' *The Age*, 6/5/1997, p. A5.

13 I. Warren, 'Soccer subcultures in Australia', in C. Guerra and R. White (Ed's) *Ethnic Minority Youth in Australia*, National Clearinghouse for Youth Studies, Hobart 1995, pp. 121-131; Hughson, J. 'Football, fold dancing and fascism: diversity and difference in multicultural Australia', *Australian and New Zealand Journal of Sociology*, vol. 33, 1997, pp. 165-186.

14 R. Hay 'A new look at soccer violence'.

15 Cunneen, Findlay, Lynch and Tupper, *Dynamics of Collective Conflict*.

16 A. Veno and E. Veno, 'Police, Riots and Public Order', in D. Chappell and P. Wilson, *Australian Policing: Contemporary Issues*, Butterworths, Sydney 1989 pp. 132-148; A. Veno and E. Veno, 'Managing Public Order at the Australian Motorcycle Grand Prix', in J. O'Hara (Ed), *Crowd Violence at Australian Sport*, Studies in Sports History, No. 7, Australian Society for Sports History, Campbelltown 1992.

17 R. Hay 'A new look at soccer violence'.

18 Although this is not to suggest that authorities and researchers should not be interested in exploring why some fans do engage in organised and deliberate acts of violence from time to time in and around sports stadia. This issue is of obvious concern in light of recent events leading up to the 1998 football World Cup in France. However, one possible explanation for the recent stabbing of a football spectator, and attempted stabbing of a referee in recent domestic competition in England could be that hooliganism has been diverted from major Premier League and international fixtures involving Britain in Europe, primarily due to the increased costs of attendance. See J. Huxley, 'Violence renews old fears' *The Australian*, 31 March 1998, p. 40.

19 Cashman, *Ave A Go Yer Mug*; Cunneen, Findlay, Lynch and Tupper, *Dynamics of Collective Conflict*; E. Dunning and K. Sheard, *Barbarians, Gentlemen and Players: A Sociological Study of the Development of Rugby Football*, Martin Robertson and Co, Oxford 1979; Giulianotti, Bonney and Hepworth, *Football, Violence and Social Identity*.

20 R. Hess, 'Women and Australian Rules Football in Colonial Melbourne', *The International Journal of the History of Sport*, 13, 1990, pp. 356-372.

21 R. Holt, *Sport and the British: A Modern History*, Clarendon Press, Oxford 1989; K. Polk *When Men Kill: Scenarios of Masculine Violence*, Cambridge University Press, Melbourne, 1994.

22 M.D. Smith, 'Precipitants of Crowd Violence', *Sociological Inquiry*, 48, 1976, pp. 121-131; Philip Mosely, A social history of soccer in New South Wales, 1880-1956, University of Sydney, Ph.D. thesis, 1987; Bill Murray, *Football: A History of the World Game*, Scholar Press, Aldershot, 1994; R. Hay, 'Black (Yellow or Green) Bastards: Soccer Refereeing in Australia: A much maligned profession', Paper delivered to the Sporting Traditions IX Conference of the Australian Society for Sports History, University of Queensland, St Lucia, 1995; Roy Hay, 'Australian Referees: How do they compare with the rest of the World', *Australian and British Soccer Weekly*, 13 December 1994, p. 13; For examples see *Sporting Globe*, Melbourne, 21 June 1933; 23 August 1933; *Soccer News*, Melbourne, 28 May 1960, p.1.

23 Cashman, *Ave A Go Yer Mug*.

24 Smith, 'Precipitants of Crowd Violence'.

25 Dunning and Sheard, *Barbarians, Gentlemen and Players*.

26 Cunneen, Findlay, Lynch and Tupper, *Dynamics of Collective Conflict.*

27 The Scottish Office, Department of National Heritage, *Guide to Safety at Sports Grounds*, The Stationery Office, London, 1997; S. Coleman, A. Jemphrey, P. Scraton and P. Skidmore, *Hillsborough and After: The Liverpool Experience*, First Report, Centre For Studies in Crime and Social Justice, Edge Hill College of Higher Education, Ormskirk, Lancashire 1990; D. Canter, M. Comber and D.L. Uzzell, *Football in its Place: An Environmental Psychology of Football Grounds*, Routledge, London 1989; L.J. Taylor, *The Hillsborough Stadium Disaster, Final Report* (April 15, 1989), Home Office, Cmnd 962, HMSO, London 1990.

28 Taylor, *The Hillsborough Stadium Disaster, Final Report.*

29 S. Coleman et al, *Hillsborough and after: The Liverpool experience, First Report*; P. Scraton, A Jemphrey and S. Coleman, *No last rights: The denial of justice and the promotion of myth in the aftermath of the Hillsborough disaster*, Liverpool City Council, Liverpool, 1995.

30 Coleman, Jemphrey, Scraton and Skidmore, *Hillsborough and After.*

31 P. Scraton, A Jemphrey and S. Coleman, *No last rights.*

32 For a specific account of this issue in the context of South African Rugby Union and the maintenance of apartheid, see J. Nauright and T.J.L. Chandler (eds) *Making Men: Rugby and Masculine Identity*, Frank Cass, London, 1996.

33 See A. Grundlingh, 'Playing for Power? Rugby, Afrikaner Nationalism and Masculinity in South Africa, c. 1900-c.1970' Nauright and Chandler (eds) *Making Men*, pp. 181-204; J. Nauright and D. Black, 'Hitting Them Where it Hurts: Springbok-All Black Rugby, Masculine National Identity and Counter-Hegemonic Struggle', in Nauright and Chandler (eds) *Making Men*, pp. 205-226; S. Harris, Political *Football: The Springbok Tour of Australia, 1971*, Gold Star Publications, Melbourne, 1972.

34 F. Brennan, *Too Much Order with Too Little Law*, University of Queensland Press, St Lucia, 1983; J. Given, 'Red, Black, Gold to Australia: Cathy Freeman and the Flags', *Sport! Changing the Angle*, Media Information Australia Journal Series, 75, 1995, pp. 46-56.

35 See S. Tsaousis and I. Warren 'Law, Language and Racism in Australian Rules Football: A Critical Analysis' *Sporting Traditions: Journal of the Australian Society for Sports History*, vol 14, no. 1, pp. 27-53; C. Tatz, *Obstacle Race: Aborigines in Sport*, University of New South Wales Press, Sydney, 1995.

36 Given, 'Red, Black, Gold to Australia'; Tatz, *Obstacle Race.*

37 D. Waddington, *Contemporary Issues in Public Disorder: A Comparative and Historical Approach*, Routledge, London 1992.

38 See D.S. Grant and M. Wallace 'Why do strikes turn violent?' *American Journal of Sociology*, 96, 1991, pp. 1117-1150; P. Green, *The Enemy Without: Policing and Class Consciousness In the Miners' Strike*, Open University Press, Milton Keynes, 1990; B. York 'Baiting the tiger: Police and protest during the Vietnam War', in M. Finnane (Ed) *Policing in Australia: Historical Perspectives*, University of New South Wales Press, Kensington, 1987, pp. 170-187.

39 R. Hay, 'British Football, Wogball or the World Game? Towards a Social History of Victorian Soccer', in J. O'Hara (Ed), *Ethnicity and Soccer in Australia*, Studies in Sports History, No. 10, Australian Society for Sports History, Campbelltown 1994.

40 Cunneen, Findlay, Lynch and Tupper, *Dynamics of Collective Conflict*; N. Mellor, 'Measures to Reduce Violence at Major Public Events: New Year's Eve', in D. Chappell and S. Egger (eds), *Australian Violence: Contemporary Perspectives II*, Australian Institute of Criminology, Canberra 1994; Warren, *Cultures of Control;* Warren, 'Soccer subcultures in Australia'; Vamplew, 'Sports Crowd Disorder'; Vamplew, 'Violence in Australian Soccer'; Cashman, *Ave A Go Yer Mug*; R. Lynch, 'A Symbolic Patch of Grass: Crowd Disorder and Regulation on the Sydney Cricket

Ground Hill', in J. O'Hara (Ed), *Crowd Violence at Australian Sport,* Studies in Sports History, No. 7, Australian Society for Sports History, Campbelltown 1992.

41 Waddington, *Contemporary Issues in Public Disorder;* G. Armstrong and D. Hobbs, 'Tackled from Behind' in R. Giulianotti, N. Bonney and M. Hepworth, *Football, Violence and Social Identity,* Routledge, London 1994, pp. 196-228; Canter, Comber and Uzzell, *Football in its Place;* Coleman, Jemphrey, Scraton and Skidmore, *Hillsborough and After*; P. Scraton, A Jemphrey and S. Coleman, *No last rights: The denial of justice and the promotion of myth in the aftermath of the Hillsborough disaster*, Liverpool City Council, Liverpool, 1995

42 Cunneen, Findlay, Lynch and Tupper, *Dynamics of Collective Conflict.*

43 Coleman, Jemphrey, Scraton and Skidmore, *Hillsborough and After*; P. Scraton, A Jemphrey and S. Coleman, *No last rights: The denial of justice and the promotion of myth in the aftermath of the Hillsborough disaster*, Liverpool City Council, Liverpool, 1995.

44 Veno and Veno, 'Police, Riots and Public Order'.

45 Cunneen, Findlay, Lynch and Tupper, *Dynamics of Collective Conflict.* This is also evidenced by the data from Trivizaz presented on page 1 of this paper: Trivizaz, 'Offences and Offenders'.

46 Veno and Veno, 'Police, Riots and Public Order'.

47 I.D. Froyland and D. Bell 'Making Police More Efficient', in D. Chappell and P. Wilson (eds) *Australian Policing: Contemporary Issues* (2nd Ed) Butterworths, Sydney, 1996, pp. 71-84; Council on the Cost of Government, New *South Wales Police Service: Review of Resource Management, Scoping Study Report,* Council on the Cost of Government, Sydney, 1996.

48 (1987) 2 All ER 839.

49 See for example *Police Regulations Act* (Vic) 1958 s. 130(1)(de) which provides that the Governor in Council can make regulations on charging for the services of any police member or policing division in Victoria; *Police Service Act* (NSW) 1990, Ss. 208-211; *Australian Federal Police Act* (Cth), 1979, s. 71.

50 Cunneen, Findlay, Lynch and Tupper, *Dynamics of Collective Conflict.*

51 This issue has been evidenced in the aftermath of the Hillsborough disaster in England, and is permeating Australian legal culture. In June 1997 it was estimated that the police would face costs for up to $(A)15m for negligence claims stemming from a raid and mass strip search of patrons in a Melbourne nightclub, and for the use of excessive force at several political demonstrations in Melbourne in the early 1990s: see J. Silvester 'Police face $15m black hole over civil claims' *Sunday Age* 15/6/1997, p. 1. Damages have also been awarded against individual police members for proven negligence in discharging firearms which has resulted in injury to members of the public: see *Zalewski v. Turcarolo* [1995] 2 VR 562.

52 See J.R.T. Wood, *Royal Commission into the New South Wales Police Service: Vols 1-3*, The Government of the State of New South Wales, Sydney.

53 A. Goldsmith 'Complaints against the police: A community policing perspective', eds S. McKillop & J. Vernon, *The Police and the Community in the 1990s*, Australian Institute of Criminology, Canberra, 1991; A. Goldsmith, (Ed) *Complaints Against the Police: The Trend to External Review,* Clarendon Press, Oxford, 1991.

54 Council on the Costs of Government, *New South Wales Police Service,*

55 Armstrong and Hobbs, 'Tackled from Behind'.

56 D. Palmer, R. Walters and G. Coventry, 'Cricket, Coppers and Cameras', *Socio-Legal Bulletin*, No. 8, 1992.

57 Palmer Walters and Coventry, 'Cricket, Coppers and Cameras'.

58 John King, *The Football Factory*, London, Vintage edition, 1997, p. 3:Today there is surveillance gear and you have to remember the cameras. But it is all a bit of a joke, because pitch invasions and riots for the cameras never compared to the

trouble away from the ground. Your actual nutters do damage miles from the stadium in a tube station or down a back street, not behind the goal with a telephoto lens shoved up their noses. This novel has a number of sharp observations about the culture of some football fans.

59 J. Bessant, 'Violence, the Media and the Making of Policy: The Closure of Richmond Secondary School', in J. Bessant, K. Carrington, and S. Cook, (eds) *Cultures of Crime and Violence: The Australian Experience*, La Trobe University Press, Melbourne, 1995, pp. 45-58; J. McCulloch and M. Clayton, 'Victoria on the Move! Move! Move', *Alternative Law Journal*, 21, 1996, pp. 103-108; Cunneen, Findlay, Lynch and Tupper, *Dynamics of Collective Conflict*; Veno and Veno, 'Police, Riots and Public Order'.

60 Armstrong and Hobbs, 'Tackled from Behind'; J. Hocking *Beyond Terrorism: The Development of the Australian Security State*, Allen and Unwin, St Leonards, 1993; Thompson (Ed) *Terrorism and the 2000 Olympics*, S. Russell, 1997, 'ASIO plan to 'defend Sydney Olympics' *Green Left Weekly*, 22/1/1997, p. 12.

61 McCulloch and Clayton, 'Victoria on the Move! Move! Move'; Cunneen, Findlay, Lynch and Tupper, *Dynamics of Collective Conflict*.

62 D. Bull & E. Stratta, 'Police-community consultative committees: a response to paramilitary policing?' *Australian and New Zealand Journal of Sociology* vol. 31, 1995, pp. 67-82.

63 Cunneen, Findlay, Lynch and Tupper, *Dynamics of Collective Conflict*; Warren, *Cultures of Control;* Warren, 'Soccer subcultures in Australia'; G. Ryle and G. Hughes, 'Secret Police Revealed' *The Age*, 6/10/1997, p. A1; G. Ryle and G. Hughes, 'The Secret Police', 6/10/1997, p. A6; G. Hughes and G. Ryle, '1200 on secret police list', *The Age*, 7/10/1997, p. A1; G. Hughes and G. Ryle, 'The Secret Police', *The Age*, pp. A6-A7; J. O'Reilly and P. Spencer, 'Force in need of urgent treatment for its paranoia', *The Age*, 7/10/1997, p. A 11.

64 Cunneen, Findlay, Lynch and Tupper, *Dynamics of Collective Conflict*; Veno and Veno, 'Police, Riots and Public Order'.

65 Cunneen, Findlay, Lynch and Tupper, *Dynamics of Collective Conflict*; Veno and Veno, 'Police, Riots and Public Order'.

66 S. Coleman, A. Jemphrey, P. Scraton and P. Skidmore, *Hillsborough and After: The Liverpool Experience*, First Report, Centre For Studies in Crime and Social Justice, Edge Hill College of Higher Education, Ormskirk, Lancashire 1990; P. Scraton, A Jemphrey and S. Coleman, *No last rights: The denial of justice and the promotion of myth in the aftermath of the Hillsborough disaster*, Liverpool City Council, Liverpool, 1995; see Green, *The Enemy Without* for detailed discussion of police relations with mining communities in Britain stemming from the intrusive order maintenance tactics adopted during the miners' strikes in the early 1980s; see also M. Keith, *Race Riots and Policing: Lore and Disorder in a Multi racist Society*, UCL Press, London, 1993 and J. Chan *Changing Police Culture: Policing in a Multi-cultural Society*, Cambridge University Press, Melbourne, 1997 for British and Australian evidence of the impact of saturation policing policies on ethnic communities in each jurisdiction.

67 C. Reynolds and P. Wilson 'Private Policing: Creating New Options' in D. Chappell and P. Wilson (eds) *Australian Policing: Contemporary Issues* (2nd Ed), Butterworths, Sydney, 1996, pp. 219-232; R. Sarre, 'The legal powers of private police and security providers', in P. Moyle (Ed) *Private Prisons and Police: Recent Australian Trends*, Pluto Press, Leichhardt, 1994, pp. 259-280; S. Tomsen, 'A Top Night: Social Protest, Masculinity and the Culture of Drinking Violence', *British Journal of Criminology*, 37, 1997, pp. 90-102; Victorian Community Council Against Violence, *Violence in and around Licensed Premises*, The Council, Melbourne, 1990; Warren, *Cultures of Control*; I. Warren, 'An Air of Uncertainty: Private Security Regulation in Victoria', *Deakin Law Review*, 2, 1995, pp. 223-253;

P. Wilson, D. Keogh and R. Lincoln, 'Private Policing: The Major Issues', in P. Moyle (Ed), *Private Prisons and Police*, pp. 281-295.

68 C. Shearing, 'The Relation Between Public and Private Policing' in M. Tonry and N Morris (eds) *Crime and Justice: An Annual Review of Research* (15th Ed) Chicago, University of Chicago Press, Chicago, 1992; pp. 399-434; L. Johnston, *The Rebirth of Private Policing*, Routledge, London, 1992; C. Shearing and P. Stenning, 'Private Security and its Implications: A North American Perspective' in A. Rees (Ed) *Policing and Private Security*, Australian Institute of Criminology, Canberra, 1983; I. Taylor, 'Crime, anxiety and locality: responding to the 'condition of England' at the end of the century' *Theoretical Criminology*, 1, 1997, pp. 53-75; I. Taylor, 'Private Homes and Public Others: An Analysis of Talk about Crime in Suburban South Manchester in the mid-1990s', *British Journal of Criminology*, 25, 1995, pp. 263-285.

69 Victorian Community Council Against Violence, *Violence in and around Licensed Premises*.

70 R. Homel and S. Tomsen, 'Hot Spots for Violence: the Environment of Pubs and Clubs' in H. Strang and S Gerull (Eds) *Homicide: Patterns, Prevention and Control*, Australian Institute of Criminology, Canberra, 1993, pp. 53-66.

71 S. Tomsen, 'A Top Night'.

72 D. Adams and M. Fyfe, 'Police to check excessive force claims at MCG', *The Age*, 29/8/1996, p. A3; Editorial, 'Wrong force', *The Age*, 31/9/1996; I. Warren, 'Block and tackle: the hardest way to move a crowd', *The Age*, 4/9/1996.

73 Sarre, 'The legal powers of private police'; Warren, 'An Air of Uncertainty'.

74 *Private Agents Act* (Victoria) 1966; Sarre, 'The legal powers of private police'; Warren, 'An Air of Uncertainty'.

75 I. Warren, 'Private Security, Law and the Cultures of Entertainment', Paper Presented at the Third Australasian Security Research Symposium, Griffith University, Mt Gravatt (Qld), 7th July, 1997.

76 Sporting authorities are not always receptive to the idea of personal security being present during athletic competition. See C. Happell, 'Armed guard for Woods ruled out of bounds', *The Age*, 15/7/1997, p. B8, which outlines the decision of the organisers of the British Open golf tournament to deny permission for an armed private security guard to accompany Tiger Woods during competition in Britain.

77 Warren, 'Private Security, Law and the Cultures of Entertainment'.

78 R. Sarre, 'Spectator Protection: The Legal Issues Confronting Sports Fixture Operators' *Canberra Law Review* 2, 1995, pp. 25-37.

79 Canter, Comber and Uzzell, *Football in its Place*.

80 J.C. Taylor, 'The War on Soccer Hooliganism: The European Convention on Spectator Violence and 'Misbehaviour' At Sports Events', *Virginia Journal of International Law*, 27, 1987, p. 603.

81 J. Walvin, *Football and the Decline of Britain*, MacMillan, Hampshire 1986.

82 The Scottish Office, Department of National Heritage, *Guide to Safety at Sports Grounds*.

83 L.J. Taylor, *The Hillsborough Stadium Disaster, Final Report* (April 15, 1989), Home Office, Cmnd 962, HMSO, London 1990.

84 See for example M. Collin & J. Godfrey, *Altered state: The Story of Ecstasy Culture and Acid House*, Serpents Tale, London, 1997.

85 'Banks questions soccer seating policy', News and Observer Net, Agence France Presse, 5 October 1997.

86 R. Hay, 'Football in Europe', Sir Norman Chester Centre for Football Research, University of Leicester and the International Centre for Sports History and Culture at De Montfort University, hosted the Football in Europe Conference at Leicester City Soccer Club, 30-31 May 1996, *Bulletin of Sport and Culture*, Victoria Univer-

sity of Technology, 8, September 1996, pp. 10-12.

87 Roy Hay, 'Violence by Players', in Wray Vamplew, Katharine Moore, John O'Hara, Richard Cashman and Ian F Jobling, eds, *Oxford Companion to Australian Sport*, Oxford University Press, Melbourne, 1992, pp. 367-368.

88 S. Greenfield and G. Osborn, 'When the whites go marching in? Racism and resistance in English Football', *Marquette Sports Law Journal*, vol 6, 1996, pp. 315-335, 1996.

89 R. Hay, 'Football, the Law and Civil Liberties', Royal Scottish Academy of Music and Dance, Renfrew Street, Glasgow, Tuesday 26 March 1996, Scottish Council for Civil Liberties and the Scottish Trades Union Congress, sponsored by the Scotsman newspaper, *Victorian Bulletin of Sport and Culture*, Victoria University of Technology, 7, June 1996, pp. 12-14; Lord Advocate's instructions to chief constables and speech delivered to the Scottish Sports Council, 1996, copy available from the author.

90 Veno and Veno, 'Police, Riots and Public Order'; Veno and Veno, 'Managing Public Order'; Mellor, 'Measures to Reduce Violence at Major Public Events'.

91 C/f 'Thousands Miss Big Matches', *The Age*, 13/4/1993; 'Footy Farce: Lockout Fury as 5,000 Miss Game', *The Herald-Sun*, 28/8/1994.

92 R. Hay 'A new look at soccer violence'.

93 Dunning, Murphy and Williams, *The roots of football hooliganism*; Holt, *Sport and the British*.

94 Nauright and Chandler (Eds) *Making Men*; Dunning and Sheard, *Barbarians, Gentlemen and Players*.

Violence, sport and the law

a critical discussion

IAN WARREN

Introduction

SPORTING CONTESTS ALLOW PARTICIPANTS and spectators to demonstrate athletic talents and partisan emotions in a controlled environment, and to exhibit behaviours which are generally highly regulated in daily life. Sport represents 'time out' from many routine aspects of social behaviour, and its relative immunity from legal regulation has long been recognised in sociological and anthropological literature on the phenomenology of leisure.[1] Plato situated sport in the context of military training and claimed that sports participants should not be made liable for homicides which occur during competition.[2] This was viewed as a positive development for the welfare of the state, and the development of an adequately trained military to guarantee protection of the citizens of ancient Greece. It was considered that specialist regulation, monitored by professional military trainers and others familiar with athletic pursuits, was required to facilitate these broader social goals.[3] These dual rationales continually emerge in discussions of the role of law in sports violence throughout history.

Athletic aggression has been a common feature of most sports since the development of organised professional and amateur sporting contests during the 19th Century. Historically, the use of criminal and civil laws to formally impose liability in cases of injury or death occurring during 'manly'[4] sporting pastimes has been minimal. However certain exceptions to this situation are dotted throughout history, particularly where the state deemed it necessary to outlaw some sports for the overall social good. In *R. v. Hargrave* (1831) a spectator was indicted, convicted and sentenced to fourteen years transportation for being an accessory to the manslaughter of a combatant in a prize fight, even though he did not participate in the fight itself.[5] The policy behind this ruling reflected the state's desire to eliminate prize fighting, due to the perceived dangers to combatants, irrespective of their consensual engagement in the activity, and threats to public order presented by spectators.[6] However, immunity from criminal regulation was the general rule in most sports. In *R. v. Bradshaw*[7] (1878) the jury failed to convict the accused for manslaughter after he recklessly jumped into an opposition player during an Association Rules football match. Matters of proof and causation aside, there appears to be a distinct public policy rationale for granting legal immunity in such culturally legitimate sports, despite the obvious risks of death and injury to participants.

Extensive criticism has been levelled at the perceived increase in the frequency and severity of sports violence in recent years.[8] This is largely associated with broader concerns about violence and its prevention in modern society.[9] Masculine cultures glorifying aggression, violence and deliberate rule breaking as 'part of the game' in many contact sports are often cited as key precipitants of this phenomenon.[10] In response, sports organisations have altered the rules of many sports to combat athletic violence. Improved training, increased public scrutiny through extensive media coverage, and the rise of athletic professionalism combine to deter deliberate violence in elite sports. However accurate quantification of the frequency of sports violence remains speculative in both professional and amateur sports.

Boxing continues to raise debate over its potentially lethal consequences for consenting athletes. The death of Lance Hobson in 1996, the sixth fatality in twelve months of international boxing,[11] and reignited public debate both for and against increased legal regulation of this sport. 'Blood sports' such as extreme wrestling attract considerable audiences in the United States, and have raised concerns amongst legislators over their impact on athletes and spectators:

> Two fighters, unarmed and barefisted, are placed in a ring surrounded by a cage fence and do battle with each other until one is knocked unconscious or surrenders. With the exception of eye gouging and biting, anything goes. Contestants are allowed to break legs, arms and ligaments. They can deliver punches to the brain stem, elbows to the kidneys and kicks to the head and face. The umpire, who wears surgical gloves, will stop the fight only if it becomes a bloodbath.[12]

Public debate on these sports is highly polarised: some claim they create career and financial opportunities for individuals otherwise marginalised from the cultural mainstream.[13] Others view these sports as antithetical to the development of civilised society.[14]

A combination of criminal, civil and administrative legal mechanisms have emerged in recent years largely in response to public concerns surrounding violence in sport. The state and private individuals that are using these measures ensure that individuals, sporting clubs, and sports leagues are brought to account for harms caused by sports violence, or to rectify procedural irregularities in sports tribunal hearings and other internal disciplinary processes.

Table 1: Smith's socio-legal typology of sports violence

Classification	Characteristics	Examples	Legal Outcomes
Brutal Body Contact	– technically within the rules, but sometimes leads to injury; – consented to by athletes.	– legal tackles, shepherds, blocks or accidental collisions during play.	– no legal liability
Borderline violence	– technically beyond the rules; – generally accepted and consented to by athletes as 'part of the game'.	– late hits; high tackles; fist fights in the heat of competition.	– seldom litigated; – may attract civil liability.
Quasi-criminal violence	– beyond the rules of the game; – not consented to by athletic culture.	– biting, kicking, spitting, cowardly hits behind play, or 'dirty play' such as 'squirrel grips'.	– litigious depending on the severity of the injury; – civil liability common. Criminal actions rare but possible.
Criminal violence	– incidental to the event; – beyond the rules of the game; – clear criminal conduct.	– assaults prior to or after completion of the event; fights in the car park or locker rooms; – deliberate incidents resulting in death or other debilitating injury such as murder, manslaughter, rape, sexual assault, assault.	– criminal liability provided there is sufficient intention or recklessness.

In Canada it is estimated that over 100 criminal prosecutions in the area of sports violence were initiated between 1970 and 1986.[15] Civil litigation, supplemented by public and private compensation funds, provide avenues for victims to obtain direct compensation for injuries sustained during athletic competition. Administrative law principles of natural justice are used by those alleged to have engaged in acts of violence on the sporting field to ensure procedural fairness and the conduct of fair trials by sports tribunals. These developments combine to erode traditional conceptions of the immunity of sport from legal scrutiny. However, each presents several difficulties in ensuring consistency and justice under the methodology of the legal system.

This paper discusses violence in sport in light of the philosophical and practical distinctions in criminal, civil and administrative law regulation. Through an examination of several recent Australian cases, the paper documents the factual and legal issues raised in each area of law, and highlights the evidentiary and procedural concerns arising in the judicial treatment of sports violence. The paper discusses these matters in the context of critical socio-legal accounts of sports violence, and posits some future directions which may impact on legal regulation in this area.

Sports violence defined

Violence in sport is difficult to define. Legal definitions of assaultive behaviour may provide some assistance, however the rules of some sports frequently permit various types of behaviours with violent or injurious outcomes as legitimate tactics or skills central to the sport in question. This may lead to contradictions between the expectations of sports participants and spectators, and legal definitions of unreasonable or illegal behaviour warranting the imposition of liability. Smith[16] attempts to resolve these difficulties by outlining a typology of sports violence based on research into several well-publicised cases in Canada and the United States. A summary of this typology is presented in Table 1 (see previous page).[17]

Smith's typology indicates that there are varying degrees of violence in sport resulting in different forms of legal regulation. However, these definitions need to be sensitive to the various socio-cultural attitudes towards violence which emerge at different historical periods, and in the context of different sports.[18] Mummendey and Mummendey have devised a supplementary definition of sports violence which acknowledges these concerns, based on four key characteristics of the phenomenon:

- there is injury affecting at least one of the parties;
- there is a degree of intention determining the level of responsibility attributable to the offender;
- there is norm deviation as judged by fellow athletes or the broader community; and
- there is an assessment of the situational context of the incident rather than the perpetrator's conduct alone.[19]

Each of these definitions assists in understanding the difficulties associated with imposing legal liability in cases of sports violence. The following examples highlight the complexity of these issues through *ex post facto* judicial consideration.

Regulating violence in sport

i) Criminal law

Under the criminal law the state initiates legal action on behalf of an aggrieved individual for behaviour which threatens social cohesion or which results in some physical harm to individuals. The police and public prosecutions departments investigate any allegations of criminal behaviour and have the exclusive responsibility for apprehending suspects, gathering evidence, and presenting cases before the courts. Several crimes are listed in the statute books which could be pursued by the state in dealing with allegations of intentional or reckless violence on the sporting field. Several recent cases highlight the issues of principle in legislative and judicial rule making which govern the imposition of liability under the criminal law.

In cases where death occurs on the sports field, charges of murder or manslaughter may be pursued. Most incidents of sports violence will involve summary[20] or indictable assaults, or associated offences including intentionally or recklessly causing serious injury, which differ slightly in each jurisdiction.[21] Prosecutions can also be brought for behaviour which endangers life,[22] negligent or reckless infliction of injury,[23] threats to inflict serious injury,[24] and a series of offences relating to attempts,[25] aiding and abetting,[26] incitement,[27] and conspiracy to commit criminal acts.[28] In each case the prosecution must prove the charge beyond reasonable doubt, and establish that the suspect intended, or recklessly engaged in the behaviour which causes harm. Penalties may include fines, community-based orders, or terms of imprisonment.

The definition of 'assault' in Victoria appears in section 31(2) of the *Crimes Act* 1958. The following matters must be proved to sustain a conviction:

- force was directly or indirectly applied to the body or clothing of another;
- the application of force was unlawful;
- force was applied intentionally or recklessly; and
- there was resultant injury, pain, discomfort or damage to another.

'Injury' includes unconsciousness, hysteria, pain and 'any substantial impairment of bodily function'.[29] Serious injury includes any combination of injuries.

These statutory definitions clearly encompass most cases of sports violence. However, the criminal law is generally reserved for cases where the violence has been peripheral to the events during the course of sporting competition, or where there has been extreme violence leading to serious injury to a victim and consequent mass public concern over the incident.[30]

Incidents of criminal violence peripheral to the events on the field of play provide few problems for judicial scrutiny. For example, *Edgecock v. Davies*[31] involved a criminal assault on an umpire by a spectator after the completion of an amateur football match in Tasmania. As the umpire walked from the field he was verbally abused, pushed in the upper body, and punched in the side of the face by an irate and drunken spectator. The victim sustained a cracked jaw and was hospitalised. Despite minor provocation from the umpire, this was a clear case of criminal assault. The match had ended, there was a clear intention to cause injury, and the victim made no effort to defend himself. This 'cowardly and vicious attack' led to a three-month term of imprisonment aimed at deterring the perpetrator and others from deliberate acts of violence against sporting officials.[32] Further, a suspension was imposed by the league preventing the offender from playing football for 15 years.

Criminal prosecutions stemming from the behaviour of athletes during competition are rare. However, a widely publicised incident involving Victorian Football League players Leigh Matthews and Neville Bruns provides one example where criminal liability was imposed at professional level. In a particularly spiteful match where five players were reported on 17 charges,[33] Matthews ran at Bruns, who was well behind play, and executed a head high, stiff arm tackle resulting in a broken jaw. Matthews maintained that the tackle was accidental and justifiable, but pleaded guilty to assault occasioning actual bodily harm after a police investigation and extensive television coverage of the incident. Matthews was placed on a $1,000 bond and a community service order but the conviction was overturned on appeal.

The issues of principle underlying decisions to convict in cases of violence during the course of play are illustrated by *R. v. Carr*.[34] Carr was charged with assault occasioning bodily harm after executing a head high swinging arm tackle in a rugby league match. The impact broke the victim's jaw. The match was particularly violent, with one player sent of for striking, and Carr receiving two warnings from the referee for previous head high tackles. Carr denied criminal liability on the basis that he had no intention to cause harm by executing an illegal tackle. Evidence indicated that Carr wrongly anticipated that the victim would receive the ball from a teammate, but was committed to executing the tackle in the circumstances, and had no prospect of pulling out. Carr claimed he intended to execute a lawful tackle directed at the chest, rather than the head of the victim. Carr appealed against the jury conviction, claiming the judge's direction placed insufficient weight on his honest belief that the victim would receive the ball. The prosecution case stressed that athletes do not consent to serious injuries which are in breach of the rules of the sport, despite the lack of intention which might characterise violent activity during athletic competition.

In upholding the conviction, the appeal court indicated that the following direction was a valid statement of the criminal law of assault in cases of sports violence:

> ... players in an intrinsically violent game (such as Rugby League) are deemed in law to consent to force of a kind and degree which could reasonably be expected to happen during a game and they are deemed to consent to the infliction of such force upon the occasions which could reasonably be expected to occur during a game ... If you thought there was a reasonable

> possibility that the accused had made a bona fide, but ... mistaken judgment ... and ... committed himself to a (lawful) tackle ... then you might find great difficulty in determining, beyond reasonable doubt, that the accused was within any breach of the rules of the game ... If on the other hand, you did not entertain such a doubt and you felt ... he was ... unnecessarily going to make a head high tackle ... then you might find little difficulty in concluding, beyond reasonable doubt, that he was in breach of the official rules.[35]

The conviction was upheld in light of the following considerations:

- the tackle was in breach of the rules of rugby;
- head high tackles are beyond the expectation of participants in a game of rugby played according to the rules; and
- players do not consent to major breaches of the rules which lead to injuries of the type sustained in this case.

ii) Civil law and compensatory based claims

Civil actions and claims under publicly sponsored compensation funds provide avenues for financial compensation for victims of sports violence. Unlike the criminal law, there is no need to prove matters such as the perpetrator's intention and direct cause of the incident at the time to a jury or judge alone *beyond reasonable doubt*. The victim will initiate the action, eroding any problems associated with state involvement in the conduct of the case. The lower standard of proof and the prospect of direct compensation, provide additional incentives for the use of these options by victims of sports violence.[36]

a) Civil assault

Civil assault involves 'the unlawful application of force by one person to another without that other person's consent'.[37] The case must be proved on the balance of probabilities, irrespective of the degree of intention in the mind of the perpetrator. In addition, actions in negligence may be brought against individual athletes, sporting clubs or sporting organisations for injuries sustained during athletic competition. It might be preferable to initiate joint actions to enable liability to be apportioned amongst several parties, and to ensure individuals are not unduly disadvantaged by a high damages payments. Two recent examples illustrate the considerations governing the imposition of liability under the civil law.

Giumelli v. Johnston[38] involved a collision between two opposing players during an Australian Rules Football match in South Australia. The victim sustained a depressed fracture of the cheekbone and required extensive medical treatment. Evidence indicated the plaintiff was gathering the ball in a stooping position when he felt a blow to the side of the face. The defendant testified that the contact was a fair hip and shoulder bump permitted by the rules, but this was contradicted by evidence presented by the victim's coach which suggested that defendant 'jumped and brought his right elbow in a thrusting action into the respondent's cheekbone', contrary to the rules.[39] The plaintiff was unable to identify the nature of the contact in the circumstances. The court inferred from the evidence that contact was a deliberate and unlawful, despite acknowledging that the high speed and intensity of a football match could lead a player to inadvertently jump and raise an elbow when attempting to spoil an opponent in accordance with the rules.

The imposition of liability hinged on the issue of consent. The court held that athletes do not consent to deliberate behaviour which is in breach of the rules and results in serious injury.[40] The issue of consent was outlined by the court in the following terms:

> Those who participate in a football match are taken to consent to the infliction . . . of such physical force as is permitted by the rules of the game . . . some bodily contact outside the rules of the game is to be expected as an ordinary incident of a football match . . . it may be accepted that the consent which a participant in a football match gives to the application of physical force to him extends to physical force . . . notwithstanding that it involves some infringement of the rules.[41]

Athletes therefore consent to most injuries which can be expected during the course of a football match, which can involve predictable and minor breaches of the rules by an opponent. In this case, contact with an elbow was deemed to be 'completely outside the scope of any consent implied from the respondent's participation in the game'.[42] This was sufficient to establish a successful cause of action in the plaintiff's favour.

Canterbury Bankstown Rugby League Football Club Ltd v. Rogers; Bugden v. Rogers[43] elaborates on these issues. Rogers was struck with a forearm to the face during a rugby match. He sustained a broken jaw requiring surgery and extensive dental work. Rogers sued Bugden for assault, and his club for failing to ensure that Bugden did not act unlawfully during the course of his employment as a rugby player. Bugden testified that he did not strike Rogers intentionally with an illegal forearm, but in a manner permitted by the rules of rugby league. This was supported by evidence from other players, but was contradicted by Rogers' coach who testified that the contact was with a prohibited forearm. Photographic and video evidence recorded by television cameras was analysed at various speeds and angles. This evidence suggested that Rogers was hit with a swinging arm contrary to the rules, thereby making Bugden liable for civil assault.[44]

The case against the club rested on the principle that employers can be made liable for the behaviour of employees during the course of their employment. Some degree of deviation from standard procedures of carrying out the employment task may result in liability being imposed against employers, provided the employee does not radically deviate from these standards.[45] Rogers claimed that Bugden was employed to tackle opposition players, but did so in breach of the rules of rugby. However, the breach was not so radical as to prevent contribution from the club. As a result, the club should be liable for not ensuring that Bugden carried out his job in a lawful and safe fashion. This argument was successful, despite Bugden's tackle being in breach of the rules governing his employment as a professional footballer. The illegality did not preclude the tackle from being considered part of a *process* which Bugden was authorised to execute in his employment as a rugby player.[46] The club was in a position to take steps to ensure that Bugden's technique was changed to accord with the rules, but its failure to do this was sufficient to warrant joint liability.

The court also canvassed the question of the use of motivational tactics by coaches. This issue arose from an allegation that the Canterbury coach 'revved up' Bugden and other members of the team and specifically instructed them to 'stop' Rogers and two other opponents. The court held that encouragement from the coach in this case was intended to generate enthusiasm rather than to encourage the use of illegal tactics to 'stop' opposition players:

> It may be that, in professionalised sport, winning, and not playing, is the object . . . If the employee, in seeking to win, uses means which are legitimate in one area but not in another, and the employer, by his attitude to winning and his motivation of instructions to the employee, creates a real risk that the employee will act illegitimately, that may assist in finding that the employer is liable for what happened.[47]

There was insufficient evidence to establish that deliberate instructions were issued to Bugden and other Canterbury players to break the rules and win at all costs. Nevertheless joint liability was imposed due to the employer / employee principles outlined above. A total of around $150,000 in damages, divided relatively equally between the defendants, was awarded to compensate for the injury sustained and associated expenses, loss of actual and some future earnings, and in order to deter similar behaviour in the future given the severity of the injury, the deliberate nature of the assault, and the extensive publicity and humiliation experienced by Rogers. A further sum of $7,500 was awarded as an exemplary deterrent against Bugden.[48]

b) Public compensation funds

A series of recent cases involve applications by victims of sports violence for compensation through criminal injuries[49] or similar public compensation funds.[50] The legal issue in most cases relates to the existence of sufficient evidence of a 'criminal action' warranting compensation through the fund.

This is generally established by adopting a civil standard of proof. Compensation may be awarded irrespective of whether the state has initiated criminal proceedings. This avenue is preferred where protracted civil action is unlikely to be successful due to insufficient evidence, where there is no insurance covering the victim, where the financial means of the claimant or defendant might influence the ability to pay for litigation or damages, or where there is no perceived benefit in pursuing a criminal trial.

Re Lenfield[51] involved a claim on behalf of a teenage boy who sustained a broken collarbone after being 'speared' whilst in possession of the ball during a schoolyard derivative of rugby league. The claimant's opponent, who was two years older and substantially larger in physique ran at him and stated 'I will get you',[52] lifted the claimant in the air and drove him head first into the ground. The victim avoided the full impact of the tackle by pivoting his head and landing on his shoulder. Six months after the incident the claimant continued to suffer from mild pain and restricted arm movement.

The issue for consideration by the court was whether the tackle was 'criminal conduct' for the purposes of granting compensation. The absence of hostile intent, combined with the expectation that such tackles might occur in playground football, eliminated the claim at first instance,[53] but this was reversed on appeal. The court referred to the prohibition on spear tackles within the rules of rugby league, and their aim in preventing unnecessary injury to rugby players.[54] As the tackle was outlawed by professional rugby, this equated with 'criminal conduct' for the purposes of awarding compensation, despite the unsupervised nature of the match, and the degree of intention to cause harm in the mind of the older boy:

> He did it deliberately although he probably did not intend to cause injury. Given his relatively greater height and weight, the tackle may have been more enthusiastic than intended. I do not believe that the rules and usages of the game of 'tackle' would sanction conduct more dangerous than that permitted in Rugby League. It follows that the tackle was outside what would be tolerated as part of the game, particularly when executed by an older, taller and heavier player than would usually be expected to participate.[55]

The court held that the only hostile intent present in the perpetrator's actions was to inflict the illegal tackle, rather than to cause harm to the claimant: the older boy had the opportunity to execute a different tackle but consciously decided to use an unlawful tackle without the victim's consent.[56] The award was made despite the failure to initiate criminal proceedings against the older boy.

iii) Administrative regulation

On the eve of the 1994 and 1996 Australian Football League (AFL) finals two significant cases challenged the tribunal procedures dealing with allegations of rule breaking violence. The players involved were threatened with tribunal investigations, and sought injunctions to prevent official hearings leading to possible suspensions. The arguments in both cases claimed that the League breached fundamental principles of natural justice by not allowing the accused players sufficient time to prepare adequate defences to the charges.

The 'Subiaco melee' occurred just prior to the half time break in a match between the West Coast Eagles and Footscray in 1994. Several players wrestled and allegedly exchanged punches in the incident. West Coast's Peter Sumich was seriously injured and rendered unconscious during the brawl after receiving an accidental kick to the head from a teammate, and being held in a headlock by Footscray player Danny Southern.[57] The umpires laid no charges at the time. The incident received widespread media coverage on the eve of the finals which were to involve both teams.[58] Controversy over melees was sparked by a similar incident two weeks previously which led to the passage of a rule prohibiting the practice. The new rule had not come into effect at the time of the Subiaco match.[59] Eight players were charged with assault[60] on the Wednesday evening after the incident. The hearing was to take place the day before the commencement of the finals series.[61]

Footscray issued writs against AFL Operations Manager and the AFL Commission alleging breach of an agreement between the parties which would allow the club to pay a fine of $20,000 in exchange for an undertaking not to proceed with the tribunal hearing. Footscray also sought temporary and permanent injunctions preventing the AFL from pursuing the hearings, relying on the principles of natural justice. The club argued that the public announcement of the charges on the Wednesday evening, plus the scheduling of the hearing the day before the commencement of the finals, gave the players involved insufficient time to prepare adequate defences, despite the prospect of a decision in their favour.[62] Further, the date of the hearing arguably impeded the club's preparation for its forthcoming final. The Supreme Court of Victoria rejected the argument over the enforcement of the agreement but awarded a temporary injunction. This allowed the AFL to pursue the case after Footscray finished its finals campaign.[63] West Coast decided not to pursue similar legal action, allowing their players to face the tribunal. No Footscray players attended to give evidence, and all Eagles players were cleared.[64]

A similar case was initiated by Sydney full back Andrew Dunkley who was charged from video evidence over an incident involving Essendon player James Hird in the 1996 Preliminary Final.[65] The AFL completed the investigation four days after the incident, and Dunkley's tribunal hearing was scheduled three days prior to the Grand Final in which he was expected to play.[66] The AFL delayed the hearing for 24 hours to enable Dunkley adequate time to prepare a defence. In the interim, the Sydney Swans issued writs for a temporary injunction to prevent the hearing.[67] The injunction was granted on the basis that the publicity surrounding the incident, and the importance of the match to the Swans and Dunkley, demanded adherence to the principles of natural justice. The delay in laying charges, the proximity of the hearing to the Grand Final, and the significance of the match were sufficient to warrant injunctive relief.[68]

However, a more recent case involving former Carlton footballer Greg Williams casts some doubt on the ability of elite athletes to use this course of action to evade the decision making process of internal league tribunals. Williams was suspended in early 1997 by the Australian Football League tribunal for a total of nine matches for interference with a field umpire. This was despite evidence tendered by the umpire in question that Williams action was non-threatening. Williams and the Carlton club appealed the decision to the Full Court of the Supreme Court of Victoria, and later the High Court of Australia, which ultimately held, on a split decision, that the tribunal's suspension was valid. Williams major arguments were similar to those of the Footscray Football Club, and Andrew Dunkley:

- first, the decision was in error, because there was too much reliance placed on video evidence of the incident when the tribunal determination was made;
- second, to suspend Williams would have severe economic consequences, going beyond the issue of match payments, and potentially affecting his income from personal endorsements; and
- the lack of an appeals mechanism within the AFL tribunal process necessitated recourse to the courts, and warranted a ruling in Williams' favour, on the grounds that existing tribunal procedures are unfair.

The High Court in particular rejected these arguments. At the time of writing the reported judgement on this case is unavailable. However, it seems that the courts in this case feel that the nature of the incident, and the tribunal procedures adopted by the AFL, do not encourage recourse to judicial scrutiny for aggrieved players as a matter of course. In other words, the courts in this case are perhaps sending out a message to the professional sporting community to respect the decisions of internal tribunals.[69] The extent to which line of reasoning this will be accepted by the football community, particularly as allegations of drug taking and the potential tampering of bodily samples under existing testing regimes present further problems for the rights of professional athletes, remains to be seen.

The use of administrative law is not confined to professional sports,[70] and allegations of procedural irregularities in tribunal hearings will not always be sufficient to warrant an injunction.[71] In *Manlio v. Mutimer and others*[72] the Essendon District Football League tribunal suspended the applicant, a highly skilled player, after an incident in a semi-final, preventing his participation in the Grand Final. It was claimed that the suspension was unjust because it prevented the applicant from earning match payments and a possible $500 award for his club's best and fairest. His club also claimed that the applicant was a vital player, his absence would reduce their chances of victory, and the suspension adversely affected the club's preparation for the final. The court rejected the claim, arguing that the financial gains to the applicant and the club were not worthy of Supreme Court relief. This was despite questions over the conduct of the hearing by the League tribunal and the effect of the suspension on the applicant's reputation.

Discussion

Despite the philosophical and procedural differences between these causes of action, the use of criminal, civil and administrative laws in cases of sports violence has important ramifications for the role of law in contemporary sport. Several matters arise from the cases which suggest that legal regulation is highly problematic in this area. The implications of these issues are briefly examined in light of the major features of legal methodology and principle to emerge in these cases.

The criminal law places almost exclusive focus on the behaviour of the suspect. The civil law could be viewed as focussing on the harm sustained by the victim. Despite these differences, and the varying standards of proof under each form of law, the principles behind these forms of liability are relatively similar. In attributing liability under the criminal or civil law, the legal rules focus on the rules of the game, the degree to which the victim actually or could have consented to the behaviour and importantly its outcome, and the varying degrees of express or implied intention in the mind of the perpetrator at the time of the incident in question. Both forms of inquiry demonstrate similar problems relating to the use of evidence and the imputation of matters of intention and fact in these cases. This results in several common difficulties, which have implications for the conduct of cases and the consistent imposition of liability under each regime.

Evidentiary matters are especially problematic in criminal and civil actions. The speed of most contact sports creates difficulties for witnesses to accurately recollect factual circumstances. This is particularly problematic in cases where testimony is taken in court as many as five years after the incident. Further, the potential for witnesses to be biased due to partisan associations with either perpetrators or victims of violence has the potential to influence findings of fact in these cases. These issues are relatively unproblematic in cases involving deliberate assaults which are ancillary to the events on the field of play.[73] However, cases such as *Carr* and *Rogers*, raise questions about the credibility of witnesses supporting either party. In *Rogers* this issue was tempered by the availability of video evidence of the point of contact which was used in conjunction with oral accounts from witnesses to the alleged assault. However such evidence will not be available in all cases. It is reasonable to assume that evidence against the defendants in both cases was preferred on policy grounds which favoured the claims of the victims. This may raise concerns about the objectivity of the evidence presented to the court for consideration, particularly where credible witnesses may have an identifiable connection with either party to the case. Further research is required to assess the issue of evidentiary bias more systematically. However the nature of sporting contests and many violent incidents during the course of competition suggests that judicial scrutiny well after the event may not result in a true representation of the facts subject to a criminal or civil claim.

The *imputation* of different degrees of consent in each case may lead to artificial results based on relative speculation and varying policy objectives. These factors may impact on the consistency of legal regulation in this area, and are complicated in cases of on field violence given the competitive atmosphere, the presence of cultures advocating 'win at all costs' imperatives, and the speed with which many violent incidents occur. The courts in *Giumelli* and *Bugden* indicated that it is impossible for victims of athletic violence to consent to the infliction of physical injury by using the rules of the game as the bench mark for imposing liability. In both cases, it was submitted that the actions of the perpetrators were beyond the scope of any imputed consent by the victim. The reliance on imputed evidence suggests that policy considerations may override factual or empirical considerations governing the imposition of liability, particularly given the time lag between these incidents and their judicial determination. Further, any discussion of the contributory negligence of the victim remains largely unaddressed in these cases.[74] This can lead to additional distortions of factual issues which may impact on the objectivity of the fact-finding process.

The rules of the game are frequently referred to in both forms of legal regulation. If injury occurs due to a breach of the rules it is likely that liability will be imposed against a defendant. This creates several problems. Written rules may not always provide insights into aspects of behaviour which occur during sporting competition. It is possible that informal cultural norms often govern the acceptance or condemnation of various behaviours characteristic in different sports.[75] Further, the norms of various sporting contests will differ depending on the ability of the participants involved. The decision in *Re Lenfield* illustrates this issue. The application of professional Rugby League rules to legal rulings on the behaviour of school children involved in an unsupervised 'scratch' match might have well-intentioned motives in the circumstances. However the use of written standards governing professional athletes might cause harsh results for criminal or civil defendants with lesser abilities. Failure to devote adequate consideration to the context of each event may lead to the courts overlooking the importance of informal customs reflecting different ethics in various levels of sport. This feature is recognised in the definitions of sports violence presented by Smith and Mummendey and Mummendey.[76] Where criminal liability and penalties, or where multiple penalties may be imposed by different regulatory methods dealing with the same act are at stake,[77] these issues become extremely troublesome for the courts. The result may be the imposition of uniform and generic standards of conduct being used to impose liability where cultural reality dictates that there are substantial differences in athletic behaviour at different levels of generically similar sports.[78]

The extension of this is illustrated by the administrative decisions discussed above. In the Subiaco and Dunkley cases the courts awarded interim relief on the basis that there was sufficient evidence of benefit to be gained from the injunction. The publicity surrounding the events, the financial remuneration, and the status to be gained from participation in finals matches, were cited in both cases as features favourable to granting interim relief against the AFL. In both cases, the court considered that a failure to grant injunctive relief would unduly disadvantage the claimants in the circumstances, despite evidence suggesting that each had engaged in violent activity which was later punished by the AFL tribunal.

These very reasons precluded interim relief in *Manlio's* case. Despite similar allegations of potential miscarriages of justice and loss to the claimant from the tribunal's suspension, the rewards for the claimant's participation in a local league Grand Final were not deemed sufficient to warrant legal intervention. This suggests that the legal system is developing gradations of legitimate intervention which preserve the significant financial and aesthetic interests of professional athletes, yet effectively deny resort to the same relief for those with fewer monetary gains or less community status. The failure of the courts to consider the contexts of each situation in detail, with reference to the *proportionate* impact of losses sustained by denying relief in each case may lead to unjust results across different levels of sport. The High Court decision in the Williams case, however, suggests that perhaps the courts are less willing to accept the arguments of elite athletes which attempt to reverse decisions of League tribunal proceedings.

These arguments suggest that the motivations for using different laws in different contexts requires further detailed examination by critical research. The compensation motive in civil cases appears to be relatively unproblematic, and awards can be geared to suit the individual circumstances of each claimant, keeping in mind the proportionate losses sustained through similar types of violent behaviour at different levels of competition. Moreover, joint liability can ensure that responsibility for the payment of damages can be apportioned amongst several relevant parties, which distributes the financial burden where high awards are made. This is particularly important given the greater revenue raising power of football clubs compared with individuals who might have difficulty absorbing the costs of high or unduly punitive damages awards. Ultimately this provides more options for claimants to ensure that they have the prospect of receiving adequate compensation to cover their losses.

The rationale behind criminal prosecutions is more complicated. Thomas Gabor suggests that criminal actions are only pursued where victims of suspected criminal violence have something to gain from prosecution.[79] Evidence from the United States[80] indicates that the social value of prosecution, the appropriateness of criminal punishments in deterring individuals and others from similar behaviours, the level of public concern over a specific incident and the availability of legal expertise or sufficient evidence acceptable in a court of law, are all factors considered in deciding to pursue legal action in cases of sports violence. However these features compete with informal cultural norms adhered to by sports administrators, coaches and players. Such norms might view criminal regulation with scepticism. Sports administrators may see the criminal law as an unnecessary burden due to the presence of 'in house' mechanisms designed to detect and punish the violent behaviour of athletes. Elite athletes and their clubs may also be able to negotiate their way out of criminal proceedings due to the higher stakes in professional sport. This might explain the low number of prosecutions initiated against professional athletes for criminal violence either on or off the sporting field. This option may not exist for those involved in amateur competition, reiterating the proposition that class, cultural, gender,[81] sexuality,[82] or any other 'minority' considerations might be influential in determining the availability of various legal options in generically similar cases.

Many of the difficulties stemming from the imposition of liability for sports violence may be resolved through a greater reliance on private insurance policies, or public compensation funds for athletes. Litigation will not always produce the desired result for victims of accidental or deliberate violence. The difficulties in establishing proof and intention in the context of athletic competition compounds the problems faced in initiating criminal or civil proceedings. Insurance schemes may guarantee some compensation for aggrieved individuals, and requirements for appropriate contribution from perpetrators of premeditated or unacceptable violent behaviour could be imposed to foster specific deterrence where this is warranted. This would help to overcome many of the difficulties associated with litigation to obtain compensation.

The administrative law cases suggest that this area of law is a significant tactic to ensure that rights of due process, or the administrative 'rules of the game', are adhered to by sporting organisations. The cases indicate that such litigation will be used where a claimant perceives tribunal procedures are unfair in the circumstances, and where external relief is considered necessary to prevent investigations and internal penalties being imposed by the leagues in an arbitrary and unfair manner. It can be alleged that this tactic can actively subvert the specialist jurisdiction of sports organisations dealing with violent rule breaking on an 'in house' basis. The injunction permits successful applicants who have engaged in acts of violence to avoid the imposition of a suspension which might deprive them from playing in future matches of significance to themselves and their clubs. However, as the *Manlio* and *Williams* cases indicate, success in these cases is not necessarily guaranteed.

Further research on each of these areas of law and the perceptions of athletes, lawyers, and interested members of the public of the efficacy of these measures in dealing with sports violence the Australian context is clearly warranted. Extensive and informed consultation with those most concerned about the problem of sports violence can help to foster a more detailed knowledge of the implications of each form of legal regulation, with a view to devising innovative solutions to overcome the procedural difficulties and inconsistencies emerging in this area.

endnotes

1 H. Cantelon and R. Gruneau, *Sport, Culture and the Modern State*, University of Toronto Press, Toronto, 1982; N. Elias and E. Dunning, *Quest For Excitement: Sport and Leisure in the Civilizing Process*, Basil Blackwell, Oxford, 1989; P. Marsh, E. Rosser and T. Harre, *The Rules of Disorder*, Routledge and Kegan Paul, London, 1978; S. Mennell, *Norbert Elias: An Introduction*, Blackwell Publishers, Oxford, 1992; M.D. Smith, *Violence and Sport*, Butterworths, Toronto, 1983.

2 See Plato, *The Laws*, translated by T.J. Saunders, Penguin, London, 1975, p. 325: . . . we don't want the competitions they hold against each other to be entirely unalarming, but to inspire them with fear and do something to reveal the brave man and the coward; and the legislator should confer honours or inflict disgrace as appropriate, so as to prepare the whole state to be an efficient fighter in the real struggle that lasts a lifetime. *In fact, if anyone is killed in such circumstances, the homicide should be regarded as involuntary, and the legislator should decree that the killer's hands are clean when once he has been purified according to law. After all . . . even if a few people do die, others who are just as good will be produced to replace them, whereas if fear dies (so to speak), he'll not be able to find in all these activities a yardstick to separate the good performers from the bad – and that would be a bigger disaster for the state . . .* (emphasis added).

3 Plato, *Laws*, pp. 320-330.

4 *R. v. Young and others* (1866) 10 Cox CC 371 at 372.

5 5 C & P 234; 172 ER 925.

6 See *R. v. Murphy* (1833) 172 ER 1164; *R. v. Hunt, Swanton and others* (1845) 1 Cox CC 177.

7 *R. v. Bradshaw* (1878) 14 Cox CC 83.

8 R.A. DiNicola and S. Mendeloff 'Controlling Violence in Professional Sports: Rule Reform and the Federal Professional Sports Violence Commission' *Duquesne Law Review*, Vol 21, 1983, p. 843; D.R. Karon, "Winning Isn't Everything, It's the Only Thing'. Violence in Professional Sports: The Need for Federal Regulation and Criminal Sanctions', *Indiana Law Review*, Vol 15, 1991, p. 147; K. Melnick, 'Giving Violence a Sporting Chance: A Review of Measures Used to Curb Excessive Violence in Professional Sports', *Journal of Legislation*, Vol 17, 1990, p. 123; D.C. Nielsen, 'Controlling Sports Violence: Too Late for the Carrots – Bring on the Big Stick', *Iowa Law Review*, Vol 74, 1989, p. 681. For Australian literature on legal regulation in sport more generally see G.M. Kelly, *Sport and the Law: An Australian Perspective*, The Law Book Company, Sydney, 1987.

9 See for instance National Committee on Violence, *Violence, Directions for Australia*, Australian Institute of Criminology, Canberra, 1990; D. Chappell and S. Egger (eds) *Australian Violence: Contemporary Perspectives II*, Australian Institute of Criminology, Canberra, 1994.

10 P. Donnelly and K. Young, 'The Construction and Confirmation of Identity in Sport Subcultures', *Sociology of Sport Journal*, Vol 5, 1988, pp. 223-240; M. Miedzian, *Boys Will Be Boys: Breaking the Link Between Masculinity and Violence*, Doubleday, New York 1991; M.A. Messner and D.F. Sabo, *Sport, Men, and the Gender Order: Critical Feminist Perspectives*, Human Kinetics Books, Campaign, 1990; D. Sabo and S. Curry Jensen, 'Images of Men in Sport Media: The Social Reproduction of Gender Order' in S. Craig (ed), *Men, Masculinity and the Media*, Sage Publications, Newbury Park 1992; M. Burton Nelson, *The Stronger Women Get, the More Men*

Love Football: Sexism and the Culture of Sport, London: The Womens' Press Lt, 1996; c.f. D. Brown and R. Hogg, ' Violence, Masculinity and Sport: Governance and the Swinging Arm', *UTS Review: Cultural Studies and New Writing*, vol 3, no. 1, 1997, pp. 129-140.

11 P. Smith, 'Death in the ring another blow to our innocence', *The Age*, 1 May 1996.

12 C. Stewart, 'Blood money', *The Weekend Australian* 17-18 Aug 1996, (features) p. 6.

13 The connection between race and racism has been central to discussions on the social legitimacy of boxing throughout American history. For a brief discussion of this issue see W.J. Baker, *Sports in the Western World*, (Revised ed) University of Illinois Press, Urbana, 1988, pp. 204-206.

14 Elias and Dunning, *Quest For Excitement*.

15 D.V. White, 'Sports Violence as Criminal Assault: Development of the Doctrine by Canadian Courts', *Duke Law Journal*, 1986, p. 1030.

16 M.D. Smith, 'What is Sports Violence? A Sociolegal Perspective', in J.H. Goldstein (ed), *Sports Violence*, Springer Verlag, New York, 1983.

17 Smith, 'What is Sports Violence?' pp. 39-42.

18 See E. Dunning, 'Social Bonding and Violence in Sport: A Theoretical-Empirical Analysis', in Goldstein, *Sports Violence*; Smith, 'What is Sports Violence?'

19 A. Mummendey and H.D. Mummendey, 'Aggressive Behaviour of Soccer Players as Social Interaction' in Goldstein, *Sports Violence*, pp. 113-114.

20 *Summary Offences Act* (Vic) 1966, ss. 23-24 which includes the offences of common and aggravated assault, generally pursued in Magistrates' courts.

21 The Northern Territory is the only jurisdiction in Australia, which has codified the common law position into its criminal law. Under s. 187(d) there is an express exemption for criminal liability for assault in cases of bodily contact in sport provided such contact is within the rules of the game in question. This definition presents similar problems to existing common law definitions discussed below: see *Criminal Code* (NT) 1983, s. 187.

22 *Crimes Act* (Vic) 1958, ss. 22-23.

23 *Crimes Act* (Vic) 1958, s. 24.

24 *Crimes Act* (Vic) 1958, s. 21.

25 *Crimes Act* (Vic) 1958, s. 321N.

26 *Crimes Act* (Vic) 1958, ss. 323-324.

27 *Crimes Act* (Vic) 1958, ss. 321G-321H.

28 *Crimes Act* (Vic) 1958, s. 321.

29 *Crimes Act* (Vic) 1958, s. 15.

30 See however 'Junior footy knife claim' *Geelong Advertiser* 25 Jan 1995, p. 1 where it is reported that the Geelong District Football League were investigating an allegation that a junior footballer was in possession of a knife hidden in his sock during play in a football match. In such a case, the intention to cause harm might have been peripheral to the proceedings on the field of play, but the offence involves actions occurring during the course of a match irrespective of whether any harm actually ensues.

31 Unreported judgement, Supreme Court of Tasmania, 3/10/1995.

32 Two months of the sentence were suspended in favour of a community-based order. The accused had several prior convictions which contributed to the sentence imposed by the court.

33 J. Dyer and B. Hansen, *Captain Blood's Wild Men of Football* (Vol 1), Brian Edward Hansen, Cheltenham, Vic, 1993, pp. 101-107; AFL *100 Years of Australian Football: 1897-1996*, Viking Press, Melbourne, 1996, pp. 300-301; 314.

34 Unreported judgement, Court of Criminal Appeal, 17/10/1990; See also *McAvaney v. Quigley* (1992) 58 A Crim R 457 involving a fine without conviction recorded for an assault during an Australian Rules Football match in South Australia; *Watherston v. Woolven* (1988) 139 LSJS 366 involving a hit behind play

in an Australian Rules match in South Australia: the victim received a broken nose. The accused was convicted at first instance but this was overturned on appeal on the basis of the accused's good previous record; *R. v. Tevaga* [1991] 1 NZLR 296 involving a conviction for assault during a fight in a rugby union match and a sentence of 100 hours of community service.

35 Emphasis added.

36 See *Rootes v. Shelton* (1967) 116 CLR 383 where the victim was awarded compensation for colliding with a stationary boat whilst water skiing. This case is the principle authority for imposing liability in negligence for activities occurring during the course of recreational activity in Australia; *McNamara v. Duncan* (1971) 26 ALR 584 involving a successful civil action for trespass to the person from an intentional blow in an Australian Rules Football match in Canberra which was an infringement of the rules and resulted in severe head injuries to the victim; *Watson v. Haines* Unreported judgement, Supreme Court of NSW, 10/4/1987, involving an award of over $2,000,000 to a fifteen year old boy rendered a quadriplegic in a school rugby competition; *Sibley v. Milutinovic* (1990) Aust Torts Reps 81-013; 67,686 where compensation was awarded to the victim of a punch in the jaw inflicted in a friendly soccer match; c/f *Pallante v. Stadiums Pty Ltd (No 1)* [1976] VR 331 where a boxer failed in a civil claim for injuries sustained in the course of a boxing match; *Hilton v. Wallace* (1989) Aust Torts Reps 80-231; 68,448 where a rugby league footballer failed to obtain compensation for an injury sustained when an opponent tried to pull him from a fight and accidentally poked him in the eye. See generally G.M. Kelly, 'Negligence Actions Between Sports Participants: The Measure of Liability', *The Australian Law Journal*, Vol 66, 1992, p. 329.

37 *Giumelli v. Johnston* (1991) Aust Torts Reps 81-085; 68.709.

38 *Giumelli v. Johnston* 68.707.

39 *Giumelli v. Johnston* 68.708-9.

40 This principle is known as 'voluntary assumption of risk' under the civil law. According to this principle, athletes consent to those behaviours, which are within the rules of the game. Behaviours which are in substantial breach of the rules are not deemed to be consented to by athletes who suffer serious injury. See above n. 36 for legal authority on this point.

41 *Giumelli v. Johnston* 68.709.

42 *Giumelli v. Johnston* 68.710.

43 (1993) Aust Torts Reps 81-246; 62,538.

44 (1993) Aust Torts Reps 81-246; 62,538 per Mahoney, J.A. at 62,543; per Giles A.J.A. at 62,548-62,549. The court noted however that the weight of this evidence was not conclusive proof of illegality in the circumstances, but the combination of this evidence. Testimony from Rogers' coach was sufficient to establish liability.

45 (1993) Aust Torts Reps 81-246; 62,538 at 62,543-62.544; 62,550.

46 (1993) Aust Torts Reps 81-246; 62,538 per Mahoney, J.A. at 62,543; per Giles, A.J.A. at 62,550-62,552.

47 (1993) Aust Torts Reps 81-246; 62,538 per Mahoney, J.A. at 62,544.

48 Mahoney J.A. argued against such an award given Bugden's financial circumstances and the detrimental effect it would have in the present and future cases. Bugden received $20,000 in annual payments from Rugby League, but player payments were withheld for a suspension from the league which Bugden incurred after the incident. Bugden was also receiving remuneration in his employment as a police officer. An award of exemplary damages was not made against the club on the basis that it did not induce Bugden to act deliberately against the rules of rugby: (1993) Aust Torts Reps 81-246; 62,538 per Mahoney, J.A. at 62,547, per Giles A.J.A. with whom Handley J.A. agreed, at 62,555.

49 See *Re Jewell & Crimes Compensation Tribunal* (1987) 1 VAR 370 which involved an unsuccessful claim for criminal injuries compensation after the victim was struck by an elbow during an Australian Rules Football match. The victim received substantial head injuries, but because the action was not in the course of an illegal tackle (the perpetrator's fist was not clenched), the act was deemed to be within the contemplation of people who participate in Australian Rules Football and was therefore not a 'criminal act' for the purposes of granting compensation.

50 See *Van Haeften v. Caltex Oil (Australia) Pty Ltd,* Unreported Judgement, NSW Court of Appeal, 4 Sept 1995 which involved a successful worker's compensation claim for an injury sustained during a touch football match organised and sponsored by the employer.

51 (1993) Aust Torts Reps 81-222; 62,249.

52 *Re Lenfield* 62,250.

53 *Re Lenfield* 62,251.

54 The court, in establishing this point, referred to *McNamara v. Duncan* (1971) 26 ALR 584; *Smith v. Emerson* (1986) Aust Torts Reps 80-022; *Giumelli v. Johnston*; *Hilton v. Wallace* (1989) Aust Torts Reps 80-231; *Sibley v. Milutinovic* (1990) Aust Torts Reps 81-013.

55 *Re Lenfield* 62,252.

56 *Re Lenfield* 62,252; C/f *Re Jewell & Crimes Compensation Tribunal* (1987) 1 VAR 370.

57 A. Scott, 'The Subiaco melee: An angle the cameras didn't get' *Law Institute Journal* Vol 68, 1994, pp. 1158-1160.

58 See 'Clubs face $50,000 fine', *The Age* 5 Sept 1994; G. Denham, and S. Linnell, 'Sumich KO'd in brawl: West Coast implicates Southern in flare-up', *The Age*, 5 Sept 1994; G. Denham, 'Injury-hit Eagles humiliate Dogs', *The Age,* 5 Sept 1994; G. Denham and S. Linnell, 'Sumich 'feared for life'', *The Age,* 6 Sept 1994; C. Happell, '12 interviewed over melee', *The Age,* 7 Sept 1994; A. Browne, 'Eagles, Dogs finals plans in chaos as eight charged over brawl', *The Age,* 8 Sept 1994; C. Happell and G. Denham, 'Eight face brawl charges', *The Age* 8 Sept 1994; P. Smith, 'Strong stance is worthy of applause', *The Age,* 8 Sept 1994; R. Connolly and G. Wright, 'The Brawl: How a Subiaco Stoush Bloodies the AFL's Nose', *Sunday Age,* 11 Sept 1994.

59 The AFL has a rule which prevents new rules from coming into effect within seven days of their passage by the AFL Commission.

60 This was an unusual move as charges normally involve striking. It is assumed that assault is a more serious charge which is harder to prove.

61 A. Scott, 'The Subiaco melee'.

62 A. Scott, 'The Subiaco melee', p. 1159.

63 G. Denham and P. Gregory, 'AFL in legal brawl', *The Age,* 9 Sept 1994; P. Smith, 'The battle of Subiaco becomes a war', *The Age,* 9 Sept 1994; A. Attwood, 'Romper-stomper football brings out the worst', *The Age,* 9 Sept 1994; 'No place for brawlers', *The Age,* (editorial) 9 Sept 1994; G. Denham, A. Browne and C. Happell, 'We had AFL deal: Dogs, Eagles', *The Age,* 9 Sept 1994; A. Browne, 'Footscray ahead in battle of court 15', *The Age*, 9 Sept 1994. Southern was the only player to be penalised from the incident, receiving a fine of $10,000 imposed by the AFL tribunal after the injunction had expired and Footscray had completed its finals campaign.

64 The AFL Investigations Officer, Max Croxford, was summoned to give evidence at the hearing. He testified that he recommended that no charges be laid by the AFL after viewing the evidence of the melee, but this was ultimately ignored by the Commission. See A. Browne and P. Gregory, 'Verdict rocks the AFL', *The Age,* 10 Sept 1994; P. Smith, 'Frivolous, fruitless and pointless for AFL', *The Age*, 10 Sept 1994; 'Football fiasco', *The Age*, 10 Sept 1994; A. Browne, 'Hawkins accuses

Eagles of cover-up', *The Age,* 10 Sept 1994.

65 M. Blake, 'Tense wait for Dunkley', *The Age*, 23 Sept 1996; M. Blake and S. Linnell, 'AFL Investigates Dunkley incident', *The Age,* 24 Sept 1996.

66 M. Blake and G. Denham, 'Eade slams the league on Dunkley', *The Age*, 23 Oct 1996.

67 P. Gregory and M. Blake, 'Finals drama as Swans go to court', *The Age,* 26 Sept 1996; P. Smith, 'AFL acts bravely over inquiry', *The Age,* 26 Sept 1996; M. Blake, 'Roo should have been reported, say Swans', *The Age*, 26 Sept 1996.

68 M. Blake and P. Gregory, 'Judge rules for Swans star', *The Age* 27 Sept 1996; M. Blake, 'Swans back on track', *The Age,* 27 Sept 1996.

69 Interestingly, in two courts where there were multiple judges, the weight of authority overall actually favoured Williams. The precise grounds for the decision are however difficult to fathom by relying on press accounts of the proceedings alone: see A. Mithen. and M. Blake, 'Williams out 9 matches', *The Age*, 3 Apr 1997, p. C 18-C 17; S. Linnell, 'Turmoil as judge lifts player ban', *The Age*, 5 Apr 1997, p. A 1; P. Smith, "I don't know much about football, but . . . " *The Age*, 5 Apr 1997, p. A 1; S. Linnell, 'AFL Tribunal review call', *The Age*, 5 Apr 1997, p. B 30; M. Blake, 'Process is out of touch, says expert', *The Age*, 5 Apr 1997, p. B 30; R. Connolly, 'Trials and tribulations', *The Sunday Age,* 6 Apr 1997, Sport 5; D. Poulton, 'AFL judicial process needs surgery', *The Sunday Age*, 6 Apr 1997, Sport 5; R. Connolly, 'Why Diesel fumes', *The Sunday Age*, 6 Apr 1997, Sport 16-17; S. Linnell. and G. Boreham, 'Kennett attacks Carlton's court move', *The Age*, 8 Apr 1997, p. A 1; Editorial, 'AFL needs an appeals body', *The Age*, 8 Apr 1997, p. A 14; S. Reilly, 'Amid the jeers, Diesel treads softly', *The Age*, 8 Apr 1997, p. B 8; S. Linnell, 'Williams action to proceed', *The Age*, 12 May 1997, Sport 5; P. Smith, 'Footy's a funny game, all right, as fortunes turn week by week', *The Age*, 12 May1997, Sport 5; S. Linnell, 'Blues won't lose points – AFL', *The Age*, 13 May 1997, p. B 10; P. Gregory, 'Blues face $1.5m loss, court told' *The Age*, 14 May 1997, p. B 16; P. Smith, 'In 3.17, out 3.21 – Diesel has easy day of it', *The Age*, 14 May 1997, p. B 16; M. Doran, 'Blues argue dollars: This time, the judge knows his footy', *Geelong Advertiser*, 14 May 1997, p. 30; P. Smith, 'Judge does his bit to lighten the day', *The Age*, 15 May 1997, p. B 8; P. Gregory, 'QC defends AFL Tribunal', *The Age*, 15 May 1997, p. B 8; J. Brasier, 'Judge wary of setting precedent', *The Australian*, 16 May 1997, p. 24; S. Linnell and P. Gregory, 'Case forces AFL's hand on tribunal', *The Age*, 16 May 1997, Sport 2; The case has ultimately led to Williams retiring from the game at the conclusion of the 1997 season: see S. Linnell, 'Blues slam AFL over Williams', *The Age*, 26 July 1997, p. B 28; P. Smith, 'Loss of face makes bile rise', *The Age*, 26 July 1997, pp. B 28-27; R. Connolly, 'Blues to High Court', *The Sunday Age*, 27 July 1997, Sport 3; R. Connolly, 'For the master, it didn't come easily', *The Sunday Age*, 27 July 1997, Sport 8-9. See also, P. Gregory, 'Bulldogs to pursue $1.3m damages', *The Age*, 5 July 1997, p. A 2 which documents the decision of the Footscray club to claim damages for losses of earnings to stop a merger between North Melbourne and the Fitzroy football club in 1996. Footscray argued that the ruling was necessary in order to compel Fitzroy, or its successor, to abide by a playing arrangement at the Footscray ground: see also P. Smith, 'High drama, pain, but it's all good for football', *The Age*, 5 July 1997, p. A 2

70 See *Boyd v. Kelly*, Unreported judgement, Supreme Court of NSW, 21 Aug 1985, involving the granting of an injunction rendering ineffective a fine imposed against a district rugby coach unable to attend a hearing to present his defence due to legitimate work commitments.

71 See *Jackson and Brooks v. Western Australian Basketball Federation Inc*, Unreported judgement, Supreme Court of WA, 23 Oct 1990; *Hollioake and another v. Western Australian Cricket Association and another*, Unreported judgement, Supreme Court

of WA, 11 Mar 1994, involving the rejection of an application for an injunction restraining a tribunal hearing on the grounds that no legal representation was permitted by the tribunal in an investigation into allegations of ball tampering.

72 Unreported judgement, Supreme Court of Victoria, 4 Sept 1986.

73 *Edgecock v. Davies.*

74 In 1994 the then St Kilda full forward Tony Lockett was suspended for a total of eight matches for a collision with Sydney defender Peter Caven. Caven received a compound fracture of the nose requiring plastic surgery. Lockett continually claimed that he was running with his eyes on the ball and there was no malice in the contact. The fact of Caven running directly into Lockett was seldom considered in the aftermath of the incident in terms of his contribution to his own injury. A similar situation occurred in 1996 when Geelong star Gary Ablett fended off a tackle from St Kilda defender Kristian Bardsley. Bardsley was carried from the field with a fractured jaw and severe concussion. There were questions as to the legitimacy of Ablett's action's, but in defending the AFL's charge Geelong argued that Bardsley was partly to blame for his unusual tackling style. Ablett was suspended by the AFL tribunal for five matches. Neither case resulted in criminal or civil action.

75 *Pallante v. Stadiums Pty Ltd (No 1)* [1976] VR 331.

76 Smith, 'What is Sports Violence?'; Mummendey and Mummendey, 'Aggressive Behaviour'.

77 This concern was raised in the aftermath of the Matthews incident. It was argued by some that Matthews paid three times for his actions: a criminal conviction, deregistration by the VFL for four weeks for conduct unbecoming to the sport; and a broken nose inflicted by a Geelong player in retaliation for his hit on Bruns. However these arguments lose weight in the context of the successful appeal against conviction by Matthews, research evidence which indicates that sports organisations traditionally impose inadequate penalties to deal with cases of athletic violence, and the notion that violence should not be used as a means to counter violence on the sporting field; see Smith, 'What is Sports Violence?'.

78 The recent British case of *R. v. Brown and others* [1993] 2 All ER 75 illustrates the complexity of referring to the rules of a particular form of conduct the subject of an action for assault. In this case, the five accused were indicted for assault which occurred as a result of their consensual undertaking to engage in various sorts of sado-masochistic behaviour. The allegations of assault involved claims that the group's behaviour, involving piercing various parts of the penis and scrotum and the infliction of cuts and wounds to the body were unlawful. The accused claimed that they consented to the behaviour, but this was rejected by the House of Lords on the grounds that it is impossible to consent to an act of harm which is unlawful: see *R. v. Coney* (1882) 8 QBD 534; *R. v. Donovan* [1934] 2 KB 498; *Attorney General's Reference (No 6 of 1980)* [1981] QB 715. One issue which emerged in this case, and was stressed by the dissenting judgement in the House of Lords, was the fact that there were informal rules which were used by those involved in the behaviour to instruct the person inflicting the pain to desist. The majority countered this claim by indicating that there was no independent umpire present during the S & M sessions to ensure that the rules were being enforced impartially.

79 T. Gabor, *Everybody does it: Crime by the Public*, University of Toronto Press, Toronto, 1994.

80 R. Horrow, *Sports Violence: The Interaction Between Private Lawmaking and the Criminal Law*, Carrolton Press Inc, Arlington, 1980.

81 See above n. 10. See also P. Bone, 'Society's values need more than a sporting chance', *The Age* 4 Sept 1997, p. A 17. Each of these sources document a range of

cases where male sports stars have engaged in criminal or offensive behaviour upon female victims in Australia and the United States. Seldom are these cases formally prosecuted in the courts, and seldom are the victims satisfied with the judgements in these cases. See also P. Conroy, 'Carey places ad to apologise to woman over club incident', *The Age*, 11 Nov 1997, p. A 3 involving a civil suit brought against North Melbourne footballer Wayne Carey for an incident in a Melbourne night club with the female victim claiming damages for physical, psychiatric and psychological injury. The victim was allegedly grabbed by Carey on the right breast and told to 'get a bigger set of tits'. The matter was settled out of court, with Carey issuing a public apology two years after the incident; S. Lunn and M. Abraham, 'Licensees who served drunk footballer face liquor bans', *The Australian*, 24 Oct 1997, p. 3, involving New South Wales Rugby League star Noa Nadruku. Nadruku had consumed more than 30 beers prior to allegedly assaulting three women at a Canberra nightclub. Nadruku was acquitted on the basis that he was too drunk to form the intention to commit the assaults. Critics of this decision point to the danger this presents for women who might be victims of such behaviour, and the potential liability for club owners for serving intoxicated patrons.

82 See R.S. Magnusson & H. Opie, 'HIV and Hepatitis in Sport: A Legal Framework for Resolving Hard Cases', *Monash University Law Review*, vol. 20, no. 2., 1994, pp. 214-270.

Is Boxing Violent?

Let's Ask Some Boxers

MICHAEL BURKE

Introduction

AN EDITORIAL COMMENT in *The Australian Weekly* newspaper supplement from 1991 posed the question:

> Who now remembers Angelo Jacopucci? Yet, thirteen years ago, for a few days in July, Jacopucci was big news. He was an Italian middle-weight who fought Alan Minter for the European championship. In the twelth round, Minter knocked him out. Soon afterwards he fell into a deep coma. One operation, and then a second failed to revive him. Like Benny Paret and Ulric Regis and Johnny Owen and Willie Classen, and dozens more, inexorably around the world, he became just another statistic: a boxer, killed in the ring. (23: p.12):

Since that time, other boxers have died or suffered irreparable damage in the ring. Following these tragedies, the debate about the legitimacy of a practice like boxing to continue gets revived, both in the popular press and in philosophical/sociological journals.

A number of authors consider that the sport should be banned for much the same reasons. One particular editor suggests "that a sport designed explicitly to inflict human pain and human injury is degrading" (23: p.12). Yet, boxing survives. Why? According to this same editor, boxing survives because of the enormous amounts of cash provided through television fees (23: p.12). But such endorsement comes at a cost to the public, because television executives are now willing to replay over and over again, because of their understanding of the public taste, the final moments of any bout which results in death. Replays may be sanitised by commentary about the public's right to know, or the courage of the poor fighter, but these replays mark a noticeable change from 1978 when the BBC decided that it would not broadcast Jacopucci's final bout *"as a matter of taste"* (23: p.12). And such overt displays of horrendous injuries, when compared with the safety of most of our lives, ironically provokes calls for the sport of boxing to be banned.

The sociological/ philosophical press (hereafter referred to as the academic press) has been no quieter in its condemnation of boxing and its calls for a ban to be placed on this dangerous, exploitative activity. Variously, the justifications for this limitation of the freedom of some members of society who enjoy boxing have been: that the practice of boxing glorifies and exacerbates violence in our community (12), that the goal of boxing necessitates the objectified and disrespectful attitude towards the opponent which permits the infliction of harm on another (2, 3, 7, 2)[1], and that the social context of fighters' lives means that any decision to box is not one that is freely taken because of the coercive influence of both the lack of other opportunities, and the obvious rewards from professional boxing (12).

This paper will bypass this discourse, because any demand for a solution to this issue is predicated on the ideas that boxing is violent and/or exploitative; that is, on the belief that 'we' [the rational people who discuss boxing] share some conception of what violent and exploitative practices are, and that boxing is an example of such a practice. It avoids this discourse because such demands try to make these conceptions essential and rational when they are, at best, contingent and democratic, and, at worst, contingent and discriminatory. Peter Donnelly explains this contingency in terms of the definition of boxing in Canada. He suggests that boxing became progressively marginalized in Canada during the 1950s and 1960s as it was abandoned by the middle and upper classes and by the educational system. As a practice of the underclass, and specific racial minorities, boxing increasingly came to be defined as uncivilised and barbaric. Donnelly argues:

> Viewed in this way, recent critiques of boxing have often carried with them either a subtle racism (e.g., there are few white professional champions and the sport's most visible participants are often implied to represent the less civilized elements or "problem" groups in society), or a deeply-rooted paternalism (e.g., minority group members are not aware of their best interests or else are susceptible to exploitation and must be protected by the state). In addition, and as a corollary to the tendencies noted above, the current attack on boxing has typically denied the existence of strategy and defense. Boxing has been deskilled through an emphasis in the media on images of fighters beating each other senseless before a crowd that is baying for blood. (4: p.77).

This paper will discuss the often-overlooked issue of whether boxers themselves understand their practice as violent or exploitative, and their relationship to their opponents in the ring as disrespectful or objectifying. In other words, can boxers hear and understand the words that the popular press and the academic press are saying about them? In line with Wacquant's study of boxing in the poor, urban areas of Chicago (24), it will be suggested that the practice community of boxers has a very different characterisation of their craft. Acts that could normally be considered violent in almost every other situation in life, cannot be so considered in boxing *because* of the contextual morality which the goal of boxing provides. That is, the goal of boxing allows boxers to see opponents with which they trade blows, in a respectful manner.[2] This turns on their heads many arguments used to support a ban on boxing, or at least a modification of boxing, because of the essential disrespect (7) and viciousness (3) between fighters caused by the goal of boxing.[3]

But moreso, what happens when the descriptions of themselves and their practice by a group of practitioners clashes significantly with the wider community's descriptions? How can the small, and relatively powerless, practice community gain a voice, so that they are not threatened with redescription by people who do not understand them in the ways that they understand themselves? Recently, Morgan (13) and Gebauer (6) have both called for practice communities to recapture control of their practice. These calls have been motivated by the observation that institutional bureaucracies have lost sight of and touch with what is important in the practice to the practitioners. The liberal "art of separation"[4] has been claimed by Morgan (13) as a useful tool so that practitioners do not suffer redescription by practice-illiterate bureaucracies. But whilst such a separation is useful in this case, it is not the only 'separation' that is important? In Wacquant's eyes, it is the context of the wider urban community that makes this sub-group of practitioners view themselves and their practice in such a way (24: p.491). That is, there is no practice of boxing that unites boxers across classes and countries, but there are 'little communities' within various pockets of urban society whose members are united by *their* understanding of what they share.[5]

Guignon and Hiley characterise part of the problem for the various 'little communities' of boxers in the following way:

> An individual's self-descriptions are realized in his or her agency in the public world, and public practices and institutions impact on the individual's capacities for self-fulfilment. It is the task of moral and social philosophy to clarify these bonds between civic responsibility and meaningful freedom (8: p.359).

In doing so, we should be aware of the impositions that altruistically driven laws, such as a ban on boxing, could have on the various little communities. This is especially the case for those who see the practice as an important space for self-description and identity formation in a life which doesn't hold many such spaces, and in a society which can't particularly hear the words and phrases that members of the little community utter to explain the importance of such spaces. The final section of this paper will look at how boxers describe themselves, and how such description may or may not be tolerated within civic society.

Phenomenological Accounts of Boxing Amongst Marginal Men: What boxers have to say about their practice

Much has been written about the brutality and barbarity of boxing and other contact sports in our society. It has been suggested that, in modern society, there is no place for these types of sport. They remind us of what we once were, and hopefully as people we have become civilised. That is, these articles give us reasons why *they* shouldn't box. Little has been written about the boxer's point of view. What has been written comes as biographies of superstar boxers. These biographies may not be particularly representative of the conditions of most boxers' lives because of the huge prizemoney and the large-scale corruption in professional boxing. Lois Wacquant (24) offers a different perspective. He engages in the culture of a semi-professional boxing gym. He becomes a small-time fighter. He uses this engagement as a means to talk to other small-time fighters. In doing so, he is able to reveal what the less famous, less wealthy practitioners think of their trade; that is, reasons why *we* do box. The point of this section is to show the importance of phenomenological studies in revealing a different type of knowledge and understanding about boxing to most that have been previously presented in the academic press.

According to Wacquant, most academic studies of boxing;

> ... focus on the negative determinants, from economic deprivation and school failure to family disorganisation and social isolation, that allegedly funnel them into the ring by constricting other options, to the neglect of the *positive attractions* that the trade exerts on its members. And it authoritatively imputes a host of individual motivations to boxers (greed, masculine pride, anger) ... but seldom inquires into the *collective dispositions* that find in this odd craft a public theatre of expression (24: p.490).

An example of this type of reductive thinking is Messner and Sabo's commentary on the position from which many boxers claim they make a free choice about their participation in the sport. They state:

> For instance, who are these men who risk life and limb for our entertainment? Most boxers are from poor, working-class backgrounds. Many are members of minority groups for whom boxing may seem to be one of the few ways out of the misery they were born into. According to Chris Dundee, a Miami boxing promoter, "Any man with a good trade isn't about to get knocked on his butt to make a dollar" [6]. But an impoverished society (such as in many Latin American nations) or an economically depressed city (such as Detroit) is fertile ground for a flourishing boxing industry. (12: pp.77-78)

Wacquant hopes to convey the passion, understood as a combined sense of love and suffering that semi-professional boxers experience (24: p.491). He locates this passion within the social and cultural context of the world of these fighters – a world of poverty in the ghetto. Hence, it is the social and cultural context that is important in trying to understand the "game frame" of boxing for these particular practitioners. Colin Tatz (22) has suggested a similar relationship between the context and the success of Aboriginal boxers, a group unified not by geographic location, but by race. He states:

> Boxing has doubtless been a vehicle of discrimination and exploitation. But the ring as such has been one of the few sources of collective pride, and the one venue in which to vanquish the oppressor. In a life in which all things black are declared inferior to all things white, winning in the ring is a matter of great moment. Many must have felt as Henry Collins [cited by Broome, 1980][7] did: "I felt good when I knocked white blokes out . . . I knew I was boss in the boxing ring. I showed my superiority . . . but they showed it outside . . . "(22: p.52)

Through interview and experience, Wacquant tries to understand the lived experience of boxing for the semi-professional boxer, living in a society in which they feel exploited and unfree in most other areas of their life.

As stated previously, Ellen Gerber argued that to do violence to another person, you must see them as an object, and not a subject (7: p.185). You must dehumanise them. Understood in this 'objective' or 'thin' fashion, the goal of boxing is to knock out your opponent. Injuries and bodily deterioration are not incidental to the game; they are the necessary outcome of proper professional exertion. There is a hypermasculine ethos that underpins its descriptions, and military and gladiatorial metaphors are abundant within the practice (24: p.496). Its practitioners generally come from a social context that is rife with violence and the objectification of others. Boxers may take up part of this idea. That is, boxers who hit below the belt may be excluded from the dominant community as unethical. They have treated their opponent as an object. They relinquish their rights of self-description and participation that are available to boxers as part of the community.

But most boxers do not see the normal practice of their sport as violent. Kenny, a 24 year-old Black middleweight, explains that "(a)nybody who feels that it teaches you violence is a person tha's really a, a real incompetent mind *I think*" (24: p.495) To reduce a multifaceted bodily occupation to a single facet (violence) is a distortion which is phenomenologically drained. It defiles and contradicts the lived experience of most boxers. In the context of the public celebration of other sports (for example, ice hockey, gridiron), of the living conditions of urban America (crime, rape, poverty) and the frequency of other addictive pastimes (drugs, alcoholism), boxing may not be experienced as particularly violent by its practitioners. Wacquant explains: "To understand what drives fighters, their quasi-sacrificial giving of themselves to their occupation, one must heed and disclose the latter's moral and sensual attractions, elucidate the experiential foreground and dynamics of prizefighting as embedded and embodied social action" (24: p.492). For these poor fighters, it is not enough to talk of financial benefits and ecological antecedents associated with boxing. For them in their social context, boxing offers many different, and many more personally significant, rewards. And it may be arrogantly misplaced of we relatively more comfortable academics and journalists to try and remove the potential to experience these rewards under the guise of trying to save who they consider to be poor, misguided, ignorant and exploited fighters.

Many fighters understand boxing "... as a skilled bodily trade, a competitive performance craft requiring sophisticated technical know-how and an abiding moral commitment that will enable them not only to improve their material lot but also, to construct a *publicly recognized, heroic self*." (24: p.501) For boxers in this context, it offers them an opportunity to create and describe themselves in their own terms, rather than be fashioned by descriptions made by other, more powerful people for them and their like. In a society which condemns these people to socially insignificant positions, boxing offers a way "... to escape the common determinations that bear upon" them (24: p.501). It is the boxer's way of experiencing personal power and freedom in a society where there is little space for poor, urban youth to do so. According to Wacquant, in the ring "boxers nearly always deny that one can be coerced ... and they vigorously claim responsibility for their fate between the ropes"(24: p.501). This infuses their life with value, excitement and accomplishment.

Whilst boxing remains a lower-class job (normally underpaid and heavily subsidised by other work), it is for the boxers a job in which they can have control over the labour process and unparalleled independence from direct supervision (unlike factory jobs). The boxer engages in a job that is highly skilful and impressively intelligent amongst his community of practitioners. "It's a thinkin' man's game" according to one boxer from Wacquant's gym (24: p.503). In addition, the boxers display a context-sensitive, free and creative, embodied competence. According to Wacquant: "Genuine commitment and love of the game are indispensable to sustain a fighter over time. In this respect, as well as in terms of both autonomy and skill, boxers resemble the artisan more than they do the classic proletariat of Marxian theory" (24: p.504). Boxing offers the practitioner the prospect, however illusory, of a career, of advancement. Other jobs, for uneducated, urban youth offer no such prospects. This is related to the discourse within boxing that persistent effort *will* be rewarded. Finally, boxing is a glamorous profession in the 'little society' of urban America. It gives public expression to the virile values (hardness, courage, determination, and strength) that are the common bedrock of working class cultures across ethnoracial divides. According to another of Wacquant's fighters: "They give you praise and glory for you to be a warrior" (24: p.505).

All these benefits of boxing, as described by the boxers themselves, should make us wary of any attempts, no matter how noble, of people trying to save the boxer from himself. It seems a throwback to Marxist descriptions of the false consciousness of the worker and the need for enlightenment about the worker's "true" position. How do we know that the boxer is unaware of the "true" nature of his practice? What is this "true" nature? Wouldn't it be a more tolerant position to assume that those people who engage in boxing are capable of deciding their own fate, of describing themselves and their practice in the way that they choose to? And isn't it also a more tolerant position for those of us outside of the practice community to respect the descriptions of those from within?

As a craftsman, the boxer's practice-specific sense of beauty and virtue lies in the combination of bodily competence and ring generalship, as directed toward a goal. Ed, a black cruiserweight fighter, explains such bodily competence as, "he {your opponent} goes through efforts to hit-an-harm you, an' he's unable to even touch you an' you're no more than . . . twelve inches away from him: that, that, it takes an art to be able to do that" (24: p. 506).[8] Mike McNamee is another who considers that boxing can be described as a virtuous craft. He states:

The virtues one might expect of boxers would include the following . . . Coolheadedness; boxing is not mere fighting. Unlike in other sporting practices it is generally agreed that boxers' performances deteriorate when they have lost control. Moreover, boxing is neither constituted merely by aggression, but rather by that disposition carefully channelled into a variety of complex techniques to be delivered at appropriate times and with appropriate force and control (11: p.54).

He goes on to consider the importance of determination, resourcefulness, tenacity and courage as those qualities which the practice community considers as virtuous in fighters, qualities which make fighters aspire to emulate boxers who are described in this way.[9] The gym is seen as a small-scale civilising machine to avoid uncontrolled violence. Muhammad Ali comments about being challenged to a fight by a person in a restaurant. After much racist provocation, Ali decided not to fight. He explains that, " I had already signed for my first professional bout. Its part of the pride of a truly professional fighter not to indulge himself, not to be caught dead or alive in a free-for-all" (cited in 24: p.500).

Yet, for all this, I have still not conveyed the passion of the commitment to the practice that Wacquant's small-time boxers had. For these men: "Fighting is not simply something they *do*, an instrumental activity, a pastime and a sidejob separable from their persona. Because it demands and effects a far-reaching restructuring of the self as well as an integral colonization of one's life-world, boxing is what they *are*"(24: p.507). Wacquant suggested a similarity to a religious allegiance that could not be simply explained by material insecurity and the prospects of a better life through boxing. Many boxers gave up jobs to fight and train professionally; they sacrificed material comfort for their allegiance to boxing. Others said that if offered a better job, they still would not leave boxing. This depth of commitment is explained in the metaphorical analogies to the love of an unbridled woman (including metaphors of boxing as the 'untamed mistress', 'divorce' from the ring in retirement, and 'cheating' on boxing if you miss training) and the quasi-religious responsibility to 'use a God-given gift' (including beliefs about their moral obligation to fight, and to use the inner treasure bestowed on them) (24: p.509).

In boxing, the fighters can achieve a sense of control through their own gifts and powers. This is important to urban youth, who may experience little power in their everyday lives. Boxing is a hyperreal space in which "a purified and magnified masculine self can be achieved" (24: p.511). Wacquant explains that:

> By entering an occupation that hinges on "the wilful undertaking of serious chances" boxers decisively realign the structure and texture of their entire existence ... in ways that put them in a unique position to assert their agency. For with risk comes the possibility of control: with pain and sacrifice, the eventuality of moral elevation and public recognition; and with discipline and commitment, the existential profit of personal renewal ... Through the ministry of boxing, fighters' ambition is to remake themselves and the world around them. (24: p.510)

And this remaking occurs in a public space. As with Shapiro's (20) account of freestyle skiing and Eassom's (5) description of mountaineering, boxers view their sport as a test in front of others that publicly establishes their fortitude and valour. It tells the truth about them as a person – about their 'inner worth'. This discourse is based on the important notion of deserving merit in the practice, of the need for sacrifice to succeed. According to Wacquant, it is understood within the 'little community' that "[s]uccess in the fistic arena hinges on the adoption of proper personal habits and conduct outside of it." (24: p.513) Discipline and sacrifice are taught as important values in the boxer's training. Boxing is a public display of oneself. There is nowhere in the ring, or in the gym, to hide from an informed community. Finally, the boxer is independently responsible for what occurs to him. No one else can do the fighting for him. The achievement (or the failure) is incontrovertibly the boxer's. This is not the case in the rest of the boxer's existence. Within this 'little community' the boxer is "not only revered for their toughness and bravery ... they are also hailed for projecting a positive professional image of hard work, discipline, and perseverance" (24: p.516). Within the urban, poor environment, such a choice to avoid the easy money of crime, and sacrifice yourself even in the face of economic hardship is a way of asserting moral superiority.

Yet, there is still ambivalence experienced toward boxing that is described by the fighters. That is, the fighters still question their practice. The interviews and discussion by Wacquant has shown that fighters see their profession as a skilled bodily craft (distanced from violence) which they gain pleasure from as a positive self-determining choice, a moral spectacle and a sensual body-experience. Far from being 'forced' to fight because of their social situation, boxing offers a space for forgetting that situation and revealing themselves in control and as a heroic hypermasculine self. At the same time, the quasi-religious link of the boxer to his craft is not without tension, and sometimes resentment, which the fighters suggest is produced by the 'barbaricness'[10] of the sport, the grind and torture of the body resulting in its breakdown, the physical abuse of self and others, and the ruthless and despotic exploitation of the boxer by his managers and controllers for the enjoyment of others. The boxers understand it as a coerced affection, a poor man's love. It is stated about boxers generally that, "had one not been born near the bottom of society and enjoyed the privilege of inheriting an aptitude and liking for school . . . one might never have put on the gloves" (24: p.521). There are no rich, white boxers in the semi-professional game. Even the great Ali expressed his ambivalence in the following way: "True, fighting was all I had ever done, but there was always something in me that rebelled against it. Maybe it was because those who profited from it didn't think of fighters as human or intelligent. They saw us as made just for the entertainment of the rich . . . Then there was the nightmarish image I always had of two slaves in the ring" (24: p.521).[11] Boxers leave parts of themselves in the ring. The body which has been trained and disciplined to perform the 'sweet craft' does not survive intact. The contradiction in this ruination of the cherished masculine body creates a further ambivalence toward boxing. As a result, the overwhelming majority of boxers in Wacquant's little community, who speak of the love of the craft, do not want their sons to follow in their footsteps.

Therefore, the boxers' passion is a skewed and malicious one. It is tainted by the idea that boxing, for all of its benefits, exacts too high a price. Wacquant concludes with: "Only by unpacking the logic of boxing's material and moral economy can one hope to disentangle how power and submission, constraint and agency, pleasure and suffering mingle and abet each other in such a manner that prizefighters may be at once their own saviours and their own tormenters" (24: pp. 523-524).

At the same time, we should question whether what we are saving the boxers from by suggesting a ban, is going to produce greater pain for these people? Are we, in trying to save the boxer from his 'false consciousness' going to remove an area of life from him that he feels he has some control in? Richard Rorty states: "Pragmatists think that if something makes no difference in practice, it should make no difference in philosophy" (cited in 18: p.5). We may wish to produce a life of unexploited opportunities for the poor urban youth of our countries, but if the first step of this journey is to remove a practice which this youth understand as free, without being able to replace it with anything better, then have we achieved anything useful in practice? Pete Axthelm, a sportswriter in America asks; "Do those of us who are well paid to cover fights – or well educated enough not to watch them – have the right to cut off the career choices of the unschooled kids who have traditionally used the ring as a step out of hopelessness and poverty?" (cited in 21: p.40) Or moreso, do we have the right to cut off opportunities for the acquisition of personally valuable goals, which are economically profitless, by ignoring the stories that these fighters tell about their practice?

Wacquant explains the problem for secure, comfortable, rich and middle-class journalists and academics, in a comment on the editorial process for his paper. He states:

> Indeed, this section [on how boxers understand boxing as a craft][12] drew the brunt of the criticism of one of the anonymous reviewers of the article, who simply could not accept that boxing might be something other (or more) than violence. So much so that he or she was willing to array her own commonsense view and standard media representations over and against the assertions of boxers. That (certain forms) of physical aggression might not be experienced as violent is profoundly repugnant to middle-class individuals, for whom the sanctity of the human body is a defining feature of the self. (24: p.527, note 25)

Wacquant goes on to suggest that, in order to discuss this topic, academics and journalists need to start from the position that, as Guttmann (1978 cited in 24: p.527) suggests "many sports include legitimate, socially sanctioned forms of violence, which is quite distinct from simply saying, with approval or distaste, that these sports are violent." What we, as academics and social commentators, should be aware of is the contingency of our position, as well as that of the boxer. This contingency of our position allows/forces us to make noises about boxing, which may be as 'irrational' to boxers, as the noises that boxers make about their craft are to us, the academic readers.

Thick descriptions must be acknowledged, because thin descriptions can't be heard by boxers

Lyotard's notions of a *differend* and a *litige*, as explained by William Morgan, may be useful in describing the problems suffered by members of a practice community, such as boxers, when they are being judged by members of another practice community, such as sociologists or philosophers, who cannot hear or understand the terms that boxers use to describe themselves. A *differend* is "a dispute in which one of the aggrieved parties, the plaintiff, becomes a victim because he is deprived of the means of making his case" (13: p.238). The idiom that is legitimate is that of the judge, and not the plaintiff. Applying this notion to this paper, boxing is described as violent (the idiom of boxing's critics), and not a craft (the idiom of boxing's supporters). A *litige* is " a litigation in which both parties agree on how to phrase the issues that led to the dispute as well as the means for resolving them" (13: p.238). How might this occur in this dispute? The idiom that is chosen must be sufficiently inclusive and tolerant, so that both parties can make their case. This will allow the dispute between parties to be solved by the better, or more persuasive, argument.

What might such an idiom look like? Morgan suggests that we socialise the judgement of disputes; that is, we let the practice community act as the judicial body that decides upon rival interpretations. Is boxing violent? The practice community will, and already does, decide on the issue. If the response to Wacquant's boxers is representative of the practice community, then we could suggest that the community has decided that boxing is not violent. If sociological accounts of boxing are representative, but the practice still seems to be well supported, then we could suggest that boxing is violent, but such violence has not resulted in a loss of patronage. Hence, the practice survives because of the support of this community, much to the dismay of some people outside of it. Morgan continues by suggesting that:

> What are required here are... the concrete presuppositions of practice-centered deliberations that set as contextual criteria of reasoned discourse, presuppositions that demand we enmesh ourselves in the fineries of sporting practices and produce thick ethnocentric accounts of them. (13: p.242)

Gebauer also suggests that the failure to recognise the perspective of the athlete is caused by a problem with the current media coverage, in that the athlete's view does "not appear to have permanent advocates in the media" (6: p.470). Such a practitioner led discourse about boxing may display the boxer's self-descriptions in such a way, that members of the academic press may take up, and, in taking up, necessitate some change to their current schema of beliefs.[13]

However, it is important not to underestimate the change that is being called for here. To change a *differend* to a *litige*, or to even hear a *differend*, involves a paradigm shift in the dominant language, and probably some relinquishment of power by members of the dominant group. Hence, such a shift is not an easy one to produce by those who suffer the injustice, because those who produce or judge the injustice do not see their descriptions as unjust. The motivation to change idioms only occurs when what was once just is revealed to be unjust through the incorporation of new words and phrases into the rational space of language; that is, what was once irrational becomes rational.[14]

One example may clarify this call to change *differends* to *litiges*. In making a distinction from the attitude necessitated by the goals of boxing, Ellen Gerber quotes Sir Roger Bannister in his description of the exhilarated state he achieved in completing the first sub-four minute mile. Bannister states:

> I was relaxing so much that my mind seemed almost detached from my body . . . There was no pain, only a great unity of movement and aim. The world seemed to stand still, or did not exist. The only reality was the next two hundred yards of track under my feet. The tape meant finality – extinction perhaps. I felt at that moment that it was my chance to do one thing supremely well. I drove on, impelled by a combination of fear and pride . . . If I faltered, there would be no arms to hold me; and the world would be a cold, forbidding place because I had been so close. I leapt at the

tape like a man taking his last spring to save himself from the chasm that threatens to engulf him. (cited in 7: p.185).

Gerber considers this description by Bannister as, whilst flawed by its dualism, a "remarkable portrayal of the lived body" (7: p.185). It involves a self-respecting athlete, losing him in the completion of his task, so that he becomes one with the task. Bannister is a model for all athletes who drive towards some inner goal. Yet, would we ever be tempted to accuse Bannister of a false understanding of himself and his practice; that, we could enlighten him by displaying the lack of freedom he had in 'obsessively' pursuing the sub-four minute mile, where his time could have been better spent in some less risky practice? Are we wary of a practice that produces the emotion of fear, the detachment of thought and the possibility of 'emotional' extinction in a "cold, forbidding place"? I think not, because the runners are able to use their own idiom to describe their practice, and members of other social practices are willing to respect such descriptions.

Would we give the same respect to the description of an exhilarated, lived body state, if fighters experienced it in a bout? Are fighters capable of becoming the athletic model of the fully experiencing person? Gerber suggests that they are not, because the goal of boxing necessitates a willingness to treat your body, and that of your opponent, as an object, rather than a person (7: p.185). But is such treatment necessary? Wacquant argues that boxers experience similar feelings to those of Bannister:

> The fight is a sensory microcosm unto itself, characterized by a drastic narrowing of one's sentient receptivity, high-speed processing of stressful stimuli under acute urgency so as to impose order on a complex and entropic perceptual field verging at times on complete chaos, and a virtual merging with the task at hand leading to the euphoric experience of "flow" and an intense sensation of self-possession. Like other "edgeworkers" such as test pilots, high-speed boat racers, and sky divers, boxers insist that fighting has ineffable qualities that cannot be captured and conveyed linguistically to others. (24: p.512)

This difficulty in conveying linguistically the sense of flow or exhilaration that boxers feel during a fight is part of the difficulty that boxers face in justifying their sport by showing its benefits. Yet, it is only part of the difficulty. Why are we more capable of accepting with respect the story of an athlete such as Bannister, yet have difficulty in accepting the local and shared vocabulary and utterances of members of the boxing community?

Perhaps it is because the particular practice communities of poor, urban boxers are not strong enough to withstand the descriptions forced on them by residents of other social practices, such as sociology, philosophy and journalism. It is here that Morgan's call for the socialised liberal art of separation may be of further use for the little community of boxers. In the postscript to his book *Leftist Theories of Sport: A Critique and Reconstruction,* Morgan suggests the role that he sees for the state in the protection of practice communities within liberal society. He argues that the liberal ideal of pluralism calls for the state "to give its members a wide range of forms of life to choose from so that each may lead an engaging and rich life" (13: p.255). Now, because no social order has the resources to sustain all forms of social practices, a process is needed to decide which practices to keep. Morgan suggests that within a liberal state, we should socialise the decision making process; that is, let the people decide which social practices they will support with enough patronage to allow the practice to survive, and which social practices they are happy to allow to wither through lack of support. For such a process to work, it is important for our state to be an "open and radically tolerant one accepting as much diversity as it can possibly handle, and being as inclusive as it can possibly be" (13: p.255). Also the state must be willing to allow the loss of social practices which the community are no longer willing to support, for any variety of reasons. In other words, the state is not allowed to interfere in the "social accretion and attrition process" (13: p.262).

What does this mean for the "little communities" of boxers? Morgan explains:

> The pluralism I speak of argues that while the state is not equipped to make such qualitative rankings [between practices][15], civil society... is so equipped, and, when left properly to its own devices... engages in these sorts of deep and normative decisions all the time.... So only those forms of life that are able to secure the democratic sanction of civil society, of the practitioners of its varied practices, will be confirmed as life-enriching ones and supported as such. (13: p.256)

We, as a liberal society, are tolerant when we let the practice of boxing survive or wither on its own terms. That is, when the practice community is able to democratically decide its own affairs, and when such decisions allow each of its members to further decide whether they wish to continue to support the practice, or to depart the practice in such numbers that the practice is no longer able to survive in its current form. What is the state's function is such an open and tolerant, pluralistic society? The state must have a "chastened" view of itself, one that delimits its role to presiding over, rather than interfering in, civil society. But secondly, the state must have some power in order to exert "influence on social forces which stifle diversity" (13: pp.259-260). Hence, the state must preside as a banal one, willing to allow the civil society to decide how its life is enriched, and not forcing the civil society to accept the prescriptions of the state about how to produce a perfect society.[16] In other words, the ideal of an open and tolerant, pluralistic civil society will be best realised when the state is neutral "regarding the different and competing conceptions of the good entertained in civil society" (13: p.256).[17]

With regards to other's self-descriptions, we are generally willing to tolerate such descriptions provided they don't threaten or intimidate our own self-descriptions or safety. Do boxers pose such a threat? From a variety of perspectives they may. As stated by Wacquant at the conclusion of the previous section, these descriptions pose a threat to middle-class society's aesthetic sensibilities about the sanctity of the human body. Furthermore, it is an overt threat, different to the threats imposed by smokers, drinkers, overeaters etc. Whilst the boxer may claim that his practice necessitates a respectful relationship towards his body, such a claim seems difficult to accept when the brutality of the competition is contrasted with the sanitation of much of middle-class life. But the boxer also poses some sort of a threat to the description many hold of sport as healthy practice. We can tolerate the injuries and deaths in other sports as the tragic accidents that sometimes occur during generally healthy activities. Yet the boxer, like the drug-taker, challenges this tolerance, for both seem to make a deliberate decision to engage in unhealthy practices in the name of sport. How best can we maintain our description of sport-as-healthy? Perhaps by removing those unhealthy practitioners from our contemplations. But in doing so, we may close off one form of self-description and expression important to some members of our society, and particularly important to some members of a group in our society that don't have many other practices in their life where they can create their own descriptions.

The Language of Boxers Embodied in Practice

In a number of papers, Roberts uses the notion of sport as a language (16, 18, 19), that creates important meanings for athletes. Certain ingredients to this concept need to be laid out before it can be used to better understand the practitioner's notion of boxing. Firstly, following from Rorty, Roberts explains that there is nothing essential, transcendental, ahistorical or foundational which grounds any language-game. Hence, "any given language-game is responsible to no higher authority than the community of users which commends it" (19: p.2) New words and phrases, and current words and phrases may be either "savoured or spat out" (19: p.9) according to the contingent whims of the group of practitioners which are affected by their use. Guignon and Hiley describe such contingency in the following way, "all problems, topics, and distinctions are language-relative – the results of us having chosen to use a certain vocabulary" (8: p.342), rather than a different one. Roberts expands by stating: "Since all criteria of truth and all standards for conducting enquiry are predefined by the language-game we have chosen to play, and since there are no vocabulary-neutral criteria for assessing different vocabularies, we are free to spin off new vocabularies whenever they might seem useful" (19: p.3).[18]

Similarly, the speaker of such vocabularies has no firm foundations to ground such choice of words and phrases. The speaker is a "more or less complex web of beliefs and desires which is continually reweaving itself" to accommodate the words and phrases uttered by other members of both the practice community and the wider society. (19: p.3) For most practitioners, such accommodation takes the form of accepting the current ways that the practice community uses words and actions. Some practitioners, who Roberts labels "strong makers" or "strong poets", oppose the common usage of words and phrases, and create new usages, which are esteemed by the community, and force a rethinking of each other members' personal vocabularies.

This image of language as going "all-the-way-down" with nothing further grounding the beliefs and desires which produce the utterances, allows us to see boxing as something which can be deeply constitutive and revealing of the boxer. It is reductive to consider boxing as merely something that boxers do. Wacquant's boxers understood their connection to their practice as something that was important in deciding who they were. Fighting is the space in their lives where these boxers describe who they are. The boxer understands his personal "inner worth" from within the vocabulary of his practice – a vocabulary that uses not only words and phrases, but also bodily actions.

But boxing, like all sports, occurs as public spectacle. Roberts explains that

> . . . the would-be strong poet-athlete's studio is the stark, public arena filled with the babbling mass frequently unfamiliar with the tradition in which she works. There, completely exposed, she must undertake her very private struggle in front of total strangers many of whom do not understand the identity of her action with her self and the consequent personal meaning that the event may hold. (17: p.104)

And this may be why the practice of boxing suffers its "litigations" in the language of others. Because, as a public spectacle, the self-descriptions of practitioners are there to be savoured or spat out by so many not completely conversant with the ways that practitioners describe themselves. This is similar to Christopher Lasch's (9: pp.406-407) lament that the advent of television coverage of sport resulted in its degradation via a reduction of the necessity for spectators to be conversant with the practitioners, and the practices, of the sport.

So what do boxers do? For starters, the boxer would do well to inform the wider, judgmental public about his deep, visceral attachment to this specific practice. But just as there is nothing foundational within the nature of man or of sport to which the media and academic analysts may point to in order to display the irrationality or immorality of boxing to the boxer, so there is nothing foundational which the boxer can use. However, what the boxer may do is tell his particular story using words and phrases which describe the pain and suffering that he endures whilst his practice is redescribed in words that do not convey the attachment he has to his craft. As Roberts states:

> [Rorty][19] thinks that most of the work of changing moral perception, including the recognition of previously unrecognised instances of injustice,

is done not by increasing our knowledge of the truth, but by expanding the inclusiveness of moral perception through the sentimental manipulation of feelings. Said differently, it is to expose the contingency and exclusiveness of our games, linguistic and otherwise (15: p.7).

Rorty would agree that because language-games are less than fully inclusive, they can be the source of the sort of injustice Geras describes: where the so-called "facts" of the victim's story are not recognised as facts and, as a consequence, neither is the victim nor the story heard (15: p.7).

Again, the use of Lyotard's notions of *litige* and *differend* is important. Paraphrasing Roberts, the boxer's stories are excluded from the judgement in two main ways: first, when the perpetrator of the damages against the boxer, in this case the academic press and journalists, turns out to also be the judge of the case; and second, when any story that the boxer tells is ignored by the judge because he/she deals in a different idiom. Rorty explains this point in the following way: " . . . victims of cruelty, people who are suffering, do not have much in the way of a language. That is why there are no such things as the "voice of the oppressed" or the "language of the victims". The language of the victims once used is not working anymore, and they are suffering too much to put new words together" (cited in 15: p.8).

And this is the cruelty that boxers must find some way of conveying, so that judges are moved to listen to their stories with new found respect for their idiom. Boxers may be described as one of the victims of cruelty perpetuated by the Western, middle-class, 'liberal' values that many people support. Far from saving boxers via the paternalistic and altruistic application of these principles, it will cause the boxer grief and suffering because of the loss of something the boxer cares for. It is better and more liberal, according to Roberts and Morgan, following the ideas of Rorty and Lyotard, to hear the victim's story in the words that they wish to use, to feel the victim's pain and suffering, and be moved to reconfigure our own rational spaces. In a tolerant liberal society, we will leave the practice community to repair the damages suffered by the victim, within its own idiom, and thus let the victim tell his story 'as it really happened.'

Of course, this is difficult for some people to stomach. Surely the physical pain and suffering that a boxer endures is far greater than any personal/phenomenological pain he suffers if his practice is taken from him. This latter pain is just the temporary loss that must be endured until the boxer finds some 'better' way to spend his time. Yet, many people have felt such positive pain and suffering, and it may be more useful to describe this, rather than any loss of the abstract notion of freedom. As Rorty comments:

. . . most people do not want to be redescribed. They want to be taken on their own terms – taken seriously just as they are and just as they talk . . . the best way to cause people long-lasting pain is to humiliate them by making the things that seemed most important to them look futile, obso-

> lete and powerless. Consider what happens when a child's precious possessions – the little things around which he weaves his fantasies that make him a little different from all other children – are described as "trash," and thrown away. Or consider what happens when these possessions are made to look ridiculous alongside the possessions of another richer child (cited in 17: p.98).

What possessions does the boxer have? His skill at his practice and the control over his own destiny in the ring seem important possessions for Wacquant's boxers. What happens when these possessions are made to look barbaric, vicious, animal-like, useless or cruel? The boxer suffers the pain and suffering of being redescribed, using someone else's words and phrases, a pain which is familiar to anyone who has suffered such a fate. This suffering is the loss of the opportunity to search for and experience private autonomy for the boxers in the social practice.[20] Such a search is explained by Blake as the need to, "... create my own system, or be enslaved by another man's" (cited in 16: p.6). Boxers risk being enslaved by the public morality of Western liberalism unless they can recapture the control of their practice and private descriptions of their craft; that is, unless the idiom of description is the one that boxers use when describing their practice.

What we lose in such a liberal state is the epistemic comfort that we are progressing somewhere in our descriptions, that we are moving closer to *the* true understanding of sports like boxing. Yet, according to Morgan, "...the price comes with a real benefit: evaluations of sport that ring true precisely because they speak directly to those lived elements of sports that make them the compelling, gripping, and, yes, flawed human affairs that they are" (15: p.122).

Conclusion: Recapturing Control of the Practice

This paper has suggested that the view of the boxer has been ignored by those groups most vocal in their condemnation of boxing as a sport. For certain "little communities" of boxers, the practice of boxing offers a number of phenomenologically important rewards. The plight of these boxers will be heard if they can regain control of the discourse in which the debate takes place. This will occur if these boxers can find some way to describe the pain and suffering they feel by being described by another person's words, and this cruelty can be empathised with by the judges in this debate.

It was stated earlier that the descriptions used in the discourse of big-time fights do not serve fighters well, whether those fighters are similar to Wacquant's semi-professional group, or whether they are the hugely successful and wealthy fighters of the professional game. These descriptions occur in an idiom that is phenomenologically drained for both groups of fighters. Boxers do not speak about their practice in these words and phrases. These are the phrases of the business and entertainment practices. And these idioms don't serve any sport well. But when taken to the excess of professional boxing, they make sports lovers, such as journalists, sociologists and philosophers, feel threatened. That is because the viciousness, greed and vanity of these idioms doesn't fit well with the discourse of liberal-humanist sport, an idiom still supported by most of these 'judges'.

But equally, most of the practice community's members do not reflect the ideals suggested by this discourse. They view their sport as a skilful craft, a practice through which they have control over the descriptions they create for themselves, and as an overt example of virtues that are important in the urban community that many of these fighters come from.[21] There is little doubt that the critics of boxing are trying to produce a better world for the boxers to live in; a world where they don't have to sacrifice their health to achieve something that is personally significant. What is questionable is whether the arguments they use to justify their paternalistic interference, taken from middle-class, comfortable, Western notions of the sanctity of the human body and respect for persons, are the ones that are most useful in the poor, urban societies that boxers come from.

As Roberts suggests about any description of the modern practice of elite sport, of which the professional fight game is a good example:

It is blind in that it has no words that can tell the stories of a peculiar ideality of elite athletic life that can sing the songs or paint the pictures of athletes consistent with how they might choose to be taken in their own terms if they were to have an effective language of their own. To the extent that the dominant language fails to do this is the extent to which it either is irrelevant, if indeed athletes do have a finely textured language in which they can tell their own rich self-creative stories, or cruel and humiliating, if the dominant language has become so oppressive that it has obliterated any language, and thereby any selves, that athletes can call their own. It may be difficult to accept that elite athletes, the paradigm of success in our culture, are the oppressed victims of a blindly cruel and humiliating language. Yet fortune, material wealth, and high social status are flimsy protection against the sort of loss perpetuated by cruel, blind redescription. (17: p.98).

But at least professional athletes normally have the time, security and wealth to try to recapture the power of self-description, if they feel enough pain at the words that are being used by others to describe them.[22] Semi-professional boxers have neither the time, nor the security and wealth, to do much more than convey the pain they suffer, and hope their critics are moved enough to listen. As the author Peter Corris wrote about the Aboriginal boxer Ron Richards: "His hardest battle was for full, dignified, human status within a prejudiced community" (22: p.131). In our terms, a "full, dignified, human status" may mean something like being able to tell your story in the words and phrases you think are most appropriate and have your judges sit up and listen. This status must be won, or defended, by people like boxers whose self-description is currently under threat from the descriptions of others.

notes

1 It should be noted that neither Simon, nor Gerber call for a ban on boxing. Gerber suggests that the sport produces an objectified view of the person, but goes no further. Simon suggests that the sport, because of the results of its goal, should be modified, though not banned. It should also be noted that Simon and Davis argue against the consequential justifications for the ban on boxing offered by Messner and Sabo.

2 Notwithstanding the recent attempts by television executives and managers in the big-time championship fights, to promote the bout by getting their fighters to talk about their hatred for each other, Wacquant's article talks about the respect and community among semi-professional fighters.

3 Thelma McCormack provides an interesting analysis of the presumed 'violence' in fight films, which are often used by social psychologists to test the response of subjects to these depictions. She suggests that violence occurs more frequently and vividly in both Western and gang films because of the lack of rules to mark the boundaries of appropriate behaviour. By contrast, "boxing is dull" (10: p.23). Boxers are shown as overcoming their volatile tempers to perform rationally within the rules of boxing. Hence, boxing films are primarily about 'jock' appeal, and only secondarily about violence (10: p.20).

4 The "liberal art of separation" is the art of dividing the organic whole of premodern society into separate spheres. Liberal theorists suggest boundaries should be formed between the various institutions of society in order to create new freedoms for individuals. For example, the boundary between church and state, enacted in Freedom of Religion Acts, creates a private sphere for individual conscience free from state interference.

5 Colin Tatz has claimed such a racially linked understanding of boxing amongst Aboriginal fighters in Australia (22).

6 Atyeo, cited in 12: p.78.

7 My insertion.

8 My insertion.

9 McNamee uses the explanation, as supplied by Pincoffs, of virtue as "qualities of persons that give us reasons for preference and avoidance" (11: p.50). This gives a practice community some contextual leeway in the description of a virtue. Virtues become the qualities of practitioners that make fellow practitioners aspire to be like them, at this point in the social practice's history. This allows for changes in the ideas of what counts as virtuous behaviour.

10 This was the term used by one of Wacquant's boxers (24: p.20). Whilst it does not appear in my dictionary, I think it conveys its meaning well, and, in the spirit of the paper, I use it with respect.

11 Colin Tatz recounts the song by Ted Egan, about the great Australian Aboriginal fighter, Ron Richards. It is worth recounting two of the verses:

> He won the national title
> So his managers brought in stars from overseas,
> Tough stuff but he was gutsy
> And one by one he demolished all of these.
> But he took such punishment in each fight
> It scrambled his brains, impaired his sight
> His managers said: 'Kid, you'll be right',
> But the hungry fighter was on the way downhill
> Yes the hungry fighter was on the way downhill

And then he lost his title
But still they matched him time and time again
And soon he gave up training
Found a couple of drinks would kind of ease the pain
His managers all stayed rich and fat
They bought him a guitar and a cowboy hat
And then a second-rater knocked him flat
And the doctor said: 'Son, give the game away,
Hungry fighter, give the game away.' (Egan "The Hungry Fighter", cited in 22: p132)

12 My insertion.

13 Douglas Booth has suggested that sporting practice communities are notoriously bad at making moral decisions because their "narrow self-interests... are rarely compatible with strong evaluation" (1, p.139). Booth sees the decision of the New Zealand All Blacks to tour South Africa, during the years of apartheid as indicative of this shallow decision making. I would suggest the decision of the Australian Olympic Commission to send a team to the Moscow games, was a similar one. Both may stem from what Booth suggests is the common belief in sport's communities of having "an inalienable right to play" (1: p.139). Further on, Booth argues:

Strong evaluators usually link issues and consider broader moral positions before making decisions. In short, the narrow self-interests of practice-communities are rarely compatible with strong evaluation. (1: p.139)

Some important points need to be made in Morgan's defence. Firstly, there is the obvious point that Booth's characterisation may just as easily apply to all social practices; that sociology and history have, at times, been practised without an eye towards broader social issues. But generally, many members of the social practice reject this type of sociology and history. Would we support legislation against such forms? I think not, because such legislation would go against one of the first examples of the liberal art of separation; the division of state and academia via academic freedom. So, what does limit such forms of sociology and history? The democratic preferences of those particular social practice communities, perhaps informed by other things such as Western society's "harm principle" or "respect for persons." But whatever the case, we would be disappointed if the understandings of our practice community of sociologists and historians were ignored because the idiom that was selected for judgement was, for example, an economic one. And imagine the screams if the idiom of judgement was a sporting one.

14 I must thank Professor Terry Roberts for this important idea.

15 My insertion

16 A common criticism of such a pluralistic state is that people do not have the capacity to choose from a wide variety of options. Yet this criticism presupposes that at least some people in power have that ability, for they will make such a choice for all people via legislation. As Morgan states in answering such critics:

Pluralism is best understood and defended not as an effort to present a dizzying array of choices to a populace befuddled by the choices, but as an argument against narrowing the good life to a select few forms of life (13: pp.255-256).

17 Roberts goes even further by suggesting that a state is likely to be more tolerant of private self-descriptions when its members are safe and comfortable. So the purpose of the liberal state is to create enough peace, wealth and freedom for its members, whilst allowing sufficient spaces for its members to work out their private self descriptions. In such a state, it is likely that "sporting practices, as many of the arts, would flourish as some of the most popular, private and ultimate

ways people would choose to make and remake themselves." (16: pp.3-4)

18 The notion of 'choice' here is ambiguous, as Roberts explains: "Our sense of who and what we are and what is worth becoming are strongly influenced and frequently entirely determined by the vocabularies that become us "all the way down" simply by our ongoing participation in an historical culture" (16: p.5). So there is only an eccentric sense in which a person may pick up or drop a certain vocabulary because of private 'choices' the individual makes which are not shared with most other members of the normal society. This is the idea suggested by Heidegger's dictum: "Man does not speak; rather, language speaks man" (cited in 8: p.345).

19 My insertion.

20 Roberts and Rorty are particularly concerned with the suffering that occurs when an individual's private descriptions are ignored because of the public idiom used by the traditional social practice. That is, when an athlete's self-description is ignored because it contravenes the dominant discourse of the practice. In this case, whilst I should be wary of the tendency of the boxing fraternity to ignore the private descriptions of its members, I am discussing the trend of one social practice to interfere in the affairs of another. In Morgan's terms; "Going for local control will also promote pluralism outside of each practice within the sphere by minimizing the intrusion of practice-communities in the *litige* of other practice-communities." (13: p.258)

21 The first two films of the *Rocky* series had a number of examples of this "little community" and its esteem for the practice of boxing. From Rocky being kicked out of the gym for being undisciplined, to the community running with Rocky in training, to Rocky's problems with accepting his wife's decision about his retirement, to remaining in the "game" as a spit-boy and many more. These early films, whilst beset with many of the worst clichés of the popularization of the practice of fighting, also conveyed some of the ideas that were important for Wacquant's boxers.

22 We may like to consider the efforts of Andre Agassi, Denis Rodman, Charles Barkley and even the imprisoned Mike Tyson as examples of athletes redescribing themselves on their own terms.

bibliography

1 Booth, Douglas. "The Poverty of Logic: William Morgan's Theory of Sport." *Sporting Traditions*, 12/1, (1995), 133-142.

2 Bredemeier, Brenda Jo and Shields David L. "Athletic Aggression: An Issue of Contextual Morality." *Sociology of Sport Journal*, 3, (1986), 15-28.

3 Davis, Paul. "Ethical Issues in Boxing." *Journal of the Philosophy of Sport*, XX-XXI, (1993-94), 48-63.

4 Donnelly, Peter. "Sport as a Site for 'Popular' Resistance." *Popular Cultures and Political Practices*. Edited by Richard B. Gruneau. Toronto: Garamond Press, 1988.

5 Eassom, Simon. "Mountaineers (and Other Athletes of the Dangerous): Philosophers of Death." *Proceedings of the P.S.S.S. Conference*, Buffalo, New York, (1982), 1-18.

6 Gebauer, Gunter. "Citius-Altius-Fortius and the Problem of Sport Ethics: a Philosopher's Viewpoint." *Sport: The Third Millenium*. Edited by F. Landry, M. Landry and M. Yertes. Sainte-Foy: Les Presses De L'Universite Laval, 1991.

7 Gerber, Ellen "My Body, My Self." *Sport and the Body: A Philosophical Symposium*. 2nd. Edition. Edited by Ellen Gerber and William J. Morgan. Philadelphia: Lea & Febiger, 1979.

8 Guignon Charles B. and Hiley, David R. "Biting the Bullet: Rorty on Private and Public Morality." *Reading Rorty*. Edited by Allen Malachowski. Oxford: Basil Blackwell, 1990.

9 Lasch, Christopher "The Degradation of Sport." *Philosophic Inquiry in Sport*. Edited by William J. Morgan and Klaus V. Meier. Champaign, Illinois: Human Kinetics Publishers, 1988.

10 McCormack, T. ""Hollywood's Prizefighting Films: Violence or 'Jock Appeal'?" *Journal of Sport and Social Issues*, 8/2, (1984), 19-29.

11 McNamee, Mike "Virtues, Values and Sporting Practices." *Discourse on Sport: Proceedings of the 21st Annual Conference of the PSSS*, Edited by S. Eassom. Bedford, UK: CASPER, 1994, 44-55.

12 Messner, M.A. and Sabo, D.F. *Sex, Violence and Power in Sports*. Freedom, California: Crossing Press, 1994.

13 Morgan, William J. *Leftist Theories of Sport: A Critique and Reconstruction*. Urbana, Chicago: University of Illinois Press, 1994.

14 Morgan, William J. " Circular Theories, 'Strong Evaluation', and Sports: a Response to Booth." *Sporting Traditions*, 12/2, (1996), 115-123.

15 Roberts, Terence J. "Language, Truth, Justice and Sporting Practice." Paper presented at the Physical Activity, Sport and Health: 1996 Pre-Olympic Scientific Congress. 10-14 July, Dallas, USA.

16 Roberts, Terence J. "Private Autonomy and Public Morality in Sporting Practices." *Ethics and Sport*. Edited by M.J. McNamee and S.J. Parry. London: E and F Spon, 1998.

17 Roberts, Terence J. "Sport and Strong Poetry." *Journal of the Philosophy of Sport*, XXII, (1995), 94-107.

18 Roberts, Terence J. "Sporting Practice Protection and Vulgar Ethnocentricity: Why Won't Morgan Go All the Way?" *Journal of the Philosophy of Sport*, XXV, (1998), 71-81.

19 Roberts, Terence J. "'It's Just Not Cricket': Rorty and Unfamiliar Movements: History of Metaphors in a Sporting Practice." *Journal of the Philosophy of Sport*, Vol. XXIV, (1997), 67-78.

20 Shapiro, Joel B. "The Subject of Risk: On the Phenomenology of Skiing." *Philosophy Today*, 36/3, (1992), 228-239.

21 Simon, Robert L. *Sport and Social Values*. Engelwood Cliff : Prentice Hall Inc., 1985.

22 Tatz, Colin *Aborigines in Sport*. Bedford Park, South Australia: The Australian Society for Sport's History, 1987.

23 "The Boxer and the Box." Editorial in *The Australian Weekly Magazine*, 145/13, 20 Sept., (1991), 12.

24 Wacquant, Lois D. "The Pugilistic Point of View: How Boxers Think and Feel about Their Trade?" *Theory and Society*, 24, (1995), 489-535.

"In the Fight"

Phenomenology of a Pugilist

BAYDON BEDDOE

IT SEEMS TO ME THAT WHENEVER BOXING becomes the subject of debate it stirs up deep emotions within people, usually of an outwardly negative nature towards the sport. It is also ironic how rational discussion about boxing can get so hostile. When I mention that I am a practitioner of the "sweet science," I'm quickly seized upon. Because boxing is viewed as being violent then, for many, it implies that the participants of the sport must be somewhat depraved or immoral. For some, the urge to box must certainly reflect some pugnacious streak in the boxer's character. For others, the fighter is seen as being thick, or so impoverished in their life that boxing is the only option for a livelihood. It is then a short step for many of these critics to argue for a ban on the sport. The line that is usually run is that boxing is exploitative, that boxing is only ever about violence and violent people, that a society that condones such violence is inhumane and uncivilised, and that naive boxers who engage in such a dangerous practice should be protected from themselves.

This sets up a situation where the anti-boxing voice becomes the dominant one in society. This discourse then commands centre ring when it comes to public policy on the matter, thereby placing those in actual boxing community in the cheap seats when it comes to decisions being made about their trade. Surely this is unjust. Boxing is placed on trial and a verdict is passed without ever having heard the stories of those directly involved – the boxers. This article will hopefully provide an insight into my experience and understanding of what it means to be a boxer. In doing so, I hope to be able to debunk some of the stereotypical assumptions that abound about the current fight game.

I sit silently in the dark labyrinth below centre ring, the noise of the cheering and jeering crowd bustling about above hardly making a dent into my calm, unperturbed state. I get up and slowly move to gather the accoutrements of my trade – the long, slender and thinly lined boxing boots, the hard bulky "ball" protector and the beautifully silky shorts. All the while I focus on the upcoming contest. I reflect upon my past fights, imaging the specific moves and tactics to counter my opponent.

I wind the bandages up and around the contours of my hand, across the knuckles and about the wrist, finishing up by tying the thumb in. All this aims to tighten the bones of hand, thus transforming it into a new entity – "the fist". I feel the cool rough edges of the bandage tug upon my hand. The limited range of motion this permits reminds me that this hand is now a fist. From here I shift my focus to my boots and start the long process of threading each lace into its slotted hole. My pulse moves up another notch as I do this. It's a sign that the fight is close at hand. I'm not nervous, but eager to get in the fight.

Then the final transition towards being a boxer: the gloves are put on. I feel the immense volume of the dense cushioning press ever so gently against the breadth of my hand. The sweet smell of the leather swells up to permeate and excite my senses. I bang the gloves together signaling that I have become the pugilist. In response to my trainer's instruction I begin a shadow box to warm up. I revel in my fleet footwork and snappiness of arms as I punch the air, each one quicker than the previous one. Continuing this dance I spin to the side, twisting and turning, avoiding a series of imagined punches from my opponent. I'm totally engrossed in this ritual, yet snap out of its hypnotic hold on me by the sharp call of the boxing director signaling me to proceed to the main arena.

I advance from the small locker room out into the great expanse of the stadium. The general hum of the audience builds to a roar but I remain transfixed by the light of the main ring. It cuts a swathe though the dark, smoky atmosphere and appears like a beacon in the night. As I approach the main stage I think of myself as a religious person might when he or she is drawn to and enveloped by the light of God. While the religious person might achieve a communion with God, mine is with "the fight".

I stand at centre ring, eye to eye with my opponent, but I stare back unflinchingly. I've grown accustomed to this ritual. I know that it is a foolish "psych" game, but I go through with it just the same. Thousands of questions rush through my head as I contemplate the fight to come. What will happen? Will I go well? What is my opponent like? I remain motionless during the trivialities of the announcer's introductions and the referee's instructions. The mixture of excitement and expectation makes the wait all the more unbearable.

It is in these few brief moments before the contest when the out-of-fight world is at its most frenzied, and I have to make an extra effort to shake its grip and focus on the fight. The crowd noise is deafening, and my handlers try to fit in the last few words of encouragement. I am longing for the comfort of "the fight". Finally the time has come. With the symbolic ringing of the bell, a new world opens up. This new realm feels different. My space and my world is clearly defined and illuminated. Time seems to be slowing down, and the experience is strong and sensual.

I leap into the fight and engage my opponent quickly. There is a brief exchange of punches as we meet and feel each other out. We break and circle away from each other. In this brief respite I analyse our first skirmish. Does he drop his right when he jabs? Is his head clear for my hook? Is the solar plexus open for a quick rip? I ponder whether there are gaps in my defense that he has exploited like catching me with an uppercut when I duck under a punch, or catching me with a punch when I move in a certain direction. Every confrontation speaks volumes about both my own and my opponent's style and little quirks in our boxing technique. In this transition period a plan is hastily formulated and a new attack is initiated.

Upon reflection, this boxing way of knowing requires me to draw upon all my previous in-fight sagacity and bring it to bear on my opponent. I search his entire being for any weakness that might have supplied me with an advantage. Through this process I believe that I achieved a closeness to him that otherwise would be impossible outside the ring. This intimate insight into my opponent also provided me with another insight. The fight can be seen as a mutual agreement where the opponent is not seen as an obstacle to be overcome, but rather as a partner there to aid in testing and drawing out my own capacities. Hyland suggests something similar when he states that sport competition can be seen as "a questioning of each other together, a striving together, presumably so that each participant achieves a level of excellence that could not have been achieved alone, without mutual striving, without the competition" (4: p. 34). It is possible then to consider that in the heat of the competition, together boxers can construct an "intense, immediate and total" friendship (4: p. 36).

The fight grows more intense, each flurry winding unto another. The fight moves in its staccato rhythms, and each attack adds to the excitement. Punches fly in a myriad of directions, some connecting, some not. Many connect simultaneously to create a multi-sensory kaleidoscope of light, aromas, sounds, tastes and pressures. The contest intensifies and my heartbeat races. I am "the fight"; my opponent is "the fight". There is no clear separation between us. I am so close to my rival now that I can feel hear his heavy breathing and feel the flecks of sweat, saliva and blood splatter across my skin. The twisting, spiraling and gyrations of our bodies

> multiply upon the other to yield a certain sensory fullness. My heart is in my mouth and my lungs burn with every available breath. I am swept up in a furious power charged emotion that we are exhibiting there in centre ring. Blow after blow, the round seems to go on forever, but like all fine things it ends with the sound of the bell. The referee steps in between us, and ever so reluctantly we disengage and head for our respective corners. I am still brimming with emotion, and eager to be reunited in the fight once again.

Sometimes in a quiet moment of reflection after a fight I savour a sense of well-being in the way that I can move deftly under punches and then respond to these challenges with my own counter-attacks. For Wacquant, boxing is a strategic and interactive contest that requires not only bodily strength and technically prowess but also moral resolve and tactical intelligence (8: p. 503). This new self-knowledge that I have gained in the sport leads me to speculate that boxing is like chess. For me, the similarities abound. Moving about in an enclosed square according to clearly defined rules of engagement, the fighter/chess-master must then conceive and then apply strategic moves in a creative and effective manner. Just as a chess player moves in a calculated manner to checkmate the opposing king, so too must the boxer advance, outmanoeuvre and entrap the opposition. For Mailer,

> There are languages other than words, languages of symbol and languages of nature. There are languages of the body and prize fighting is one of them. A prizefighter speaks with a command of the body which is as detached, subtle and comprehensive as any exercise of the mind. (cited in 5: p.255).

Just as there can be clumsy and ingenious encounters in chess, so too can boxing be awkward or inventive. In both cases the game or sport "conversations" can be crude or highly articulate.

> I am in the action again, pressuring my opponent, weaving and bobbing in and out of his reach. I'm quickly caught up in the fight but I don't even realise that I am fighting. There is no stopping, no analysis, just the continuous steady stream of action. I am in some form of trance. Yet, at the same time, I feel that I am in complete control.

This description is very much like what phenomenologists would call the "lived body" experience or what Csikszentmihalyi refers to as the "flow state". The flow state, as described by Csikszentmihalyi, is "the wholistic sensation present when we act with total involvement" (1: p. 43). The flow state consists of a subset of factors that can add up to the total intrinsically rewarding experience. These factors include the merging of action and awareness, centring of attention, loss of ego, control of action and environment, and demands for action and clear feedback (1: p. 41).

When I am in "the fight" I am not cognisant of the fact that I am boxing. In giving myself over to the fight, any self-consciousness is lost. I see myself developing a oneness with the fight that, in phenomenological terms, means a passing over of any body-as-object or body-as-object-for-others perspective to one of full engagement as body-as-subject. As a result, I am aware of the punches I throw but in a dim sort of way. All else ceases to exist as my whole essence becomes focused on my competitor and all his movements. This focus is crucial, as it allows me to see and respond to his slightest moves.

> The round ends again and I collapse down on the stool, my handlers quickly rush in and hastily begin to prepare me for the next round. They rip my gum shield out, fill my mouth with refreshing liquid, spray my face with water and finally wipe my face. It is during this moment I get to reflect on the round. I am "outside" my performance now, and for some reason, the memories of past fights come streaming back. This has the effect of energising me. I want more than ever to re-enter the contest and the comfort of the fight.

Crucial to the flow experience is the presence of "interludes" (1: p. 45), that is, momentary breaks that help in recovering from the extra-normal intensity required to maintain the flow. Boxing is one of the few sports in which there are regular rest breaks (about every 3 minutes). These breaks not only assist recovery, but also provide the chance to re-gain focus for the next round. The risk and danger involved in boxing also makes it easier to get back into the flow once the fight resumes. In many ways when my opponent and I are so fully engaged and animated, so focussed on each other's actions, so challenged by what each offers up, we evoke each other's flow state.

> I bounce off the ropes, my opponent circling away from me. I feel the fatigue. The pressure in my legs reaches a point where it is like a dam ready to burst its walls. I know in myself that in order to reach my full potential I must push beyond the fatigue or somehow contain it. To achieve this I cut the ring down on my opponent. Like a hunter stalking its prey I manipulate my environment to trap my opponent in a corner. I know my opponent much better now, and I can anticipate his every move. I sense that the fight is clearly going my way.

With the training and preparation needed to go into a fight, added with the testing of the self in the ring, I can bring about what Wacquant calls an "ontological transcendence"(8: p. 510). Through no discernible division of the mind and body, I create a new way of being. It reflects who and what I want to be. The boxing experience for me overcomes what might be considered personal and social alienation. That is, it can be an antidote to the type of alienation that is based on the subjective feeling that the world that is falls short of the world that should be (4: p.58), or the feeling of emptiness that can come from fragmented, repetitious and scientifically managed labour.

When I box, ecstasy, pain, fear and freedom intersect. When I am fighting, I know that it is something that I have control over compared to most jobs that I have had. With boxing, the correlation of success and effort is much greater. The hours that I spend punching the bags, the litres of sweat that I have perspired, the undying dedication to living a "clean" life and a steadfast devotion to the sport have tangible rewards. Wacquant expresses this sentiment well when he claims that "Boxers are bound to their trade by a profound, multifaceted, sensuous relationship of affection and obsessive devotion. (8: p.507)

In spite of the dangers of the sport, and maybe because of them, the boxer is drawn to fight. While boxing can be a lucrative trade, the lure of money cannot entirely explain a fighter's motivation to don the gloves. For me, and I suspect for many others, there is a deeper and more meaningful motive at stake here in the pugilistic experience. For Wacquant "You have to experience in your own flesh the coeval anguish and excitement of "going toe-to toe" as the culminating trial of weeks of taxing training to grasp fully boxing's sensuous magnetism. (8: p. 512)

> Our bodies collide and interweave. Perspiration occasionally shaded by a tint of crimson, rolls down glistening flesh. Chests heave and bones ache with the "thud" of well connected "hits." It's a heady and chaotic, clear and purposeful world, all at the same time.

I am drawn to the exhilaration of dancing on the knife-edge. Risk, danger and possibly death are not only acknowledged or accepted, but also seen as almost integral to an authentic existence. I become an edge worker treading a fine line between life and death, between "what is possible and what is not possible" (3: p. 58). However, it is not a case of total reckless abandon, but rather a controlled risk. I recognise the dangers, and only after careful tactical preparation, fortified by hours upon hours of training, will I step into the ring.

When I box, I have to lift myself up and find a strength within or face not only a defeat marked by points lost or by being knocked out, but a much broader ruination of character, that is, as Wacquant puts it, "being branded with a mark of infamy and suffer a veritable symbolic death" (8: p. 495). This angst of having to test my limits in this way is captured well by Shapiro's notion of being on the edge. For him, "It was the fear that I would not be able to achieve that unbearable intoxication that comes from pushing the edge of the envelope and, perhaps even more, the fear that I might achieve it"(7: p. 238).

The possibility of facing death in boxing is not only symbolic; it's real. On Eassom's existentialist account of death, if we acknowledge that we are going to die, then we should reorder projects to-be, or live in the actuality (2). Put differently, "Man is forever striving to add years to his life, without thinking of adding life to his years" (2: p. 4). This is similar to the choice played out by Achilles in The Iliad. According to Mueller,

> Achilles has a choice between a long and inglorious and a short and glorious life. The motif translates into the narrative of an individual life, the condition of the warrior's existence. He cannot acquire glory without the risk of his life. The risk increases with the degree of excellence, and at the highest level the certainty of great fame is balanced of certainty of early death. (6: p. 31)

In taking risks, Hyland notes that we would sometimes say, we "put ourselves on the line," but riskful situations can individualise us, offer an occasion in which "find out who we are in the midst of becoming who we are (4: p. 36). When I box I risk all: self, body, consciousness and life. However, it is in the process when I face my opponent and, more importantly, myself, under the pitiless lights of the ring for all to see, I will define myself.

We are in a clinch now and I can feel and hear my opponents laboured panting. We are ordered to break. I struggle to disentangle myself and move a few paces back, ready to fight again. The punches seem slower and more awkward now as we both grapple with the onset of fatigue. I am weary and sore in these last stages of the fight, but I know that we are not far from the end.

Finally the bell tolls and the fight is over. We embrace in a hug. The decision is passed in my favour, but it's not the winning that excites me. I am not simply a prizefighter. Something more meaningful has been won – the chance to be "in the fight". On the path to the dressing room I am met with applause, pats on the back and handshakes. Once inside I plunk myself down on one of the chairs in the changing area and proceed to separate my drenched equipment from my pleasantly aching body. My old man comes up to me, smiles and hands me a beer. I gulp slowly. We talk.

bibliography

1 Csikszentmihalyi, Mihalyi. "Play and Intrinsic Rewards," *Journal of Humanistic Psychology*, 15 (3), (1975), 41-63.
2 Eassom, Simon B. "Philosophers of Death." *Philosophic Society for the Study of Sport Conference Proceedings*, (1982) 1-20.
3 Fairchild, David L. "Creative Sports: Antidote to Alienation." *Journal of the Philosophy of Sport*. V, (1978), 57-62.
4 Hyland, Drew "Competition and Friendship." *Journal of the Philosophy of Sport*, V (1978), 27-37.
5 Lowe, B. *The Beauty of Sport: A Cross-Disciplinary Inquiry*. New Jersey: Prentice Hall. 1977.
6 Mueller, M. *The Iliad*. London: George Allen and Unwin, 1984.
7 Shapiro, Joel B. "The Subject of Risk." *Philosophy Today*, 36 (1992), 236-237.
8 Wacquant, Loïc J. D. "The Pugilistic Point of View: How Boxers Think and Feel About Their Trade" *Theory and Society*, 24 (1995), 489-535.

Her Beauty and Her Terror

Australian Football and the Community

MARGARET LINDLEY

ONCE UPON A TIME, the world was simpler. We suppose. There were at least fewer people with fewer means of communication between them. Those people understood, or believed they understood, most of what they observed and used.

In the last years of the twentieth century much of what we observe and most of what we use is only dimly understood, if it is understood at all. Complexities overwhelm us. So long as the sun, the rain, the car, the computer produce the desired results, we leave the comprehension to the experts – to our scientific and technological priests.

Sport has become one of the few features of our life that we can, more or less, understand. If the games we watch and play do not always produce the desired result, they are at least comprehensible. They are, in that sense, psychically soothing. As more and more of our world becomes a bewildering battleground, a playing field which is horribly uneven, sport restores some sense of moral balance. The importation of sporting metaphors into entirely inappropriate economic and political environments tells us something of the ethical order sport is meant to represent; is still able to represent.

In a combative world it is in the sporting arena that combat is most unabashed, most honest; least likely to be overlaid or disguised with claims that what is occurring is something other than a clash of wills. And the clash of wills at least interests, often fascinates, at times obsesses all of us from the time we are about two and discover to our horror that the will exists in the plural.[1] The discovery of the other is inseparable from the discovery of the other's will: it is the other's will that separates, marks an entity off/from, indicates that the world is not, is other than an extension of self.

There are those who never recover from this shock, who spend their energies in an attempt to return to existence before the awful and unacceptable Discovery.[2] By and large, however, human beings accommodate themselves to the clash; find their allies, endure their opponents, enjoy their victories and tolerate their defeats with what grace they can muster.

Sports play out the clash before us, invite us to identify with a 'side of the question', and in a few hours (or days in the case of the great saga that is Test cricket) demonstrate for us successful and unsuccessful strategies. The players live to play again, to show us the consequences of their responses, usually over a period of some years in what may be hundreds of tests.

Most of us have played something called a sport. Some of us continue to play a sport, the rest direct their sporting energies elsewhere. A few (less than one might imagine) avoid anything smacking of sport – that is, of open, undisguised competition of wills. A precious handful become demonstrators of sport for the rest of us: put on uniforms, and before the eyes of cameras and reporters 'play' for critical comment in the public arena.

In Australia the demonstrators of sport who have attracted most interest and attention have been men playing Australian Football, men playing cricket; and women and men running, swimming or cycling quickly or with exceptional endurance.[3] The crowds turn out for displays of men combining wills in a common purpose; the greatest attention is paid to the men who play Test cricket, which first showed us how to best Mother England, and to those men who play Australian football, the Australian cultural product *par excellence*.

Australian football is the home-grown equivalent of opera or ballet, ill-treated by academics precisely because it is so dramatically effective; relegated to the sidelines of history or any other serious intellectual investigation, either for fear of contamination by its unashamed display of wills in conflict or by fear of exposure of the degree to which one is already contaminated. Will they guess that I love it? That I have not been able to stand apart from and implicitly above it?

Those academics who, *à la* Manning Clark, stand unashamed in the outer, tend to wear their involvement in Australian football as a badge signifying membership of 'the people'; they argue that the game does matter; but are not always sure of how to write of it without writing, embarrassingly, of themselves.[4]

Rugby may dominate newspapers, radio and television in New South Wales and Queensland (and lately the Australian Capital Territory) to a degree similar to the domination of Australian football elsewhere. It has never been able to attract comparable numbers of supporters to its games. In recent years, the Sydney Swans and Brisbane Lions have been able to attract bigger attendances than rugby matches in states dominated by a pro-rugby media and without a tradition of Australian football. The game is peculiarly attractive to the Australian public.

It has been suggested, unkindly, that outside Australia it is simply regarded as peculiar: a wild, lawless, free-for-all. It is not, of course, lawless. In fact, at the highest level the game requires the constant vigilance of seven umpires to uphold its many rules, with possible recourse to others off-field, and periodic suggestions that more are required. It appears lawless because it seems, compared to other footballing codes, to be wild, free-for-all, even when players are not breaking the laws.

Australian football is closer than any other variety of codified football to the proto-football of village communities, reported in England from the twelfth century. It is played on a ground of no specific proportions – on a space which is 'big enough' and 'oval'. The ovalness of the oval varies from ground to ground: fat ovals, thin ovals, ovals with bulging pockets, even lop-sided pockets.

There is no offside rule. Players go where they damn well like, risking only the coach's wrath for tactical foolishness. The ball's bounce cannot be reliably predicted, allowing for sheer luck to disrupt the mastery of the more highly skilled, and it may be moved forward in any way the player pleases (unless the player transgresses into rugby by throwing the ball or by tucking it under his arm and running with it). Or it may be moved backwards, or sideways – any way, but keep it in play, keep it fast, keep it flowing.

Any attempts by wily coaches to disrupt the flow, to dam it, bring it under control, are met by rule changes. If the ball is to be swamped by players at the centre-bounce, the numbers at that bounce will be restricted by law.[5] If players are to be slung to the ground in order to slow the game down (rather than to alter ball possession, when slinging to the ground is not only legal, but rewarded), the offenders will be penalised with sufficient severity to deter all save the most savage or stupid.

The region within which a score may be registered is unusually wide, and high. The scoring is also stubbornly pre-decimal. Base six, not base ten rules. And, most notably, and importantly, there is no specific body-type better suited than others to playing Australian football. Heights of successful footballers vary from just above five feet to just below seven: in fact, the game calls for players of differing heights. Although a notably muscular frame is considered important, it is not absolutely necessary. The game accommodates the thin, the wiry, the heavy, the fast and the slow of the village. Provided, at the highest levels, that they bear male genitalia. So far.

With eighteen of your lads and eighteen of our lads gathered on the ground of no particular dimensions in no particular positions (for all the precision suggested by names like left-half-forward-flank), the ball is bounced by one of three umpires, running about in the colour of truce, preventing traffic jams, ensuring flow (or meant to do so), and offering some measure of protection from the more unscrupulous.

From the opening bounce, the game, to a degree which has invited scorn from some rugby supporters, becomes airborne. There are few footballers who do not, at some point in the game, leap into the air – and some of them leap very high indeed.

One of the more unaccountable omissions from *The Australian National Dictionary* is the word 'specky'. You will find 'ruck' and 'follower' there, in their footballing variants. You will not find 'specky'. Not in any spelling. For the uninitiated, a specky is a 'spectacular' – not a speck or a spectacle – a spectacular mark or catch, a leap which is spectacular, a juggling which is spectacular, a spectacular feat by an Australian Rules footballer in relationship to ball and air. A footballer may not be a specky; he may only take or do a specky. And so they do, week after week, year after year, across the country.[6]

The specky is a punctuation mark in a game of constant motion. It is the creation of individual skill and/or daring; the spectacular catch of cricket become so familiar that it has acquired a nickname. Some players 'fly' so often that the crowd anticipates their speckies, drawing in breath as they begin their approach.[7]

The specky, or the desire or possibility of taking one, takes Aussie rules closer to ballet or dance than any other football. The great high-flyers hang in the air as a Nijinsky or a Nureyev did; sit on shoulders with the poise, but not the demeanour of a ballerina. Once, such feats were followed by a suitable interval for applause, as the player – as modestly as possible – paused for his kick. Now, although he may still do so, he is as likely to race on, or dispose of his right to kick with a handpass to a team-mate running past. The trend was evident from the later sixties, as the handpass began to disrupt set positions and positional play to the extent that they were traditionally followed.

The solo 'dances' of ballet are known as variations, following upon the musical sense of variations upon a theme. In classical ballet, they last a little more than a minute, perhaps as long as two minutes. No Australian footballer would ever be allowed to possess the ball (with which all variations must be performed) for more than thirty seconds of rapid improvisation, during which, as Malcolm Blight (a notably graceful performer) puts it, 'danger comes from the four points of the compass.'[8]

The variations of Australian football are collective, *un pas de dix-huit* at most, but more usually of three, four or five. They end only when a score is registered, and the leaps (which may be horizontal as well as vertical) are integrated into a flowing series of manoeuvres, an improvised choreography, *un spettacolo*: a scene, a play, a show.

Australian Football is a drama in four acts. The extreme liberty allowed for player improvisation is contained within strictly disciplined time. There shall be twenty minutes of actual 'play' in each act: twenty minutes of variations. The quality of these variations is all-important. In 1994 the quarters were reduced from twenty-five to twenty minutes in order to maintain standards of artistic excellence without testing players' bodies beyond acceptable limits.

Those standards are evaluated by spectators from the opening bounce and they apply to umpires as well as to players. Scorn is directed at umpires who do not bounce well, with mastery of their art. A good bounce is high and does not deviate from a vertical line. Proud umpires approach the task (performed as many as sixty times in a game) with care and a precise sense of style: the ball is not easy to control, and on some surfaces must be thrown into the air if an unsightly failure is not to be recorded. Australian football umpires are supposed not only to be just and observant, but at least moderately graceful and skilled: either with a ball or with flags.

Boundary umpires attract less scrutiny than field umpires, but their throw-ins require some skill, sending the ball in a high arc backwards over their heads. Concentration is required to do it well. Goal umpires, less athletic, are expected to demonstrate goals with some degree of panache, quite apart from judging them accurately. Affection is expressed for those who approach this task with particular energy, but all goal umpires invest their role with a sense of drama. Excessive drama, an overly long display, is frowned upon by purists.

A wider range of skills is required from players (though it should be pointed out that I have not exhausted the list of physical skills of umpires, which include the ability to run backwards without appearing silly). A high leap may require more than judgement and courage, as players manoeuvre for position in the midst of or on the backs of other players. There is also the problem of the descent. From time to time stories appear of young or inexperienced footballers who seriously injure themselves, who break their necks, because they do not know how to land from the heights to which they are encouraged to fly.

Films of high marks, beloved of television editors and of audiences, show an extraordinary variety of leaps. Some leapers sit in the air, both legs outstretched; knees may be bent or straight; bodies at any angle; arms held high, curved, or just held. One or more players may act, unwillingly and unwittingly, to propel the player higher: the great high marks (a player may be a great high mark, thus taking on the character of his most distinguished feat) judge their runs to perfection to take advantage of the upward movement of others.

One of the curiosities of Australian football is that, technically, many high marks might be judged illegal, because the player attacks another player's back. It is not lawful to attack a player's back, but the umpires get around the problem where high marking is concerned by explaining that the player flying for the high ball has the ball as his object. There is a problem in this. Any player penalised for attacking another's back would probably be able to argue that the ball was also his object – that he was not so much attacking a back, as encountering a back between himself and his object.

There can be no doubt that the player who finds the high flyer's knees in his back has suffered interference in his own attempt to mark, but it is understood by even the most pernickety of umpires that if the flyer succeeds in taking the mark (that is, securing possession of the ball) he will suffer no penalty. If he fails to mark, he might well be punished for his infringement, though such punishment is usually thought unfair, particularly if the attempt was a spectacular one.

Any mark requires judgement and many require considerable strength. All are satisfying to those supporting the players who take them, the fortunate or skilled ones who capture the ball in outstretched palms (or, in a feat which attracts considerable admiration, a single palm). For Kevin Sheedy, the ball is 'the challenge'. That is what it represents, what it symbolises.[9] Whatever else it might be, that is fundamental; all representations refer back to that signification. The mark always signifies success in facing challenge; the kick sends it; the handpass links those who take on challenges.

Any ball in any ball game may be so constructed, of course: the kick and the mark have their equivalents in the throw and the catch. But in no ball game are challenges presented as freely and diversely as in Australian football; in no other ball game are players permitted as wide a range of responses to challenges. Even where there are restrictions (as in the distance a player may run with the ball without touching it to the ground in some manner), those restrictions are meant to be 'interpreted', rather than imposed with anything approaching mathematical precision.

The issue of interpretation provides spectators with the possibility of an unusual range and degree of disagreement with umpiring decisions. The most frequently asked questions at Australian football matches begin with the words, 'How can you call that'.

It is not altogether clear what a mark is, whether or not a kick is of requisite marking length, whether or not a player has infringed. Spectators can and do feel themselves entitled to offer their interpretations as counter-interpretations to those of the umpires (and not necessarily, though usually, in their own team's favour).[10]

Players are required to learn quickly how a particular umpire interprets rules on any given day. If it is wet, they may be indulged where marking is concerned. If they are playing an interstate team away from its home, they may be indulged where tackling is concerned, in the absence of a large number of dissenting voices from the outer.[11]

Players will tell you that they love it – love it all. At the highest level, that of the Australian Football League, they will be well-paid for their love. More than seven hundred men are listed as AFL footballers, have the opportunity to run out before crowds of up to one hundred thousand, soar as the crowd gasps, raise their arms in triumph as thousands cheer. They suffer for this: they risk serious damage to knees in particular, and they experience pain every week: intense, sharp pain and dull, bruising pain that may last them for days or weeks.

But theirs will be the glory, the honour and the fame – and that may last them the rest of their lives. No one outside Australia will know them, but that will have no effect on their position within Australia. When a dying Ted Whitten was taken around the Melbourne Cricket Ground to hold up his arms to crowds he could not see, people across Australia wept. When he died he was accorded a state funeral, and people around the country stood silently in their grandstands and in the outers as the seagulls wheeled and cried.

Their fame may outlive their deaths. No Australian sporting song is better known than "Up there, Cazaly!" – the song based on the cry of crowds in the early years of the twentieth century as Roy Cazaly soared to mark. It was the cry Australian soldiers took with them into battle in the first World War.

There are those who read much into that; who argue that certain kinds of sport offer a training, a preparation for war. The playing fields of Eton are meant to have had something to do with the creation of a British empire; masculine violence generally is seen, by many feminists, as something encouraged and developed by sports in which male bodies clash brutally.

There can be little doubt that bodies clash brutally in Australian football. A good deal, but not all of the pain endured by footballers is a direct or indirect result of those clashes. Players cannon into each other, quite legally; players damage their joints twisting away from those legitimate collisions. Nervous officials suggest from time to time that the level of violence deters youngsters (or their parents) from commitment to the game. Soccer is seen as a threat because it does not permit the violent clashes inherent in Australian football.

Much has been done (some would argue too much) to eliminate those clashes not seen as "part of the game". The brawls and altercations for which the game was once notorious are almost eliminated from the game at the highest level. In the nineties violence outside the rules is policed very much more thoroughly than before. Punishment for uncontrolled, illegitimate violence is more likely than at any time in the game's history.

Which leaves the legitimate, controlled, inherent violence. In Australian football a player may still strike another player with his body in such a manner as to cause that player to leave the ground unconscious, on a stretcher, without suffering any form of punishment at all. In the 1997 season, West Coast Eagles' captain, John Worsfold, a notably skilled practitioner of such violence (and a mild-mannered pharmacist off the field), dealt such a blow to a Collingwood player. He endured some minor booing from the crowd, but no penalty of any description. Mr Worsfold had not broken a rule.

What are we to make of Australian football's lawful violence? Is the game a disturbing remnant of colonial thuggery, or, worse, a defiant glorification of masculine aggression?

Supporters of the game are fond of pointing out that there is far less violence amongst spectators at Australian football matches than there is from soccer crowds. All sorts of amateur psychologists and sociologists suggest that soccer spectators enact the violence they are deprived of seeing on the field, and that Australian football supporters go home to peaceable pursuits because their violent instincts are played out before them by men trained and willing to do so.

Perhaps. But perhaps it is also true that little boys in particular learn, from sports like Australian football, to hurl opponents to the ground, to run through, rather than negotiate a path. In that respect, Australian football may well be one of the entertainments which demonstrates and reinforces notions of strength and efficacy which have advantaged men and disadvantaged women.

Australian football, however, like all complex forms of entertainment, teaches a number of things simultaneously. One of the things it displays before its public is courage. The courage is raw, physical, vividly obvious. Bodies hurtle towards other bodies with daring which appears fearless even if it is not.

The apparent fearlessness, or the triumph over fear, subverts the docility, the timidity increasingly encouraged as the twentieth century draws to a close. Michel Foucault has spoken of bodies rendered docile, tractible by the insertion of a power to punish, the internalisation of dread of punishment; and Brian Massumi has asked, "What aspect of life, from the most momentous to the most trivial, has *not* become a workstation in the mass production line of fear?"[12]

At the end of the twentieth century we are taught to be frightened of the sun because it will give us cancer; frightened of the rain because it may be acid; frightened of the computer because of its radiation; frightened of the car because we may die in it; frightened of the food we eat, the words we use, the job we might lose.

Fear, says Massumi, is a part of "setting social boundaries, . . . erecting and preserving hierarchies, . . . the perpetuation of domination".[13] Australian football defies fears, flirts with boundaries, challenges domination. Although it erects hierarchies, it does not preserve them. Today's premiers might well be tomorrow's also-rans. In defiance of economic trends which see the wealthy becoming wealthier while the poor become poorer, Australian football clubs are required to observe a salary cap which prevents a wealthy club from dominating competition.

Australian football is not a workstation in the mass production line of fear. It teaches triumph over fear. It disrupts conventional patterns of domination. And it does so because of its peculiar relationship to the community it serves.

Australian Rules footballers belong to us. Although players are bought and sold, de-listed and swapped, they belong to their club's members and supporters, not to a set of owners or managers. They represent us, not Nike, or BHP. Their courage, their boldness in the face of the obvious and immediate danger the game's violence presents is ours, at our service, of us and for us. They are not the hired gladiators of company-owned teams; the hirelings of robber barons.

It is complained that capitalism has put its grubby paws onto football, as though it would not. But it is largely in the arena of team-sports, particularly in Australian football, that a pre-capitalist sense of community is conserved.

When Andrew Jarman exercised his individual, free-economic-agent right to refuse to play for the Adelaide Crows one week because he preferred to play for Norwood, Australian football supporters were horrified. The fine imposed on him was considered inadequate and would have been whatever the amount. The moral universe of Australian football was not restored until the new coach, Malcolm Blight, declared that Jarman was no longer required, and no, he did not wish to speak to him.

I am a member of the West Coast Eagles, which each year asks its members if they are happy with the services provided, what we like and dislike about the club, what suggestions we have to improve it. Children who are members receive each year a signed birthday card from the club. If they should be hospitalised they will be visited by a player – without cameras. When a young cousin of mine died, players from her club, Carlton, wore black armbands for her.

When I attend 'functions', like all members of all clubs, I will be able to converse with the coach and any players present. Indeed, that is the purpose of 'functions'. I am not only entitled to talk to the coach about the team's performances – he is expected to listen to me.[14] Weary players limp through supporters to be patted on the back, and to discuss the game yet again, with men and women they have never met before who call them 'Bluey' and 'Woosha' and 'mate'.

A few months ago, at yet another 'function', I spoke with the injured Chris Mainwaring. Mainwaring is thirty-two years old, and recovering, like so many of today's players, from a knee reconstruction. He assured me that he would play again. He had two years' football left in him. As I patted him reassuringly on the back, I was moved by his determination – and struck, again, by the strange siting of the footballer, his body and his public.

I had never met Mr Wainwaring. I am not in the habit of patting young men at first acquaintance – no matter how attractive they are (and Chris Mainwaring is famously attractive). He was not in the least disconcerted to be patted. As a supporter, I had certain rights with regard to his body – to knowledge of its condition, and to affectionate touching of agreed areas (the back is the favourite, but the arms are okay too).

They are our heroes. We send them out in our colours to thrill and inspire us; to show what courage, determination and skill can do. We expect them to show us how to learn from mistakes, how to triumph over adversity.

We expect our clubs to be run not as gambling dens, like northern rugby league clubs, but as organisations which show respect for children and the elderly. We expect the clubs to survive in the world of late twentieth-century capitalism, and we like them to do so as honourably as possible. A Hawthorn 'merger' with Melbourne was dishonourable and Hawthorn members knew it and rejected it; ignored the corporate advice and their own board for all that it was headed by the once-mighty Peter Hudson. Seeing their club under threat, supporters by the thousand became members – pledged and gave their money as well as their voices.

Our clubs have objectives which are intelligible to us and acceptable to us. Whatever explanations for failure are offered, we may have our own ideas – we, after all, are there. In an Australian community so 'rational' that none of us can understand it any more, our football clubs make sense.

Around the fences women and girls are as welcome as men and boys, as self-confident and as accepted. In more than thirty years of energetic expression of my opinions at Australian football matches I have never been rebuked on the ground of gender. At the football I cease to be female and become the colours I wear.

The colours are my signs of membership of a community more vibrant and more democratic than any other of the communities to which I belong. In the footballing community I rub shoulders, or at least pass in the aisles, those I would have encountered in the long-gone villages where we once fought cheerfully over a ball on a common. I sit with company directors and market gardeners, with priests and prostitutes.

Alphonso Lingis tells us that 'Before the rational community, there was the encounter with the other, the intruder. The encounter begins with the one who exposes himself to the demands and contamination of the other.'[15] In Australian football the intruder runs to the encounter in a quite considerable band: at least twenty run onto the field, may exhibit their speed and some of their skills, but always display their cohesion.[16] The other is met fairly and squarely. We rage and shout, but by and large we leave the encounter on good terms. Before us, strong young men leap, swerve, and run. They soar to breathtaking heights; they dash down long curving flanks. They meet challenges with swift, bold courage. When the game is done, they will shake the hands of the opponents whose bodies have crashed into theirs.

Their bodies have crashed with their consent. Players crash into the bodies of those prepared and able to withstand the blow. To equate the physical contact of sports like Australian football with the physical contact of the battery of women (or frail men), children and the elderly by an unconsidered use of the term 'violence' is nonsensical. Abuse of power and violence are not necessarily synonymous.

I am an enemy of abuse of power. I do not oppose violence in sport. I would rather celebrate the strong, beautiful, healthy and noble. Lingis says of the servile that they are 'those who understand evil', whose 'morality is built around the notion of evil': 'The evil one for them is the one who is strong, that is, violent; beautiful, that is, vain; healthy, that is, lascivious; noble, that is, domineering.'[17] I have heard the carping of the servile: footballers are violent, brutal, egotistical, conceited 'animals', aggressive oafs.

They are, implicitly and inevitably, stupid. The slightest signs of inarticulateness (even from a player interviewed after an exhausting game, whilst still panting for breath) are seized upon – particularly by sedentary intellectuals – as indications of a mental defectiveness which compensates for excessive physical competency. No listing of footballers who have doctorates or who work in the higher professions will convince the resentful that those bodies bear brains.

I have heard the strong, beautiful, healthy and noble, and those who watch them, mocked – such expenditure of effort and emotion over a scrap of inflated leather. Australian football is not about leather, of course – inflated or otherwise. It's about struggle, wills in conflict, courage, love, triumph, sorrow and joy.

It is as free and unbounded as we wish ourselves and our lives to be – or it appears to be. As we are taught, more and more, to be isolated, fearful individuals, kept firmly under our own or other's control, Australian football teaches us community, union, and fearlessness in the face of danger. Its wild fierce beauty is an inspiration, a delight, and a national treasure.

endnotes

1 Up to this point the will is perceived as desire, which may or may not be satisfied, but which is not understood as being contingent for its gratification on the desires of others. On differing concepts of desire see Elizabeth Grosz, *Volatile Bodies: Toward a Corporeal Feminism*, Sydney 1994, p. 120n1.
2 Such personalities are usually labelled according to some form of 'pathology', suffering which has been designated as errant because it has not chosen one of a variety of acceptable paths of relief.
3 I am considering Australia as a whole, if that can be done. In two of Australia's three major cities, more attention is paid to rugby players.
4 The academic writing about sport of any kind steers awkwardly between condescension towards folk pastimes and the kind of smug, slightly twee parochialism which tends to infest local histories; between two opposed senses of belonging. Above all, writers about sport strive to create the impression it does not matter to *them* who wins or loses; that the matter is to them 'purely academic'. A good many academics who are fascinated by 'the game' will not write of it precisely because they know that a loss by their team can seriously impair their weekend, and either do not know how to or do not care to conceal the fact.
5 Hawthorn's tactics under Kennedy of massing numbers at the centre-bounce brought about the innovation of the centre square or diamond, entry to which is limited until after the ball has been bounced. Ron Barassi suggests that the size of the square may need to be increased further, in order to provide for a 'clean' bounce and clearance (Interview, July 17, 1995).
6 And at all levels of competition, as the immensely popular television programme, *The Footy Show*, has demonstrated. Denied permission by Channel Seven to show film of games at the top level, the programme's only speckies are those produced at lower levels of competition.
7 The specky is also known as a 'screamer' (another omission, in its footballing variant, from the *Australian National Dictionary*), though the crowd gasps and roars rather than screams. It is generally understood that all spectators should applaud the specky, though Australian football, as played today, rarely leaves time for a sustained display of appreciation.
8 M. Blight, Interview, June 20, 1995.
9 K. Sheedy, Interview, June 23, 1995.
10 Umpires are widely suspected of awareness of their own more dubious interpretations and of a tendency to make amends by making an equally dubious interpretation to the benefit of the offended party.
11 Interstate teams, over a period of years, receive less free kicks than their opponents; and home teams are generally favoured in free-kick statistics.
12 M. Foucault, *Surveiller et punir: Naissance de la prison*, Editions Gallimard, Paris, 1975; B. Massumi, Preface, in *The Politics of Everyday Fear*, (ed. B. Massumi), (University of Minnesota Press, Minneapolis, 1993), p. viii.
13 B. Massumi, *ibid.*
14 David Parkin receives dozens of letters when Carlton loses. The letters are not abusive. They offer suggestions on how to improve the team's performance, and he answers them. About half the letters are from women, whose suggestions are as likely to be helpful as those of the men, and whose recommendations are treated as thoughtfully (Interview, D. Parkin, June 21, 1995).
15 Alphonso Lingis, 'The Other Community', in *The Community of Those Who Have Nothing in Common*, (University of Indiana Press, Bloomington, 1994), p. 10.
16 In AFL matches they run through banners, advertising their fame (and their sponsors) and displaying their determination.
17 A. Lingis, 'Faces, Idols, Fetishes', *op. cit.*, p. 57.

All Part of Whose Game?

A Violence and Sport Commentary

Dennis Hemphill

Introduction

CONTEXT, CONTEXT, CONTEXT. What comes out loud and clear in many, if not all, of the papers in this collection is that the incidence, acceptability and management of violence in sport is largely dependent on the historical-cultural contexts within which sports are organised, participated in, reported on and policed. From the beginning I declare that I am not embarking on some grand synthesis. I will not be snipping off loose ends or smoothing over rough edges in an attempt to make the papers fit into a neat tapestry. Neither will I engage in a systematic critique of each paper, as there are several research disciplines with which I am not familiar to do so properly. Rather, I hope to act more as a "critical friend," to question assumptions, pose questions and draw out implications, the purpose of which is to stimulate further discussion on the issue of violence and sport.

In one way or another the papers in this collection point to the benefits of adopting a more local perspective when it comes to making sense of and judging violence in sport. Whether it be for ascertaining the meaning and legitimacy of violence, or for making policing, judicial and public policy decisions, the papers stress the need to look at local sporting cultures and the communities they serve. Of the various discourses and metaphors I've detected, for instance, sport as war, sport as patriarchal institution, sport as business, and sport as art, some will be shown to be dominant, some as emergent, and some as submerged. Taken together, they jostle and nudge each other in ways that reveal how social interests come to be embedded in the descriptions of violence and sport, and to what effect.

The Truth is Not Out There

Roy Hay's paper "A New Look at Soccer Violence" encourages us to take less of a comparative approach and more of an Australian, and even more local community approach when we look at the incidence, evaluation and management of violence in soccer. His paper does well to make the point that close historical description can show how something as local as an umpire's misinterpreted hand signal or a federal/state politician taking sides in an international ethnic issue, can raise community tensions and precipitate local soccer violence. Ian Warren and Roy Hay, in their paper "Order and Disorder at Sporting Venues," carry this approach further when they identify and assess the range of local factors that should be taken into account when sport managers and policing bodies try to predict the incidence of violence and organise appropriate interventions. Warren's paper "Violence, Sport and the Law: A Critical Discussion" asks us to consider that interpreting and applying criminal, civil and administrative law in matters of sport violence always has to be considered in light of the growing business orientation of sport, local community values and sporting ethos.

For instance, support for this more contextual approach is clear in Warren's claim that,

> Many incidents of collective deviance are glorified in spectator folklore, or are the subject of considerable media publicity or political debate. This can distort the way in which each incident transpires in its specific context, and may lead to unduly negative or uninformed political decisions and community perceptions about the nature of spectator behaviour in certain sports.

Warren attributes to Hay the suggestion that certain media descriptions of European "hooligan" culture permeating Australian soccer have the potential to "distort our understanding of the true frequency of spectator violence of various sports, and our perception of the causes of, and the factors which might contribute to these incidents".[1]

I could not agree more that when it comes to explaining something like violence in sport, using a European, or North American perspective for that matter, to make sense of Australian sport violence can slant interpretations in a certain way. While we can certainly learn something by looking at global trends in research and public policy on violence in sport, informed Australian public policy on the issue would be lacking if it wasn't sensitive and responsive to local cultures and sporting practices. I think that this is the gist of what Warren and Hay are saying.

However, they could have taken this contextual argument further. That is, to suggest that certain representations of sport violence may "distort" our judgment and our understanding of the "true" frequency and perceptions of violence simply begs the question as to what "the" undistorted and true judgements, understandings and perceptions really are, and how we might know them to be so. Judging by the content and tone of their papers, I don't think that Warren and Hay would support the idea of there being an objective position from which an undistorted or true version of sport violence can be gleaned. But once they make the move to suggest that a multi-perspective, local investigation leads the way to a less distorted, undistorted or true version of violence in sport, they back themselves into a corner.

A way out of the dilemma would be to push the contextual position a bit further and simply acknowledge that no particular spokespersons, whether global or local, have a monopoly on truth or some undistorted reality or value position. It may simply be the case that one perspective is as "one-eyed" as any other when it comes to making sense and evaluations about violence and sport. In other words, local and specific descriptions about the incidence, meaning and management of violence are no less contingent than comparative or general ones. It may have been safer for them to say that if there are to be angles, distortions, slants in our sense making about violence in sport, at least let them be local ones rather than European ones. The trick would then be to ascertain what social interests or understandings are served or sacrificed by the various local descriptions of sport violence.

The Contingency of Legitimacy and Meaning

It appears that the main employment of a contextual orientation is for establishing the specific circumstances when a so-called violent action is thought to be acceptable or not. It seems very useful to employ historical description and figurational approaches in order to distinguish what is considered "legitimate" or "illegitimate" violence in sport, not to mention what is considered "expressive" or "instrumental," or "borderline," "quasi-criminal" and "criminal" violence. Where the lines are drawn can have a huge bearing on the way the game is played, the careers that hinge upon them, the social values that are supported or jeopardised by them, and the degree to which public intervention and control can be exercised over sport. It allows us perhaps to look at those social interests and forces that drive certain forms of so-called violence out of the game or transform them into more acceptable forms.

As useful as this is, there still seems to be an unwillingness to take the contextual approach back to the meanings of violence in the first place. For example, in his paper "Sporting Violence: History, Theory, Context and Figurations", Hutchins recruits a number of authors to support the idea that violence is "polymorphous in its forms and meanings" and that "What is perceived as 'violent' in one sport may not be in another, and tightly defined forms of social reference help negotiate the variations". This would seem to suggest that a contextual analysis of some description would be useful to sort out when an action is perceived to be violent and when it is not. Yet, shortly thereafter Hutchins paraphrases Dunning and Sheard's example of mid 1800's rugby football as "an extremely disorderly and violent game where 'stiff-arm' tackles and 'hacking with iron-tipped boots ('navvies') were ... just an accepted part of playing a 'manly' game of rugger". The example begs the question as to who made the judgement that "stiff-arm tackles" and "hacking" are violent. If Hutchins, following Dunning and Sheard, is assuming that they are, then the conclusion that we are forced to accept is that rugby violence in the mid 1880's was simply an acceptable part of the game. I thought, though, that it was the very point of a more contextual analysis, as stated above, to detail the local culture of rugby at the time to ascertain its perceptions and judgements as to whether "stiff-arm tackles" and "hacking" were considered violent or not. If Hutchins has overlaid his own, perhaps "our" cultural understanding of what violence means, he has in effect hijacked the very thing that a contextual analysis was meant to do.

A similar concern arises with Martin Crotty's paper "'There's a Tumult in the Distance, and a War-Cry in the Air': Violence and Sport in the Australian Public School of the Late Nineteenth and Early Twentieth Century."(5) While he doesn't claim to be doing sociological history, Crotty demonstrates quite well how in the space of a few short decades at the turn of the century, "violent" sport in the Australian public schools went from being roundly condemned to celebrated, depending on the particular religious, educational or militaristic/ nationalistic priorities of the time. Yet, we are left not knowing whether it is Crotty or those in the schoolboy sporting culture who regard certain sporting or sport related actions as violent. This is where our history colleagues can shed considerable light on how athletes, coaches, officials, journalists and sport followers in particular historical periods and circumstances describe themselves and their sporting practices. In other words, the historians can give us the 'nitty-gritty' of the language used by those at a particular time to describe their sporting activities. For example, when I asked Crotty if the word "violent" was ever used in the descriptions of Australian schoolboy sport at the turn of the century, he said, "No, they did not, or rarely at best. (They) used 'danger', 'roughness,' 'clash,' and the like."[2] A further look at Crotty's paper shows that the type of actions either condemned or praised were described in the words of the day as "boyhood rough and tumble," "upper class larrikinism," and the like. So I am left wondering whose voice is being heard in this instance.

There is a similar situation in Hay's paper "A New Look at Soccer Violence." In it, he cites Vamplew's operational definition of violence among players in soccer as including foul language, racial or ethnic abuse, sexual harassment, verbal abuse of officials, physical abuse of officials, verbal abuse of other players, kicking, eye gouging, punching, biting, elbowing, head high tackles and tripping. Again the concern is not so much with what makes these legitimate or not, and subject to appropriate controls, but with the social interests that constitute narrow or broad meanings of the term "violence" itself. It is quite clear that Vamplew's cited definition is quite broad, the inclusion of racial, ethnic or sexual (verbal) harassment being relatively recent concerns in terms of access and equity in sport. The upshot of this point is that if a description of violence can be stretched in some circumstances, then it is plausible to suggest that it can be narrowed in others, depending on whose social agenda is being pushed.

There is yet another instance of perhaps historical bias, this time with Smith's socio-legal typology of sport violence cited in Warren's paper "Violence, Sport and the Law: A Critical Discussion." Under the general heading of violence, Smith categorises certain forms of body contact as legal in sporting terms and acceptable to players (Brutal Body Contact); as beyond the technical rules, but acceptable (Borderline Violence); as both beyond the rules and not acceptable (Quasi-Violence), and finally as incidental to the game, beyond the rules and clearly criminal (Criminal Violence). While Warren argues correctly that each of these "types" needs to be understood in the context of local conditions, I am curious as to why Smith added the adjective "Brutal" in the classification of body contact, otherwise described as legal tackles, shepherds, blocks or accidental collisions during play. Perhaps Smith felt compelled to add a pejorative word like "brutal" to make body contact fit better as a sub-category of violence. As with the example above, certain descriptions of sport can broaden the notion of violence to included actions that might, in another context, appear quite acceptable.

I raise these points in order to suggest that all definitions of "violence" are operational ones. They are put together in certain historical-cultural circumstances already laced with various political, ethical or aesthetic commitments and interests. The descriptions and redescriptions serve to delimit and define the understandings in important ways, and lay out a foundation for evaluating practices and recommending policies. So if we can agree that the social goes all the way down in constituting reality, truth and value claims, then we have to push the contextual approach back to this level. I don't think that it is good enough to claim that some sports, especially contact ones, are "inherently" violent, or that "violence" is part of the "competitive logic of sport." The social interests at work, that is, the social interests spoken by certain vocabularies here go beyond simply the conditions of acceptability and unacceptability of actions considered violent. It goes to the very social constitution of the action as violent in the first place.

Perhaps the question is not what a particular description of sporting action as violent *means*, but rather what it *does*. The term "violence" tends to be a pejorative one. Violence is usually something that "we" don't want to expose our children to, something "we" don't want glorified, something many fear will be increased by watching it on television, and so on. I suspect that when the term is used by current sport historians, philosophers or sociologists to refer to actions that occurred a century ago in different circumstances "we" just might be carrying some baggage with us in our characterisation of certain sporting actions as violent. Recall Warren and Hay's warning that carrying some European baggage might distort our sense making and evaluations about Australian soccer violence. I would think then that the discourse of violence that speaks "us" may or may not be the discourse that speaks "them." This then leads the investigation to exactly what "us" and what "them" we are talking about, and the influence their descriptions of violence can have on sporting matters.

Other(ed) Voices

It is quite clear from the papers above that some of the dominant discourses on violence operating in and through sport deal with the militarism, nationalism, ethnicity and a dubious type of masculinity that may underpin them. We can now ask whether there are voices that have been marginalised, some lurking under the surface, and others excluded altogether. There are several.

For Crotty, the "intellectual, the idle and religious" were marginalised in the Australian public schools at the turn of the century by discourses of sport that favoured robust athleticism, hard work, manliness and militarism. Crotty could have also included women and the womanly in this "othered" category. His paper is replete with examples of headmasters recommending vigorous sport as a "safeguard against effeminacy", and scorning tennis as "effeminate" and idlers for the likelihood of them being "selfish old women" when they become men. A letter to the editor cited by Crotty chastised overly protective parents, suggesting that those fearful of injury to their "darlings" should "put frills on their limbs and send them to ladies' seminaries". One editor at the time suggested that "the lad who can take and give blows in an hour of excitement and trial is likely to make a stronger man . . . than the one who has been carefully nurtured on the lines beloved by old maiden aunts".

On this account, women and the so-called feminine come up as not only "other", but "negative other." This is still very much the case today. When it comes to differences between the genders, and between "straights" and "gays/ lesbians," the masculine and the heterosexual in our society usually come out on top. Competitiveness, aggression and violence, along with the urge to master and control are thought to be masculine characteristics embedded in the culture of sport. Being feminine, being gay or lesbian, inside or outside of sport, is considered by many to be not only different, but inferior. The "other" in sporting culture is often harassed and vilified; reference to the feminine, the "poofter" and the "dyke" are often used in ways to discredit certain athletic performances and discount certain persons.

The idea that sport is a patriarchal institution is picked up by Hutchins in his discussion of the "media-sport production process." He highlights how the entrenched media discourse of aggression, force and violence in sport has contributed to what Yeates refers to as the "ex-nomination" and Hall refers to as the "symbolic annihilation" of the female experience in sport. While I wholeheartedly support a critical feminist perspective when it comes to making sense of sport, I do have a concern. It has to do with the moral closure that may come about when we speak of force, aggression, violence and masculinity in the same breath. While linking these terms may broaden the field of solidarity when it comes to defining and condemning what is considered to be violent, the result may be a growing uneasiness to talk constructively about anything that hints at vigorous, forceful and perhaps injurious body contact.

As mentioned above, the word violence is a pejorative term, and we have already seen an instance where a definition of violence was broadened to include racial or sexual verbal harassment. I suspect that the motive for expanding the notion of violence to include verbal vilification on gender or racial lines may be to enhance the moral force of the condemnation. But is verbal vilification violent and condemnable in the same way as a "king hit" behind play in rugby? The exercise of physical force can be seen to be objectionable when viewed in light of other objectionable characteristics of "manly" culture," such as male aggression and domination in the home. There is no denying that many women have suffered greatly under the hands of men largely because of men's ability to exercise greater physical force. This is especially the case in cultures where it is believed that "a man's home is his castle," thereby, and regrettably, granting men a perceived immunity of sorts. Yet, do we want to say that the exercise of force in sport is condemnable in the same way as that in a domestic violence situation?

In some circumstances the indiscriminate lumping together of words like physical force, aggression and violence might be a case of "throwing out the baby with the bathwater." In the paper "Her Beauty and Her Terror: Australian Football and the Community," Margaret Lindley recognises the association of football violence with militarism and the domination of women, but, in her words, "to equate the physical contact of sports like football with . . . the battery of women . . . by an unconsidered use of the term 'violence' is nonsensical". While Lindley's claim that this is "nonsensical" sounds a bit strong, there may be instances where the expression of physical force, and the rough and tumble of sport, can be described without it being linked to sexist, misogynist or homophobic violence. For example, describing sport as an aikido or zen-like "oneness with," a "connecting up to," a "struggle with," an "extension or redirection" of, natural forces and personal powers, calls up a host of different images. Similarly, the use of metaphors of sport contests as a "loving struggle" (2) or "Socratic dialogue" (1), stand in stark contrast to popular metaphors of sport as "war," or as a Darwinian "survival of the fittest," and so on.

I am not offering up an apology for violence, or at least for certain understandings and forms of it. Rather, I am operating on the assumption that sport is open to a number of social readings, each of which presumably grounded in dominant, subordinate, receding or emergent social interests. As a result, I am suggesting that we can talk about forceful exertion, robust athleticism, and aggressive tactics without necessarily subscribing to a hyper-masculinist and "illegitimate" violent sporting agenda. However, this may require the recognition of alternative descriptions of sport, perhaps by other so-called marginalised or discredited voices.

This is where Rorty's idea of speaking differently rather that arguing well might be useful. For Rorty, social change comes about by redescribing "lots and lots of things in new ways, until you have created a pattern of linguistic behavior which will tempt the rising generation to adopt it, thereby causing them to look for new forms of nonlinguistic behavior, for example, . . . new social institutions"(3: p.9). It may also be a case of having to listen differently, opening up to more and more "unfamiliar noises" until something strikes a chord, that is, makes a connection with our ethical or aesthetic sensibilities, and evokes sympathy. In other words, we might be able to achieve a measure of solidarity with abject others when we can start to recognise ourselves in their self-descriptions.

Michael Burke, in his paper "Is Boxing Violent? Let's Ask Some Boxers" asks us to listen to the stories of those he thinks have been excluded from the violence and sport debate, the boxers themselves. Both Burke's and Baydon Beddoe's paper "In the Fight: Phenomenology of a Pugilist" attempt to have us recognise the intimacy and artistry of boxing from a boxer's point of view.

It is quite clear that boxing has been and still is under attack on a number of fronts. Medical statistics about the number of deaths and injuries related to the "inherently" violent sport are cited time and time again to support calls for a ban on boxing. In addition to the claims that boxing is dangerous, there are also moral claims about boxing being dehumanising because the central aim of the sport is seen to inflict injury or incapacitate the opponent. Critics also claim that boxing is exploitative, that boxers are victims of false consciousness, that boxing encourages violence among children, and so on. This is all very powerful ammunition used in the assault on boxing.

The strategy that both Burke and Beddoe employ is to have us consider the contingency of the notion of "violence." Both are suggesting in their own ways that morality needs to be understood in a contextual manner, not a universal one. For Burke, the popular and academic press may be demonising boxers and rendering abject the practice of boxing. Those who proclaim the immorality of boxing are really speaking from subject positions shaped by certain ideas and values that define themselves as separate from those who don't share them. Critics may be "one-eyed" and acting paternalistically when they call for a ban on boxing. Worse yet, on this account, banning the sport on grounds that only a dominant group in society finds acceptable may be cruel and unjust to boxers in so far as they are denied a means of self definition.

Let's put aside for a moment the fact that there are a number of dangerous sports where participation may result in injury or death, yet are not subject to calls to be banned. Burke wants us to hear stories, and Beddoe wants us to hear his, about whether boxers see themselves or what they do as violent. It is quite clear from the stories cited by Burke and the one offered up by Beddoe that many boxers see themselves as part of a noble martial craft requiring the cultivation and demonstration of a number of virtues. Boxing-intelligent action requires discipline, technical expertise, tactical prowess and creativity, responsive openness to opponents, and the like. Boxers on this account are presented with an opportunity for self-expression, personal responsibility, identity and social recognition, features that may be denied to them in much of their everyday lives. Described in these terms, boxing requires virtues and recognises professional expertise and judgement in ways not unlike a number of other practice-intelligent actions.

Margaret Lindley tries to counter what may be seen as objectionable features of football by recontextualising it. Lindley suggests that many may feel uncomfortable with the sheer clashing of wills in sport. While she claims that in sport "combat is most unabashed, most honest; least likely to be overlaid or disguised with claims that what is occurring is something other than the clash of wills", Lindley makes ample use of the ballet metaphor for football. As an artistic or aesthetic experience, football is replete with examples of flow, grace, poise, style and panache. For her, football involves drama, improvised choreography and artistic excellence, the latter being embodied most poignantly in the "specky." One might now ask whether this rendering of football by Lindley, or boxing by Burke and Beddoe, might make footballers and boxers appear less foreign or abject.

In addition to requiring athletic judgement, timing and determination, football excellence, for Lindley, also requires courage and daring, all of this of course in the face of possible severe injury. "Courage and daring for what?" I ask. As we saw with Crotty's paper, "violent" sport at the turn of the century served the ideological function of promoting manly assertiveness, vigour and heroism in preparation for war. It might be said that we have come full circle with Lindley's paper. Her "New Vitalism" pits courage, vigour and community identity against contemporary, but no less formidable foes: the merchants of health and those of corporate football. On this account, health-scare merchants render us docile by packaging and selling the fear of illness, injury and death; the merchants of corporate football undercut team loyalty and collective identification.

There are two extensions to the "health panic" idea and the "sport as business" metaphor that might shed additional light on the subject of violence and sport. Lindley suggests that the public disapproval of violence may have something to do with the brute clashing of wills. I suggest that it might also have a lot to do with the clashing of bodies. While she doesn't elaborate on this, I take this to mean that so-called civilised society expects to have brute or blunt face-to-face encounters mediated in some way by manners, ritual, tactfulness, decorum, protocol, and diplomacy.[3] The praise of "down-to-earthness" by some may be condemned as blunt rudeness by others.

Maybe the discomfort with clashing bodies is more of an aesthetic than a moral concern. It may be the case that what is objectionable is the sheer clashing and intermingling of bodies. When more and more of our social interactions are mediated by phone calls, faxes, and emails, when "reaching out and touching someone" is more than ever a metaphor, when direct "hands-on" teaching, coaching and therapy needs to be increasingly mediated by liability wavers, informed consent forms and witnesses, arms-length social relations can appear "normal." Perhaps some then are uncomfortable with the sheer physicality of body contact in sport, the close proximity with another body and its associated smells and fluids. Along the lines suggested by Lindley, we may be growing more fearful of the possible exchange of sweat, saliva, mucous, snot, blood and other body fluids. Image and hygene-obsessed and HIV/AIDS-fearful society, where body odours, textures and fluids come under closer scrutiny and management, may make the vigorous body contact between athletes appear all the more disturbing, even grotesque, to participants and spectators.

The rising discourse of sport as business and athletes as entertainers can have a number of effects on the understanding and management of violence in sport. In the past two or three decades the descriptions of sport as business may have overshadowed the notions of sport as skilful, artful performance, especially when much of the media was capitalising on chauvinistic rivalries in sport and highlighting sensational examples of "illegitimate" violence.[4] Yet, there are signs of change. Hutchins suggests that competing in the marketplace for broader (especially television) audiences, is forcing sport leagues to deal with the more "illegitimate," rough edges of sport, making it more palatable to larger, especially younger audience members. As part of this sport as business discourse, athletes are also making greater use of criminal and civil law in cases where "illegitimate" violence has reduced their earning capacity as athletes.[5] The sport as business discourse may also have the unintended effect of athletes coming to describe themselves as unionists, the solidarity of which perhaps encouraging a concern for safer work conditions and job security. Taken together, they show how the sport as business discourse may have a moderating effect on what many consider "illegitimate" violence in sport.

Conclusion: Truth, Justice and the Australian Way

I hope that the critical review of the papers presented in this collection has gone some way to make the case that, or at least speak differently about, how certain participant, spectator, media, political or other social interests can come to dominate public perceptions and social policy with respect to sport. They may do so probably always at the expense, for better or worse, of other social interests. It was also shown that local, more ethnocentric approaches appear to be preferable to global ones when it comes to ascertaining legitimate and illegitimate violence, and the appropriateness of policing, judicial and social policy decisions. When we push this contextual approach right back to uncover social meanings of the term "violence" itself, the notion of "truth" about violence starts to sound more like the truth as "we" make it rather than as something that is "inherent" in sport or fundamental to its "competitive logic." In the end, "the" meaning of violence and the normative effect various descriptions of violence can have depend on whose (language) game we are really talking about.

The cultural pluralism many seek for Australia can be reformulated in the context of sport. Sport is an arena where class, gender, sexuality, race/ethnicity and a host of other social interests play themselves out. In turn, they shape what we understand violence to be, what tends to be accepted and not, and how we might regulate it or leave it alone. In describing violence in the various ways that we do, we may be saying as much, or even more, about ourselves than about those we seek to condemn or defend. Hearing from those who have been excluded by one discourse or another may lead us to ask whether there is enough room, enough tolerance, for a number of voices to be heard before deciding the fates of the persons and practice-communities these voices sustain. On this account, justice starts sounding more like how inclusive sport can be when it comes to the number of social interests it can accommodate.

notes

1 In Warren's paper "Violence, Sport and the Law: A Critical Discussion," he also makes the claim that judicial scrutiny of a case of sporting violence well after the event may not result in a "true representation of the facts" subject to a criminal or civil claim, and, further, that the failure of the courts to address contributory negligence in cases of sport violence can lead to additional "distortion of factual issues" which may impact on the "objectiveness of the fact finding process". This also sounds like "the truth is out there" talk, when I would think that the notions of "truth" and "fact" have particular meanings in a legal language game.

2 This question was raised and answered in personal correspondence with the author.

3 This point is also addressed in Hutchins' paper.

4 I am reminded here of the promotional video that preceded the Australian Football League tour of Canada and the UK in the late 1980s. The video featured some of the most notorious "striking" charges in the game, perhaps with the (misguided?) idea that it would somehow appeal to North American fans brought up on a steady diet of "contact" gridiron and ice hockey. It may only be coincidental that the AFL demonstration matches during the tour resulted in a number of bench-clearing melees.

5 Yet, even here, there are excluded voices. Recall the Manlio and Dunkley cases cited by Warren, Each sought to gain relief from possible League suspensions on the basis of the perceived financial and sporting stakes involved; but the rewards for Manlio's participation in a local league Grand Final were not deemed sufficient to warrant legal intervention. For Warren, this suggest that the legal system is developing gradations of legitimate intervention which preserves the significant financial and aesthetic interests of professional athletes, yet denies resort to the same relief for those with fewer monetary gains or less community status. The failure of the courts to consider the contexts of each situation in detail, with reference to the proportionate impact of losses sustained by denying relief in each case, may lead to unjust results across different levels of sport.

bibliography

1 Hyland, Drew. "Competition and Friendship." *Philosophic Inquiry in Sport*. Edited by W. J. Morgan and K. V. Meier. Champaign, Illinois: Human Kinetics Publishers, 1988.

2 Meier, Klaus. "The Kinship of the Rope and the Loving Struggle: A Philosophical Analysis of Communication in Mountain Climbing." *Journal of the Philosophy of Sport*, III, (1976), 52-64.

3 Rorty, Richard. *Contingency, Irony and Solidarity*. Cambridge: Cambridge University Press, 1989.

Violence and Sport

A Select Bibliography

ROB HESS

THIS BIBLIOGRAPHY IS A SELECT COMPILATION of the reference material used by the authors in this anthology. It does not include the large number of newspaper articles, interviews, specific legal cases, parliamentary reports, or conference papers referred to by the authors, although citations for this type of material may be found within the individual articles. Much of the bibliography is concerned with violence in the Australian sporting context, although where the authors have referred to major debates and relevant literature from other countries this has usually been included. As such, the bibliography represents a useful starting point for academics and students wishing to begin research in the area.

Theses

Hughson, J. E., 'A Feel for the Game: An Ethnographic Study of Soccer Support and Identity', Unpublished Doctoral thesis, Sydney: University of New South Wales, 1996.

Hutchins, B., 'Five Yards, a Cloud of Dust and a Bucket of Blood: Australian Rugby League Violence, 1970 to 1995', Unpublished Masters thesis, Canberra: University of Canberra, 1997.

Mosely, P., 'A Social History of Soccer in New South Wales, 1880-1956', Unpublished Doctoral thesis, Sydney: University of Sydney, 1987.

Warren, I., 'Cultures of Control: Law, Enforcement and Public Order at Sporting Events: A Comparative Approach', Unpublished Masters thesis, Melbourne: University of Melbourne, 1996.

Journal Articles

Adair, D. and Vamplew, W., 'Not So Far From the Madding Crowd: Spectator Violence in Britain and Australia: A Review Article', *Sporting Traditions*, vol. 7, no. 1 (November 1990), pp. 95-103.

Bredemeier, B. J. and Shields, D. L., 'Athletic Aggression: An Issue of Contextual Morality', *Sociology of Sport Journal*, vol. 3 (1986), pp. 15-28.

Bryson, L., 'Sport and the Maintenance of Masculine Hegemony', *Women's Studies International Forum*, vol. 10, no. 4 (1987), pp. 349-360.

Cunneen, C., 'An Historical Analysis of Police/Spectator Conflict at the Bathurst Motorcycle Races', *Sporting Traditions*, vol. 3, no. 2 (May 1987), pp. 217-238.

Csikszentmihalyi, M., 'Play and Intrinsic Rewards', *Journal of Humanistic Psychology*, vol. 15, no. 3 (1975), pp. 41-63.

Davis, P., 'Ethical Issues in Boxing', *Journal of the Philosophy of Sport*, vol. xx-xxi (1993-94), pp. 48-63.

Dunning, E., '"Culture", Civilisation" and the Sociology of Sport', *Innovation in Social Sciences Research*, vol. 5, no. 4 (1992), pp. 7-18.

Fairchild, D. L., 'Creative Sports: Antidote to Alienation', *Journal of the Philosophy of Sport*, vol. 5 (1978), pp. 57-62.

Finn, G. T. P., 'Racism, Religion and Social Prejudice: Irish Catholic Clubs, Soccer and Scottish Society – I The Historical Roots of Prejudice', *International Journal of the History of Sport*, vol. 8 (1991), pp. 72-95.

Finn, G. T. P., 'Racism, Religion and Social Prejudice: Irish Catholic Clubs, Soccer and Scottish Society – II Social Identities and Conspiracy Theories', *International Journal of the History of Sport*, vol. 8 (1991), pp. 370-397.

Grant, D. S. and and Wallace, M., 'Why do Strikes Turn Violent?', *American Journal of Sociology*, vol. 96 (1991), pp. 1117-1150.

Greenfield, S. and Osborn, G., 'When the Whites Go Marching In? Racism and Resistance in English Football', *Marquette Sports Law Journal*, vol. 6 (1996), pp. 315-335.

Hay, R., 'Report on Football in Europe Conference', *Bulletin of Sport and Culture*, no. 8 (September 1996), pp. 10-12.

Hay, R., 'Report on Football, the Law and Civil Liberties Conference', *Bulletin of Sport and Culture*, no. 7 (June 1996), pp. 12-14.

Hess, R., 'Women and Australian Rules Football in Colonial Melbourne', *International Journal of the History of Sport*, vol. 13, no. 3 (1996), pp. 356-372.

Hughson, J., 'Football, Folk Dancing and Fascism: Diversity and Difference in Multicultural Australia', *Australian and New Zealand Journal of Sociology*, vol. 33 (1997), pp. 165-186.

Hutchins, B. & Phillips, M., 'Selling Permissible Violence: Australian Rugby League and Commodification, 1970 to 1995', *International Review for the Sociology of Sport*, vol. 32, no. 2 (1997), pp. 161-176.

Hyland, D., 'Competition and Friendship', *Journal of the Philosophy of Sport*, vol. 5 (1978), pp. 27-37.

Jamison, B., 'The Sandgate Handicap Riot: Sport, Popular Culture and Working Class Protest, *Sporting Traditions*, vol. 12, no. 2 (May 1996), pp. 17-48.

Lewis, R. W., 'Football Hooliganism in England Before 1914: A Critique of the Dunning Thesis', *International Journal of the History of Sport*, vol. 13, no. 3 (1996), pp. 310-339.

Lynch, R., 'Disorder on the Sidelines of Australian Sport', *Sporting Traditions*, vol. 8, no. 1 (November 1991), pp. 50-75.

McConville, C., 'Football, Liquor and Gambling in the 1920s', *Sporting Traditions*, vol. 1, no. 1 (November 1984), pp. 38-55.

McCormack, T., 'Hollywood's Prizefighting Films: Violence or "Jock Appeal"?', *Journal of Sport and Social Issues*, vol. 8, no. 2 (1984), pp. 19-29.

Moorhouse, H. F., 'Football Hooligans: Old Bottles, New Whines?', *The Sociological Review*, vol. 39, no. 3 (1991), pp. 489-502.

Moorhouse, H. F., 'Scotland Against England: Football and Popular Culture', *International Journal of the History of Sport*', vol. 4, no. 2 (1987), pp. 189-202.

Mosely, P., 'European Immigrants and Soccer Violence in New South Wales, 1949-1959', *Journal of Australian Studies*, vol. 40 (1994), pp. 14-26.

Pilz, G. A., 'Changes of Violence in Sport', *International Review of Sport Sociology*, vol. 17, no. 4 (1982), pp. 47-72.

Roadburg, A., 'Factors Precipitating Fan Violence: A Comparison of Professional Soccer in Britain and North America', *British Journal of Sociology*, vol. 31 (1980), pp. 265-276.

Roberts, T. J., 'Sport and Strong Poetry', *Journal of the Philosophy of Sport*, vol. XXII (1995), pp. 94-107.

Sarre, R., 'Spectator Protection: The Legal Issues Confronting Sports Fixture Operators', *Canberra Law Review*, vol. 2 (1995), pp. 25-37.

Sharp, M., '"A Degenerate Race": Cricket and Rugby Crowds in Sydney, 1890-1912', *Sporting Traditions*, vol. 4, no. 2 (May 1988), pp. 134-149.

Smith, M. D., 'Precipitants of Crowd Violence', *Sociological Inquiry*, vol. 48 (1976), pp. 121-131.

Smith, M. D., 'Sports Violence: A Definition', *Arena Review*, vol. 5, no. 1 (1981), pp. 2-8.

Wacquant, L. D., 'The Pugilistic Point of View: How Boxers Think and Feel About Their Trade?', *Theory and Society*, vol. 24 (1995), pp. 489-535.

Yeates, H., 'Women, the Media, and Football Violence', *Social Alternatives*, vol. 11, no. 1 (1992), pp. 17-20.

Young, K., 'Violence, Risk, and Liability in Male Sports Culture, *Sociology of Sport Journal*, vol. 10, no. 4 (1993), pp. 373-396.

Book Chapters

Armstrong, G. and Hobbs, D., 'Tackled From Behind', in R. Giulianotti, N. Bonney, and M. Hepworth (eds), *Football, Violence and Social Identity*, London: Routledge, 1994, pp. 196-228.

Bessant, J., 'Violence, the Media and the Making of Policy: The Closure of Richmond Secondary School', in J. Bessant, K. Carrington and S. Cook, (eds), *Cultures of Crime and Violence: The Australian Experience*, Melbourne: La Trobe University Press, 1995, pp. 45-58.

Dunning, E., 'Social Bonding and Violence in Sport', in N. Elias, and E. Dunning, *Quest for Excitement: Sport and Leisure in the Civilising Process*, Oxford: Blackwell, 1986, pp. 224-244.

Dunning, E., 'The Social Roots of Football Hooliganism: A Reply to the Critics of the Leicester School', in R. Giulianotti, N. Bonney, and M. Hepworth (eds), *Football, Violence and Social Identity*, London: Routledge, 1994, pp. 128-157.

Finn, G. P. T., 'Football Violence: A Societal Psychological Perspective', in R. Giulianotti, N. Bonney, and M. Hepworth (eds), *Football, Violence and Social Identity*, London: Routledge, 1994, pp. 90-127.

Grundlingh, A., 'Playing for Power? Rugby, Afrikaner Nationalism and Masculinity in South Africa, c. 1900-c. 1970', in J. Nauright and T. J. L. Chandler (eds), *Making Men: Rugby and Masculine Identity*, London: Frank Cass, 1996, pp. 181-204.

Hay, R., 'British Football, Wogball or the World Game? Towards a Social History of Victorian Soccer', in J. O'Hara (ed.), *Ethnicity and Soccer in Australia*, Campbelltown, Australian Society for Sports History, 1994, pp. 44-79.

Hay, R., 'Violence by Players', in W. Vamplew *et al.* (eds), *Oxford Companion to Australian Sport*, Melbourne: Oxford University Press, 1992, pp. 367-368.

Hobbs, D., 'Tackled From Behind', in R. Giulianotti, N. Bonney, and M. Hepworth (eds), *Football, Violence and Social Identity*, London: Routledge, 1994, pp. 196-228.

Lynch, R., 'A Symbolic Patch of Grass: Crowd Disorder and Regulation on the Sydney Cricket Ground Hill', in J. O'Hara (ed.), *Crowd Violence at Australian Sport*, Campbelltown, Australian Society for Sports History, 1992, pp. 10-48.

Marsh, P., 'Life and Careers on the Soccer Terraces', in R. Ingham, *et al.*, *'Football Hooliganism': The Wider Context*, London: Inter-Action Inprint, 1978.

Mosely, P., 'Balkan Politics in Australian Soccer', in J. O'Hara (ed.), *Ethnicity and Soccer in Australia*, Campbelltown, Australian Society for Sports History, 1994, pp. 33-43.

Nauright, J. and Black, D., 'Hitting Them Where it Hurts?: Springbok-All Black Rugby, Masculine National Identity and Counter-Hegemonic Struggle', in J. Nauright and T. J. L. Chandler (eds), *Making Men: Rugby and Masculine Identity*, London: Frank Cass, 1996, pp. 205-226.

Redhead, S., 'Football and Youth Culture in Britain', in J. Williams and S. Wagg (eds), *British Football and Social Change: Getting Into Europe*, Leicester: Leicester University Press, 1991, pp. 145-159.

Stokvis, R., 'Sports and Civilization: Is Violence the Central Problem?', in E. Dunning and C. Rojek (eds), *Sport and Leisure in the Civilising Process: Critique and Counter-Critique*, Toronto: University of Toronto Press, 1992, pp. 121-136.

Taylor, I., 'Soccer Consciousness and Soccer Hooliganism', in S. Cohen (ed.), *Images of Deviance*, London: Penguin, 1971, pp. 134-164.

Taylor, R., 'Walking Alone Together: Football Supporters and Their Relationship to the Game', in J. Williams and S. Wagg (eds), *British Football and Social Change: Getting Into Europe*, Leicester: Leicester University Press, 1991, pp. 111-129.

Vamplew, W., 'Sports Crowd Disorder: An Australian Survey', in J. O'Hara (ed.), *Crowd Violence at Australian Sport*, Campbelltown, Australian Society for Sports History, 1992, pp. 79-111.

Vamplew, W., 'Ungentlemanly Conduct: The Control of Soccer Crowd Behaviour in England, 1888-1914', in T. C. Smout (ed.), *The Search for Wealth and Stability: Essays in Economic and Social History Presented to M. W. Flinn*, London: Macmillan, 1979, pp. 139-154.

van der Brug, H. H., 'Football Hooliganism in the Netherlands', in R. Giulianotti, N. Bonney, and M. Hepworth (eds), *Football, Violence and Social Identity*, London: Routledge, 1994, pp. 174-195.

Veno, A. and Veno, E., 'Police, Riots and Public Order', in D. Chappell and P. Wilson (eds), *Australian Policing: Contemporary Issues*, Sydney: Butterworths, 1989, pp. 132-148.

Warren, I., 'Soccer Subcultures in Australia', in C. Guerra and R. White (eds), *Ethnic Minority Youth in Australia*, Hobart: National Clearing House for Youth Studies, 1995, pp. 121-131.

Books

Allan, J., *Bloody Casuals: Diary of a Football Hooligan*, London: Famedram, 1989

Armstrong, G. and Giulianotti, R. (eds), *Entering the Field: New Perspectives on World Football*, Leamington Spa: Berg, 1997.

Bessant, J., Carrington, K. and Cook, S. (eds), *Cultures of Crime and Violence: The Australian Experience*, Melbourne: La Trobe University Press, 1995.

Brennan, F., *Too Much Order With Too Little Law*, St Lucia: University of Queensland Press, 1983.

Brimson, D. and E., *Everywhere We Go: Behind the Matchday Madness*, London: Headline, 1996.

Buford, B., *Among the Thugs*, New York: Vintage Departures, 1993.

Cantelon, H. and Gruneau, R., *Sport, Culture and the Modern State*, Toronto: University of Toronto Press, 1982.

Canter, D., Comber, M. and Uzzell, D. L., *Football in its Place: An Environmental Psychology of Football Grounds*, London: Routledge, 1989.
Cashman, R., *'Ave a Go Yer Mug!: Australian Cricket Crowds From Larrikin to Ocker*, Sydney: Collins, 1984.
Chan, J., *Changing Police Culture: Policing in a Multi-Cultural Society*, Melbourne: Cambridge University Press, 1997.
Chappell, D. and Egger, S. (eds), *Australian Violence: Contemporary Perspectives II*, Canberra: Australian Institute of Criminology, 1994.
Chappell, D. and Wilson, P. (eds), *Australian Policing: Contemporary Issues*, Sydney: Butterworths, 1989.
Cohen, S. (ed.), *Images of Deviance*, London: Penguin, 1971.
Connell, R. W., *Gender and Power*, Cambridge: Polity Press, 1987.
Craig, S. (ed.), *Men, Masculinity and the Media*, Newbury Park: Sage Publications, 1992.Creedon, P. J. (ed.), *Women, Media and Sport: Challenging Gender Values*, California: Sage, 1994.
Cunneen, C., Findlay, M., Lynch, R. and Tupper, V., *Dynamics of Collective Conflict: Riots at the Bathurst 'Bike Races*, Sydney: Law Book Company, 1989.
Davies, P., *Twenty-Two Foreigners in Funny Shorts*, New York: Random House, 1994.
Dunning, E., Murphy, P. and Williams, J., *The Roots of Football Hooliganism: An Historical and Sociological Study*, London: Routledge, 1989.
Dunning, E. and Rojek, C. (eds), *Sport and Leisure in the Civilising Process: Critique and Counter-Critique*, Toronto: University of Toronto Press, 1992.
Dunning, E. and Sheard, K., *Barbarians, Gentlemen and Players: A Sociological Study of the Development of Modern Rugby Football*, Oxford: Martin Robertson & Co., 1979.
Dyer, J. and Hansen, B., *Captain Blood's Wild Men of Football*, Volume I, Cheltenham: Brian Edward Hansen, 1993.
Elias, N. and Dunning, E., *Quest for Excitement: Sport and Leisure in the Civilising Process*, Oxford: Blackwell, 1986.
Finnane, M. (ed.), *Policing in Australia: Historical Perspectives*, Kensington: University of New South Wales, 1987.
Giulianotti, R., Bonney, N. and Hepworth, M. (eds), *Football, Violence and Social Identity*, London: Routledge, 1994.
Goldstein, J. H. (ed.), *Sports Violence*, New York: Springer-Verlag, 1983.
Grosz, E., *Volatile Bodies: Towards a Corporeal Feminism*, Bloomington: University of Indiana Press, 1994.
Guerra, C. and White, R. (eds), *Ethnic Minority Youth in Australia*, Hobart: National Clearing House for Youth Studies, 1995.
Hargreaves, J. (ed), *Sport, Culture and Ideology*, London: Routledge and Kegan Paul, 1982.
Harris, S., *Political Football: The Springbok Tour of Australia, 1971*, Melbourne: Gold Star Publications, 1972.
Hocking, J., *Beyond Terrorism: The Development of the Australian Security State*, St Leonards: Allen and Unwin, 1993.

Holt, R., *Sport and the British: A Modern History*, Oxford: Clarendon Press, 1989.
Horne, J., Jary, D. and Tomlinson, A. (eds), *Sport, Leisure and Social Relations*, London: Routledge, 1987.
Horrow, R., *Sports Violence: The Interaction Between Private Lawmaking and the Criminal Law*, Arlington: Carrolton Press, 1980.
Ingham, R. *et al.*, *'Football Hooliganism': The Wider Context*, London: Inter-Action Inprint, 1978.
Keith, M., *Race Riots and Policing: Lore and Disorder in a Multi-Racist Society*, London: UCL Press, 1993.
Kelly, G. M., *Sport and the Law: An Australian Perspective*, Sydney: The Law Book Company, 1987.
King, J., *The Football Factory*, London: Vintage, 1997.
Lingis, A., *The Community of Those Who Have Nothing in Common*, Bloomington: University of Indiana Press, 1994.
Lowe, B. (ed.), *The Beauty of Sport*, New Jersey: Prentice Hall, 1977.
Marsh, P. E., Rosser, E. and Harre, R., *The Rules of Disorder*, London: Routledge and Kegan Paul, 1978.
Mason, T., *Association Football and English Society, 1863-1915*, Sussex: Harvester Press, 1980.
Massumi, B. (ed.), *The Politics of Everyday Fear*, Minneapolis: University of Minnesota Press, 1993.
Messner, M. A. and Sabo, D. F. (eds), *Sex, Violence and Power in Sport*, Champaign: Human Kinetics, 1990.
Messner, M. A. and Sabo, D. F. (eds), *Sport, Men, and the Gender Order: Critical Feminist Perspectives*, Freedom: Crossing Press, 1994.
Morgan, W. J., *Leftist Theories of Sport: A Critique and Reconstruction*, Urbana: University of Illinois Press, 1994.
Morris, D., *The Soccer Tribe*, London: Cape, 1981.
Mosely, P., *Ethnic Involvement in Australian Soccer, 1950-1990*, Canberra: Australian Sports Commission, 1995.
Murray, B., *Football: A History of the World Game*, Aldershot: Scolar Press, 1994.
Murray, B., *The Old Firm: Sectarianism, Sport and Society in Scotland*, Edinburgh: John Donald, 1984.
Murray, B., *The World's Game: A History of Soccer*, Urbana: University of Illinois Press, 1996.
National Committee on Violence, *Violence, Directions for Australia*, Canberra: Australian Institute of Criminology, 1990.
Nauright, J. and Chandler, T. J. L. (eds), *Making Men: Rugby and Masculine Identity*, London: Frank Cass, 1996.
O'Hara, J. (ed.), *Crowd Violence at Australian Sport*, Campbelltown, Australian Society for Sports History, 1992.
O'Hara, J. (ed.), *Ethnicity and Soccer in Australia*, Campbelltown, Australian Society for Sports History, 1994.
Pearson, G., *Hooligan: A History of Respectable Fears*, London: Macmillan, 1983.

Polk, K., *When Men* ... bourne: Cambridge Unive...
Scraton, P., Jemphrey, A. and Coleman, S., *No Last Rights: The Denial of Justice and the Promotion of Myth in the Aftermath of the Hillsborough Disaster*, Liverpool: Liverpool City Council, 1995.
Smith, M. D., *Violence and Sport*, Toronto: Butterworths, 1983.
Simon, R. L., *Sport and Social Values*, Englewood Cliff: Prentice Hall, 1985.
Smout, T. C. (ed.), *The Search for Wealth and Stability: Essays in Economic and Social History Presented to M. W. Flinn*, London: Macmillan, 1979.
Tatz, C., *Obstacle Race: Aborigines in Sport*, Sydney: University of New South Wales Press, 1995.
Thompson, A. (ed.), *Terrorism and the 2000 Olympics*, Canberra: Australian Defence Studies Centre, 1996.
Vamplew, W., *Pay Up and Play the Game: Professional Sport in Britain, 1875-1914*, Cambridge: Cambridge University Press, 1988.
Vamplew, W., *Sports Violence in Australia: Its Extent and Control*, Canberra: Australian Sports Commission, 1991.
Vamplew, W. *et al.* (eds), *Oxford Companion to Australian Sport*, Melbourne: Oxford University Press, 1992.
Vance, N., *The Sinews of the Spirit: The Ideal of Christian Manliness in Victorian Literature and Religious Thought*, Cambridge: Cambridge University Press, 1985.
Waddington, D. P., *Contemporary Issues in Public Disorder: A Comparative and Historical Approach*, London: Routledge, 1992.
Walvin, J., *Football and the Decline of Britain*, Hampshire: Macmillan, 1986.
Ward, C., *Steaming In: Journal of a Football Fan*, London: Simon and Schuster, 1989.
Watt, T., *The End: Eighty Years of Life on the Terraces*, Edinburgh: Mainstream, 1993.
Williams, J. and Wagg, S. (eds), *British Football and Social Change: Getting Into Europe*, Leicester: Leicester University Press, 1991.
Williams, J., Dunning, E. and Murphy, P., *Hooligans Abroad: The Behaviour and Control of English Fans in Continental Europe*, London: Routledge and Kegan Paul, 1984.